THE WINTER SAILOR

Fig. 1. Francis R. Stebbins. (Lenawee County Historical Museum. Used by permission.)

The Winter Sailor

Francis R. Stebbins on Florida's Indian River, 1878–1888

Edited by

Carolyn Baker Lewis

THE UNIVERSITY OF ALABAMA PRESS

Tuscaloosa

Typeface: AGaramond

∞

The paper on which this book is printed meets the minimum requirements of American National Standard for Information Science–Permanence of Paper for Printed Library Materials, ANSI Z39.48-1984.

Library of Congress Cataloging-in-Publication Data

Stebbins, Francis Ranna, 1818 or 19–1892.
   The winter sailor : Francis R. Stebbins on Florida's Indian River, 1878–1888 / edited by Carolyn Baker Lewis.
       p. cm.
"Fire Ant books."
   " . . . consists of Stebbins's articles for the Adrian Daily Times and Expositor and the Florida Star, three letters written on the road by two traveling companions, and contemporary newspaper announcements and commentary about Stebbins's trips"—Introd.
   Includes bibliographical references and index.
   ISBN 0-8173-1422-9 (cloth : alk. paper) — ISBN 0-8173-5129-9 (pbk. : alk. paper)
   1. Indian River (Fla. : Lagoon)—Description and travel. 2. Stebbins, Francis Ranna, 1818 or 19–1892—Travel—Florida—Indian River (Lagoon) 3. Florida—Description and travel. 4. Florida—History, Local. I. Lewis, Carolyn Baker, 1946– II. Title.
   F317.B8S74 2004
   975.9'27—dc22

                                                                    2004002836

For Clara Hunziker Baker,
in gratitude and admiration

Contents

Illustrations

FIGURES

MAPS

Preface

There was nothing extraordinary about how I came upon Francis R. Stebbins's Florida adventures. It happened in the usual way. I was looking for references to nineteenth-century Florida, and they figuratively reached out and grabbed me. At the time I was working through the Library of Michigan's microfilm collection of Michigan newspapers that I had previously identified as a treasure trove of contemporary writing about postbellum Florida. The first Stebbins article I found was useful in itself. Then more and more pieces by the same talented author came to light. When it became clear they formed a series spanning ten years, I was overjoyed and astounded. It was an exciting discovery to find a gem like Stebbins's travelogues. The collection was so complete and so cohesive that it immediately suggested a book. In the beginning, I was lulled into thinking that transforming the articles into a manuscript would be a short-term project.

Various distractions and emergencies taught me how wrong I was, and the Stebbins project languished for a while. But after I returned to it, I felt rewarded for perseverance, for then a surprisingly large amount of pertinent information about Stebbins, his family, his traveling companions, and his Florida trips surfaced. The new data added crucial detail to and closed some gaps in Stebbins's story. In the end, *The Winter Sailor* benefited from the delay.

Stebbins's corpus is indeed a gem. It is nothing less than a new major primary source for postbellum Florida history, arguably the state's most defining period and certainly its most neglected. It is filled with new data, new analysis from an expert contemporary observer, and a perspective new to modern historians. Perhaps its most unexpected feature is its readability. Stebbins aimed his travelogue at a general audience and strove to entertain as much as inform. He imbued his text with his own humor and delight. Fate added an ending that turned his travelogue into a story. It is easily on par with such well-known nineteenth-century books as George M. Barbour's *Florida for Tourists, Invalids, and Settlers,* Sidney Lanier's *Florida: Its Scenery, Climate, and History,* and Silvia Sunshine's *Petals Plucked from Sunny Climes,* all of which were deemed sufficiently meritorious to reprint for the nation's bicentennial.

Stebbins's approach to Florida differs from theirs in ways that make his work invaluable to researchers. First, he was not a paid writer assigned to

promote the interests of the state of Florida. He was a private citizen express-
ing his personal opinions, some of which would horrify Florida's boosters.
Stebbins represented Northern tourists' response to the state. Their views
tended to be more mixed than those of supporters and state businessmen.
His observations and evaluations provide the tourist's reaction to Florida and
its voluminous promotional literature, something that until now has been
missing from the equation. Second, Stebbins's travelogue has a strong regional
focus. While he did record his travels throughout east Florida—the primary
tourist destination of the day—and one Gulf Coast visit, he devoted most of
his attention to the Indian River–Lake Worth area. His annual excursions
occurred before Henry Flagler pushed rail service through Indian River to
points south and changed the region's character. Stebbins thoroughly documented the Indian River country in its final frontier years and furnished readers with an unparalleled study of the land and its people. Third, and most
important, is the long consecutive time span his articles cover. Stebbins left a
moving picture lasting ten years, not the typical one visit snapshot. The advantage of his long-term portrayal of the Indian River–Lake Worth area is
that now change and growth in frontier Florida can be more easily chronicled
and the rate of settlement expansion and its impact on the natural environment better determined. There is no other late nineteenth-century Florida
account that affords modern scholars this degree of time depth.

A word about the editing is in order. Because Stebbins's fifty articles are
complete in themselves and his personality pervades his style, it seemed
best to make as few changes as possible. I limited myself to removing the
attention-grabbing subheadings the contemporary newspaper editors added
to his text, excising only two extraneous passages, noting typographical errors,
and correcting misspelled names. Because of the frequency with which he
used two misspelled words, *cavalli* and *cocoanut,* I substituted their modern
spelling, *crevalle* and *coconut.* My principal editorial decision was to include
additional material.

The Winter Sailor consists of Stebbins's articles for the *Adrian Daily Times
and Expositor* and the *Florida Star,* three letters written on the road by two
traveling companions, and contemporary newspaper announcements and
commentary about Stebbins's trips. I also included in the notes extracts from
another companion's later published article that dealt with bird life he saw on
Indian River. I do not consider combining Stebbins's pieces with others un-
necessary gilding of the lily. The surviving letters home by those sharing Stebbins's experiences are an integral part of the narrative as are the relevant passages in L. W. Watkins's article. The editorial glosses are equally essential.
Aside from the supplemental information they supply, they firmly establish
the context of Stebbins's writing and give his modern readers a good, long look

at his original audience for whom he tailored the tenor of his columns. They emphasize the basic interregional character of his work, for communications about one place to another are naturally interregional. The various editors' remarks may be regarded as a proxy for typical readers' responses to Stebbins's Florida reports, and, in this role, they provide historians with the rarely seen other half of a dialogue. It is singular good fortune that they are available. The fact that Stebbins's corpus appeared first in a country newspaper rather than as a published book is a major advantage for scholars. Untidy as their format is, newspapers divulge a community's life and vitality and recall the immediacy of time and place in a way few other historical documents do.

In *The Winter Sailor*, I have separated Stebbins's corpus into chapters according to the year they appeared in print. Each chapter is organized chronologically with Stebbins's articles, editorial glosses, and letters by traveling companions in sequential order. Thus in the chapters, Stebbins's columns are introduced, occasionally separated, and concluded by contemporary editorial commentary as they were originally. Stebbins composed his pieces as a series of journal entries, chronologically arranged and labeled by place and date. I have followed his lead in integrating the newspaper glosses into the narrative by identifying each item according to its publication place and date. This is not a perfect system due to the lag between Stebbins's composition dates and the actual publication dates. Further, while the *Adrian Daily Times and Expositor* was a daily newspaper, the other contributing papers were on weekly schedules that accentuated the temporal gap. Though these caused some irregularities in the date sequence, the narrative's natural progression is preserved by this ordering of its elements, and retaining the narrative's sense is of paramount importance. It would be disruptive to adhere rigidly to one time line or the other. By compromising yet making clear the actual component dates, confusion is held to a minimum.

It is my pleasure to acknowledge the help I have received with the Stebbins project over the years. I wish to thank the staff members of the Clarke Historical Library of Central Michigan University, the Western Michigan University Archives and Regional History Collections, the Michigan State University Archives and History Collections, the Orange County Regional History Center, the Bentley Historical Library of the University of Michigan, the Lenawee County Historical Museum, the Shipman Library of Adrian College, the P. K. Yonge Library of Florida History, the Estate Division of the Lenawee County Probate Court, the Adrian Public Library, the Library of Michigan, and the Tecumseh Area Historical Society for assistance in searching their collections. In particular I thank Elizabeth Alexander, Bruce Chappell, Opal Dickinson, Shirley Ehnis, Noelle C. Keller, Charles N. Lindquist,

Marian J. Matyn, Tana M. Porter, and Doris C. Trowbridge for their interest in and efforts on behalf of the Stebbins project.

Many people have contributed their time and expertise to locating illustrations for *The Winter Sailor*. I am indebted to Beth Bowen, Cynthia Cardona, Daniel Clark, Susan Duncan, Pat Foreman, Patricia C. Griffin, Dawn Hugh, Craig Likness, Charles N. Lindquist, Dot Moore, Joan Morris, Debi Murray, Joanne Norman, Susan R. Parker, Dick Punnett, Yvonne Punnett, DeeDee Roberts, Leslie Sheffield, Anne Sinnott, Diane Vosatka, Judith Watt, Debra T. Wynne, and Michael Zaidman for footwork and guidance. I owe thanks to Peter Berg and Gerald Paulins of Special Collections, Michigan State University Library, for their help in copying images from the collection's original issues of *St. Nicholas* magazine and to the Lenawee County Historical Museum and the Loxahatchee River Historical Society for permission to use original photographs from their collections. I am grateful to Kenneth E. Lewis for doing the illustration photography and to the Cartographic Research Laboratory at The University of Alabama.

I would like to express my gratitude to all those who read the entire manuscript or parts of it. I thank Kenneth E. Lewis, Patricia C. Griffin, Susan R. Parker, Iwao Ishino, and two anonymous readers whose insights and critiques improved the final draft. Jennifer Backer, who copyedited the manuscript, deserves recognition for her good work in turning the manuscript into a book.

Here I wish to pay tribute to Kenneth E. Lewis, the person who never lost faith in a seemingly endless project. Among other things, he made the rounds of archival institutions with me, assisted with data collection, participated in the hunt for illustrations, took all the necessary photographs, offered helpful tips with the maps, read and critiqued the prologue and epilogue several times and facilitated the indexing. Over the years, he served as adviser and sounding board, but I am grateful most of all for his unflagging encouragement.

Lastly, I must acknowledge Francis R. Stebbins's input into the editorial process. A couple of years ago, I made a trip to Adrian in search of illustrations and material to tie up loose ends. While Ken and I were examining the holdings in the Adrian Public Library's local history room, I noticed a stack of dusty and aged folios tucked behind packing boxes. They were unprepossessing yet warranted a closer look. Ken investigated and found the top volumes were ancient store ledgers. Continuing down the pile, he came to a scrapbook. He opened it and read the inscription: "Scrapbook of F. R. Stebbins." I recognized the handwriting as his own. After the jubilation subsided somewhat, we scanned the contents, which consisted of some of his newspaper articles. A few of his Florida columns were present and mounted, and the last of the loose clippings was titled "Resolution to the Memory of A. Worden." These were familiar, but there was one surprise, a Florida article I'd not seen before ("From Florida Home," 1878). It was a wonderful but somewhat embarrassing moment, and indeed I took the hint. Later while tracking down the article's date, I checked the entire run of Stebbins's pieces in the *Adrian Daily Times and Expositor* for any others I had overlooked. It was not a useless exercise. Still the "new discovery" held another pointer from Stebbins. He had circled an incorrect name and squeezed the proper one into the margin. I carefully followed his instructions. I trust he is now content.

Prologue

One early March day in 1878 two travelers from Adrian, Michigan, saw their plans to visit Cuba dashed as they stood before a steamship company ticket window in New Orleans. It was the first trip south for Francis R. Stebbins and Frank W. Clay, and before leaving home they had widely broadcast their intention to visit strife-ridden Cuba. They were keenly disappointed to learn American citizens were required to have passports to go to the Spanish colony, which could only be obtained in Washington, D.C. The two men revised their itinerary hurriedly; they did not consider returning to Michigan so soon after arriving in the South. After witnessing Mardi Gras and spending a few days exploring the city, Stebbins and Clay lost their initial interest in New Orleans and were ready to continue their southern tour.

F. R. Stebbins cast about for a substitute destination. Indian River in Florida sprang to mind. He recalled, "Indian River Lagoon, as I had seen it on the map during my school-boy days, always brought to my imagination a romantic charm of strange and tropical beauty, which I longed to explore, but never dreamed I should enjoy. . . . [T]his Indian River romance took possession of me, and I said: 'Let us go over to Florida,' and my friend said, 'all right.'"[1] Stebbins and Clay booked passage hastily to Cedar Key, Florida, that day to avoid waiting a week for the next steamer. They journeyed toward their new destination over the Gulf of Mexico, inland across Florida to Jacksonville, and south down the St. Johns River. They were told no one ventured south of Lake Monroe and Sanford. But Stebbins was resolved to continue: "I had started to look upon Indian River, and as Luther said about his journey to Worms, I was determined to go if all the 'devils' of the vermin creation stood in our pathway."[2] The pair pressed on to Titusville and beheld their objective. However, the next day they started north, returning to Jacksonville by way of St. Augustine, and thence home. This brief visit to the Indian River country in 1878 was the beginning of F. R. Stebbins's ten-year fascination with the region. Bringing along various traveling companions, he returned nine more times and added to the burgeoning numbers of northern tourists intending to recover their health and amuse themselves in Florida.

Prior to boarding the train in Adrian, Michigan, for New Orleans, Stebbins arranged with Tom S. Applegate, editor of the *Adrian Daily Times and*

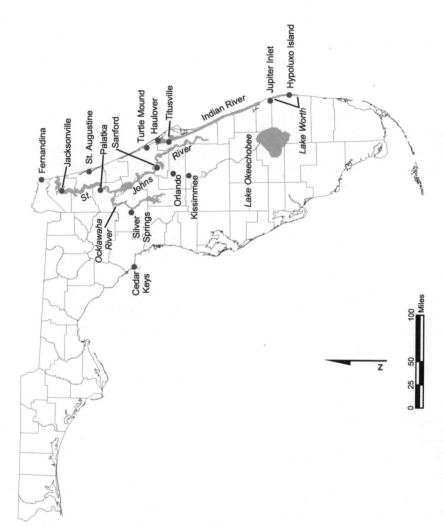

Florida locations visited by Francis R. Stebbins.

Expositor, to write occasional articles about his trip for the paper. He would describe the countryside through which he passed and give an account of the people he met, any interesting events that occurred, and his own movements. Stebbins was no amateur. Between 1837 and 1860, he had edited several newspapers in New York and Michigan and subsequently reinvented himself as a travel writer.[3] His original intention in going to Cuba may have been to report on conditions there at the recent end of a ten-year internal struggle. The Cuban situation was a continuing front-page story in the major New York City newspapers, and Stebbins may have wanted to try his hand at it. If so, he was thwarted. Instead, he forwarded the paper articles chronicling his progress toward Indian River and home. The substitution proved entirely satisfactory. Stebbins had found a place with limitless material, and Applegate had found a Florida correspondent in his own backyard.

In the 1870s Adrian, Michigan, like the rest of the North, nursed a case of "Florida Fever," one that became more intense in the next decade when Stebbins wrote the majority of his travelogues. The subject matter's continuing popularity with readers ensured that Stebbins' work would be welcomed as long as he cared to produce it. Florida stories sold newspapers. This was true from the major national journals of New York City down to the local weeklies. Each fall Florida articles, anecdotes, and advertising materialized on newspaper pages across the land and usually faded out by late spring. It became customary for New York City papers to sponsor special traveling correspondents to cover the Florida scene during "the season." In their turn, writers from large regional newspapers, responding to the increased interest in Florida in their areas and imitating the New York City newspapers, rushed south to provide their own journals with descriptions of the land of flowers. Even editors of smaller newspapers throughout the Northeast and Midwest found it profitable to combine a winter vacation with a research trip to Florida. As the editor of the Titusville *Florida Star* expressed it, "So many Northern people are residents of Florida, and so many Northern people pass the winter season in this state that Northern papers find it to their interest to give a good deal of attention to Florida matters."[4]

This environment substantially influenced the body of literature F. R. Stebbins built up year by year about Indian River. Stebbins was not the first tourist to winter on Indian River, nor was he the first to supply a periodical with vivacious articles based on his observations and activities there. He followed a well-trodden path. His columns, which began to appear in the *Adrian Daily Times and Expositor* in 1878, marked an increase in intensity of Florida coverage from the 1870s to the 1880s. Starting when the national press had already advertised Florida widely, Stebbins's work demonstrated its effectiveness. His winter pleasure trips to the Indian River came at the optimum time to capitalize on the fad.

Stebbins organized his Indian River articles in the conventional format of a travel journal. He told his tale chronologically and recorded events under the day of their occurrence. Because he spent most of his time away from tourist centers, his travelogue was atypical. It fell into the category of outdoor adventure, which, while a literary staple, was a far less common genre than accounts of or guides to northeast Florida, where the important tourist destinations were situated. Stebbins wrote for his own and his readers' enjoyment and was not rigidly constrained by custom or an editor's dictates. This permitted him to focus on his own experience and to stress topics dearest to him. Once in Florida, he and his traveling companions regularly pursued favorite pastimes: hunting and fishing, acquiring items for his personal natural history museum, and digging into Indian mounds for relics. He based his narrative on these amusements and worked all other thoughts, expositions, and occurrences around them. They became his central motifs running through his Indian River corpus, and he referred to them repeatedly.

The former editor and current contributor knew full well what his Northern readers wanted addressed in a Florida travelogue. They expected to learn about Florida's warm climate, its strange native and ornamental flora, and the state's unusual fauna, particularly the alligator. They wanted descriptions of orange groves, banana plantations, and any other tropical fruit operations the writer could find. If the reporter included accounts of social life at St. Johns River resorts and portrayals of St. Augustine's antiquities, all the better. And the most anticipated feature was an assessment of the state's agricultural potential, especially regarding citrus cultivation. Stebbins met his audience's expectations by weaving these familiar topics into the exposition, but he never allowed them to dominate his articles. It suited him better to fit the predictable matter into the framework of his own interests and activities.

As a practical journalist attuned to public penchants, Stebbins realized his pieces would be more widely and entirely read if he extended his attention to such popular topics. Therefore, he expounded on Indian River's natural beauty and exotic, tropical character. He also documented the scattered communities and dwellings he found on his travels along the lagoon. Here he seamlessly inserted the information on economic development that engrossed his Northern readers. Along with straightforward description, Stebbins unhesitatingly added his evaluation of social as well as economic conditions. This was common practice in travelogues of the day, and his audience not only anticipated but demanded it as an integral part of his report. He was the townspeople's expert witness on the scene and, being one of their own, could be relied on for accuracy and truthfulness. Although Stebbins followed the lead of other travel writers by acceding to majority preferences, he deviated from them in his contradictory portrayal of Indian River.

F. R. Stebbins was enthralled by the Indian River and every visit further entranced him. While home in Adrian, he subscribed to at least one Florida east coast newspaper to follow events there and, from time to time, contributed items to Titusville's *Florida Star*. He continuously voiced his admiration for the "fair lagoon" in all that he wrote for the Michigan as well as the Florida press. Yet this same Indian River eulogist painstakingly and sometimes abruptly interjected denigrating statements about some portion of Florida into every year's installments. In nearly every instance, he coupled his criticism with a warning against emigrating to the southern state. He seems to have feared even one family would decide to relocate on the basis of his articles. Over and over he stressed Indian River's remoteness, the isolation of its residents, its lack of comfortable and refined homes, and the absence of schools. He argued that compared with all the basic community services readily available in the North, Florida was a poor trade for a man with a family. His wife would pine for her old friends and myriad activities, and his children would suffer with no schools. After shooting these alarming salvos at his readers, Stebbins would just as swiftly collect himself, stand down from his figurative podium, and resume his lighthearted vacation narrative. He might further astound his reader in the next paragraph by countering the points just made about crude Florida life with an eyewitness report showing the opposite conditions. Stebbins's obliviousness to such inconsistency combined with his random cautionary interruptions interjected a distracting unevenness into his Indian River articles.

Stebbins's presentation of Florida was most unusual. It is true not all Northern tourists were delighted by Florida, though a majority were. There were many who felt it was a good place to pass the winter but not to live permanently. Stebbins sided with this last group; however, he carried the idea to the extreme. To him it was not merely a commentary but an injunction to enforce. He was passionately devoted to Florida and especially Indian River as a winter recreation destination, but he fought fiercely to prevent Northerners from removing there. He labored to avoid even the appearance of promoting Florida to possible Lenawee County emigrants. His behavior begs the question why.

There are several possible reasons. He could have genuinely believed his arguments about Florida's poor homestead potential. He might have been sure the rosy picture boosters painted for the future of the state's citrus and other tropical produce would not materialize. He also may have seen removing to Florida as a far greater financial risk for northerners than moving west because of the differences between Northern and Floridian agriculture and economic development. Adjusting to a strange situation would consume too much precious time. He certainly was convinced that the civic values of Michigan and Florida were widely divergent. Therefore, he may have felt merchants, professionals, and craftsmen would prefer areas where familiar approaches to business and social organization prevailed. Perhaps he even sought to preserve Indian River's wildness by slowing settlement there, but this alone is not likely. But these points are moot.

One can locate a more compelling motive in Stebbins's personal situation.[5] When he began his Indian River cruises at age sixty, he had long been a member of the socioeconomic class most likely to suffer should there be excessive emigration from Lenawee County. As the owner of an established and prosperous furniture manufacturing and retail firm, he had a vested interest in the vitality of his city and the region. Stebbins had spent his lifetime building up a financially sound business. His store and manufactory supported not only his household but also those of his adult children who resided in Adrian. He and his wife had considerable social standing, and, as pioneers who had "grown up with the country" and succeeded economically, their opinions were sought and heeded. But too much emigration from Lenawee County and the rest of southern Michigan would threaten Adrian's security and his success.

Stebbins implied that emigration would be an irrational choice for himself and his family and this colored his view of its appropriateness for others. At this stage in his life, he would not give up the comforts, conveniences, and community connections he had built up over forty years to emigrate anywhere and assumed everyone else had similar advantages or knew they were readily attainable where they were. Indeed, most of his business and social associates were also city leaders and well off. Their families' futures, too, were assured. Though Stebbins had participated in building up Adrian, he now wanted no part of pioneering. Had he the strength for the task, there would be no point in it. He had already achieved in Michigan all that he and his family could desire.

However, when Stebbins wrote his Indian River articles for the *Adrian Daily Times and Expositor* in the 1870s and 1880s, there was widespread restlessness in Lenawee County and throughout southern Michigan. He was acutely aware of it and probably intended his anti-Florida remarks to stifle local interest in that direction. At this time, the frontier had moved well beyond southern Michigan, which was now covered with farms, thriving villages, and growing cities and was an adjunct of the settled East. Other areas undergoing development now targeted Michigan's population for immigrants and held out the promise of economic advancement. The opportunities from which the first landowners profited were no longer available to late arrivals or successive generations; these people found farmland largely taken up and expensive to buy when it came on the market. This created dissatisfaction as the population grew. Tight money that stifled investment, periodic depressions that reduced income and savings, and the lures of cheap lands and a new start combined to dissolve local ties and persuade Michigan residents to seek their fortunes elsewhere. Simultaneously, expanding midwestern cities drew people from their hinterlands to growing urban manufacturing and financial enterprises. So much opportunity and competition encouraged continued mobility and presented new problems to established regions.[6]

Adrian business and community leaders became concerned about the effects of out-migration on current and future area prosperity. F. R. Stebbins and other members of Adrian's establishment felt uneasy about losing citizens and knew they were regularly bombarded with promotional literature touting advantages elsewhere. Even more tempting were the enthusiastic letters written home by pleased migrants, who encouraged their family members and former neighbors to join them. In the 1880s Kansas, the Dakotas, and, to a lesser extent, Texas held the attention of potential Michigan emigrants. Lenawee County editors, who served as one-man chambers of commerce, carefully noted the railroad carloads of emigrants passing through their towns heading west. They also nervously monitored the level of area preoccupation with out-migration. In 1883 when "Dakota Fever" seemed especially virulent to Scovel Stacy, editor of the *Tecumseh Herald,* he lamented, "[R]ight here we are not exempt from emigrants, who are looking toward the West. Even in Southern Michigan, where there are as fine farms as anywhere in the world, men are giving them up and starting west. A good farm in southern or northern Michigan is good enough, if the people would but realize it." He then gleefully predicted, "There will be lots of sick, poor people walking back from Dakota in the course of a couple of years."[7] All editors could do to restrain potentially footloose citizens was to print dire warnings or letters showing "actual conditions," which portrayed frontier hardships as insurmountable. Their counteroffensive, though it amounted only to a war of words with promoters, was frequently a community's best weapon in the contest for area inhabitants.[8]

Everyone who worked for or read a newspaper in the 1870s and 1880s also knew the power of "Florida Fever." Created and fed by a legion of publicists, it reached an annual peak during the winter months when Northerners dreamed of escaping the ice, snow, and howling wind. Glamour surrounded Florida. There was no mystique to the Dakotas, though they and the rest of the West certainly pried more settlers from Michigan than did Florida.[9] But no one went to the Dakotas for their balmy winter climate. Nor did the Dakotas produce oranges or any of the other semitropical fruits for which Florida was renowned. Instead, it was the lure of perceived easy fortunes from orange

growing that enticed Northern immigrants to Florida. People from every social stratum came to the southernmost state with high expectations of acquiring wealth through orange growing. Florida also drew on the swelling numbers of winter visitors for potential immigrants. In the 1870s and 1880s, more
and more Northerners traveled annually to Florida, spending as much of the
winter there as they could. Once in the state, they were targeted by land
agents, and many succumbed to their sales pitches and purchased orange
groves of varying ages and sizes. Some kept them and returned to spend each
winter on their property. Quite a few Lenawee County citizens followed this
pattern. Their movements were covered by the Adrian and Tecumseh papers,
which gladly printed their observations and impressions of Florida.

Stebbins was not the only Florida correspondent sending copy back to the
Adrian Daily Times and Expositor. Aside from occasional travelers mailing a
spate of individual letters to the editor each winter, others sent the Adrian
papers multiple items. In particular there was Mary Howell, wife of a prominent local judge, who spent several winters in east Florida to improve her
health. With only slight prompting from editor Tom Applegate, she became
an entertaining and informative reporter.[10] There was also B.C. Adams from
Fairfield Township. The sometime college professor, art teacher, and newspaper
editor sent the *Adrian Daily Times and Expositor* occasional descriptive pieces
through the 1880s.[11] Howell passed through Florida as a tourist, but Adams
became a permanent Southern resident and bought grove land. As an owner
of a Florida orange grove, Adams was the more dangerous of the two in Stebbins's eyes.

But more serious Florida promoters lurked among the Lenawee County
newspaper contributors. In 1882 Adrian College professor Dr. John Kost began
wintering in Tallahassee, Florida, where he zealously worked to establish
Florida University, the state's first university. During the institution's short life
span, Kost staffed its faculty with many Michigan professionals. Through the
1880s, he used Adrian's newspapers to advertise his several educational endeav-
ors in the state and extol north Florida's advantages.[12] Another local Florida
promoter was Dr. Elmer Hause, a popular Tecumseh dentist, who, due to a
horrendous incident on the eve of emigrating to Kansas in 1879, lost the use
of a hand and was left unable to practice his profession. After a trip to Florida
in 1883, Hause started selling citrus properties to support his family. He solicited purchasers from around the county and escorted them to Sorrento in
central Florida to inspect the country and select orange groves. Hause's annual excursions ran throughout the 1880s and were extremely popular.[13] The
Tecumseh papers covered his activities extensively and printed his numerous
letters from Florida. The *Adrian Daily Times and Expositor,* in retaliation for
his successful stoking of "Florida Fever" among county citizens, seldom men-

tioned Hause's enterprises. Applegate, however, gladly published a lengthy poem by an anonymous woman disclosing the harsh conditions in Hause's purported paradise and poking fun at the men who followed him there and dragged along their reluctant families.[14]

By convention, editors Applegate and Stacy could harangue their readers freely on the general evils of emigration. They could and did seize any and all opportunities failed colonizing attempts offered to lecture their readers on the uncertainties and risks of life in unsettled places. But they could not so much as hint at discrediting a fellow citizen's rhapsodic remarks about the latest Eden. Nor could they refuse a well-written article from such a person. To do the first would shatter the paper's goodwill within its community, and to do the second might cost the paper a chance to hold or increase its readership. While editors were constrained in how they could control out-migration, a man like F. R. Stebbins was not. He was allowed to be direct and specific while they were not. As a correspondent, he could address readers frankly and warn them against settling on Indian River or anywhere else in Florida. He hoped to foil the promotions of other area correspondents through reporting the state's disadvantages, and he relied on his local reputation for accurate analysis to sway his fellow citizens.

Though Stebbins was quite willing to stand with his finger in the dike to deter emigration from Lenawee County, it was hardly the main purpose of his annual travelogues from Indian River. His primary aim in composing his Florida articles was to entertain himself and his readers. Above all else, F. R. Stebbins enjoyed writing and found abundant subject matter on his Indian River cruises. Part of the pleasure for him was diverting an audience. Clearly, he would not have written continuously about Indian River's appeal to him had he gone there exclusively to discredit the country. It would serve that purpose better not to have sent a word to the *Adrian Daily Times and Expositor* about Florida. Likewise, Tom Applegate, guardian of Lenawee County's interests, would not print material sure to send the populace flying south, never to return. Neither saw an intrinsic threat in Stebbins's travel accounts, nor did the editor view anyone else's travelogues, even those advocating emigration elsewhere, too subversive to publish. Public interest in them was too great and selling newspapers was, after all, his business. Stebbins's Florida adventures were an enormously valuable property, and Applegate fully appreciated their worth in his daily competition with other Adrian journals. Everybody, including those mulling over emigrating, read them first for entertainment. Since their author intended his travel tales to amuse, he felt freed to please himself by composing them providing he periodically invoked his talisman, the disparaging remark.

The primary tenor of Stebbins's Indian River articles is hardly censorious but exceedingly affirmative, full of his wonder and delight in what he found along the shores of Indian River. Their great appeal lay in the opportunity they afforded readers to participate vicariously in all that the traveler saw and did. Everyone knew his principal and overriding theme was his personal discovery of Florida. His favorite pursuits—hunting and fishing and collecting natural history specimens and ancient American relics—for all their frequent mention, were only secondary leitmotifs. Their function was to enhance the sense of place. For us, they mark a specific era as well.

The popularity of Stebbins's writing stemmed from its mainstream quality. He voiced the preconceptions and the reactions of the average midwesterner, and his readers felt entirely comfortable with his attitudes. In this regard, he represented the typical Northern tourist. To some extent, these articles fall under the heading of classic nineteenth-century travelogues. Yet they possess a distinguishing characteristic. They are remarkably private for newspaper copy. Stebbins wrote as a friend communicating with his friends. He was always mindful of the worldview he shared with his audience, and his constant playing to their perspective permits modern readers a glimpse into Northerners' response to Florida.

Stebbins used the first person masterfully. It was the secret of his success and how he imbued his writing with a strong immediacy. In 1879 he spoke to his local history society specifically on the subject: "It is perhaps very commendable in a recital of personal recollections, to keep one's self as much concealed as possible; but are not these histories seriously shorn of great interest, in an over-sensitive reserve which leaves to other historians, who never knew of the incidents of our own lives, a record of events, with our own recollections left out."[15] Without resorting to other literary devices, he swept his readers along with him to warm, distant, and fascinating Indian River. They were, for a while, no longer in winter-locked Michigan but cruising through the tropical south Florida wilderness. To the immense appreciation of his audience, Stebbins did realize his goal "to picture to the readers of the *Times* the great enjoyment of this roving life under the summer skies and semitropical air, over the ocean beaches, and beautiful lagoons of southern Florida."[16] And for latter-day readers of his Indian River opus, Francis R. Stebbins performs the additional feat of transporting them through time to Indian River as it was.

THE WINTER SAILOR

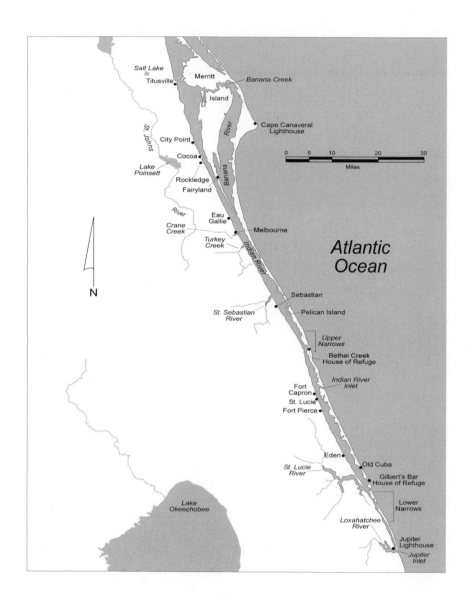

Indian River locations visited by Francis R. Stebbins.

1   Indian River Longings

In this clime of snow I'm longing
For the balmy air of June,
As it breathes thro' all the winter
O'er thy waters, fair Lagoon.

In the silent hours I'm dreaming
Of thy song birds, everywhere,
Singing out their heaven-born music
On the orange-scented air.

Ne'er did earth hear sweeter music
Since the Christmas song of old,
Than thy morning songs, oh! wild birds,
In your robes of red and gold.

Oh! what gladness! oh! what rapture
Did thy swelling throats outpour,
From the tall pines and palmettoes,
As we sailed along the shore.

Memory brings it all back to me;
And I live those hours again;
When all time from morn to evening
Was one song of glad refrain.

I can hear the palm leaves rustle;
I can see the old pines sway,
As the soft wind bloweth gently
Thro' their foliage day by day.

I can see the proud banana
Vestured like a tropic queen;

And the oranges, and lemons,
Rich in form and golden sheen.

I am dreaming of our boat life;
I am sailing down the shore,
By the curious Mangrove islands—
Ne'er had life such charms before.

I can see the cranes and herons,
With their plumage white as snow,
And the pelicans, and eagles,
As they ever come and go.

Fair the winds and blue the wavelets;
Serving us as willing slaves;
While from o'er the narrow lowland
Comes the roar of ocean waves.

Down by Fabers; on by Rockledge;
Merritt's Isle, home of the deer;
Past St. Lucie; thro' the narrows;
Lo! the Light of Jupiter!

At Jupiter we moor our boat
Safe in a sandbar sheltered cove,
And many a pleasant hour we stroll
O'er shell strewn beach or thro' the grove.

Now in the ocean surf and foam
We cast our lines with sinewy strain,
And the sea bass and cavali
Struggle on our hooks in vain.

Now a shark and now a bluefish,
Land we on the shore with glee;
Thus we vary daily pastime,
In our boat life by the sea.

The days have passed and sleet and snow
Are tapping on the window pane;

But in my room, with fire aglow,
I live those joy days o'er again.

And while I live in sun, or storm,
In forest camp, or gay saloon,
I'll ne'er forget the days we sailed
On thy blue waves, O, fair Lagoon.[1]

2   1878 From Far Florida

Adrian, March 1.—For New Orleans, and Perhaps Farther.—To-morrow afternoon, Messrs F. R. Stebbins and F. W. Clay, of this city, start for a trip to New Orleans.[1] They go all the way by rail, taking the Toledo & Wabash road at Toledo, and following out the line of the Canada Southern excursion party to New Orleans. After doing the Crescent City, they propose, if the spirit so moves them, to extend the trip to Havana. And just now, as we are threatened with a cold eastern storm, those of us who are chained to desks and counters will especially envy these fortunate excursionists.[2]

WAY DOWN SOUTH

New Orleans, March 6.—Thirteen hundred miles by rail on a Pullman car is by no means a task as severe as it looks to be, and the last half of it was to us one of new and varied interest. We crossed the "great river" at Columbus, about daylight, and the day's panorama of negro cabins, with the doors and yards always decorated with black diamond jewels, from the merest "chip" grading up to the mother "Kohinor," [sic] all the shining darkness embellished with the whitest ivory, always enlivened with the happy smile of those sons and daughters of Africa, kept us well occupied. Through Mississippi, almost the entire population seems to be of the colored people. Many of them have small but good and painted tenements, but there are also very many hovels of logs.

It would do even the eyes of a Lenawee county farmer good to look upon the vast expanse of those cotton and corn lands of Mississippi. As far as the eye could reach, we saw the long furrows stretched away, on both sides of the road, of black, rich soil, some of it already thrown into ridges for cotton and corn, the rest dotted over with colored men and women, with three mules and light ploughs, while in advance the children were gathering and burning the last year's corn stalks. The corn is raised on ridges with only one stalk in a place. Grass is only just beginning to start, even at Mobile, but near New Orleans we saw peas in the open field, a foot high.

We arrived at this city just thirty minutes before the procession of Mardi

Gras started, and had a fine view of it. It was immense, but the display in the evening was beyond all attempts to describe in a short letter. The cars and their decorations must have cost thousands of dollars apiece. Over 200,000 people were in the streets, and the illuminations were gorgeous beyond description. In one of them there were red, white and blue gaslights, in number over 600. And all Canal street, which is 150 feet wide, was ablaze with these lights, and every balcony filled with ladies.

The levee is covered with cotton, oats, cotton-seed, etc., and lined with river and ocean steamers, and sailing vessels, as far as you can see. A Liverpool ship has just put in 6,000 bales in her hold.

The temper of the people seems to be fair. One man said to me, "I am a Democrat, but I had rather have an honest negro in office than a thieving white man." An old planter who had been ruined by the war, said to me, "The only and best way is to educate and elevate all the classes." We are obliged to leave the city to-night, as the only steamer for Florida for a week or more leaves now. We find no one who is an American citizen can visit Cuba without a passport. Not from Spanish objection, but from our own government; and passports are only issued at Washington.[3] Therefore we decide to go to Cedar Keys and Jacksonville, Florida. We hope to take another look at this city on our return.

I find groves of the same pines, between here and Mobile, that grow on our Grand Lake property—the same form of trunky limbs, and bark and foliage. They looked like old friends, but the great beds, under them, of the "Spanish bayonet," did not look like home, and the dead cane reeds in the swamps, killed by an unusual frost this winter, remind us of fish poles. This same frost, they say, has killed a large portion of the sugar cane in Louisiana.

We expect to pass the jetties at the mouth of the river, to-morrow morning by daylight.[4]

NOTES ON THE GULF

Steamer *Margaret,* 60 miles below New Orleans, March 7.—We left New Orleans at 2 a.m. this morning, and daylight finds us at this point, moving down the turbid Mississippi, between low shores fringed with a few willows, with an occasional cabin and orange grove, now and then a sugar plantation, and over and beyond marshes and canebrakes as far as you can see.

9 a.m.—The air is cool, and overcoats comfortable on deck. We have just passed Forts Jackson and Phillips, where the river is contracted to about a half mile in width. Below the forts it widens to about three-fourths of a mile.

1 p.m.—At the heads of the three main passes of the river, piles have been driven across a part of the east and west passes, throwing a larger quantity of water into the central channel. This raises the main channel one or two feet higher than the others. Below the conjunction of these passes the channel is about 300 feet wide, as I estimate it. The main jetties are at the mouth of this central pass, and consist of piled and filled wings jutting out into the river on both sides, thus throwing the current and volume of water into a contracted centre channel, thus creating a stronger current, and this tearing out the mud at the bottom and carrying it out to sea; thus from the old depth of eight feet, it is now increased to twenty-two feet.

Pelicans and gulls have been flying over us, and songs of many birds come to us from the shores, on our way down.

We have just steamed out into the gulf, 110 miles from New Orleans, and we have before us a ride direct 350 miles more to Cedar Keys.

20 miles out.—The water of the gulf is still yellow with the mud of the river. It requires no little pluck for one accustomed to pure water to drink water from a mudpuddle, wash in water yellow and thick with mud, and look out upon a river of mud from which is made your tea and coffee; and I suspect the first thought in making the black coffee of this region was to hide the mud of the water, and thus it has become the custom here to make coffee like a bitter solution of tar.

8th—On the Gulf—About noon yesterday a heavy wind from the southeast met us, and the huge swells of the water set our boat to bobbing and pitching so that no one could walk without holding on to something; and as darkness settled down upon us the scene was one not a little testing [of] one nerve's and confidence. We can brag and strut around in our fancied greatness and independence, with solid earth beneath, and fair skies over us; but find yourself a hundred miles out from land, in a small steamer, with dark clouds over you, the wind blowing a gale, the huge black waves crested with white phosphorescent light rolling upon your boat, making her quiver like a wounded bird, breaking over your bows, and rushing by with this peculiar seething, hissing surge of angry waters, with your boat rolling and pitching in the foaming turmoil of the great deep, and then turn into your narrow berth, and while you listen to the roar of the tempest, you will feel how small an item and atom you are in God's great universe. Happy the man who can look upward and claim with confidence the care of One mightier than wind and waves. When we turned in last night we knew not but the *Times* might write of us:

"LOST IN THE GULF OF MEXICO"

but the gale settled down before morning into a steady, strong trade wind, and we have been running against it all day, with a heavy sea. I have since learned that the old boat was shamefully overloaded and in danger of foundering had not the storm abated. I had suspected it from a low-voiced conversation between the mate and engineer and purser at the table. Of course most of our passengers are not hungry. I have missed no meals yet. Those beautiful little sailors, called "Portuguese men-of-war," have been passing us in numbers today. They are a kind of cuttle fish, which rise to the surface, and spreading a fan-shaped filmy fin, sail with the wind.

9th—Still out of sight of land, and the same steady, but lighter head winds; we hope to reach Cedar Keys before night.

4 p.m.—We have had a beautiful day. The invalids have all appeared on deck, and enjoyed the sunshine and beautiful blue waters of the gulf. At one time we were visited by a large school of porpoises, and they kept just alongside the boat and around our bows, directly under our vision for some time, affording a fine display of agility in aquatic maneuvers.

Cedar Keys, March 10.—We landed here at nine this morning, having laid at anchor all night some five miles from shore, and came ashore in a sail boat. On our way in, we passed a sawmill where a large part of the red cedar for Faber's pencils is prepared and shipped in boxes, to be leaded in New York. The cedar is found on this coast in great abundance.

We got our first sight of the cabbage palm, which grows an enormous bud, which is edible. In this land of oranges, we could not find one for sale in a town of 400 inhabitants, except on a transient coast schooner at the dock.

Several beautiful islands, called Kays or Cays by the Spaniards, and Keys by the English, are in sight, and we intend to visit some of them before we move on.[5]

CEDAR KEY AND JACKSONVILLE

Cedar Key, March 12.—We leave this morning for Jacksonville, 120 miles by rail. Yesterday we chartered a little schooner and ran over to see Horse Key, about two miles out. The water all around these islands is shallow, and the channel to the town very crooked. We had a fine stroll around the shore of this island, picking up various kinds of shells, investigating the wonderful construction of the shrub palmetto, the cabbage palm, and huge cactus plants with spines an inch long, and very sharp and strong, which we found to our cost in attempting to push our way through the thick shrubbery.

On the beach we would occasionally come upon an army of "fiddlers," a species of crab only about an inch and a half in size; but they swarmed along the smooth sand beach in countless numbers. The beaches all around this section, and much of the interior soil, are almost pure white sand. We found on one part of the sand bluffs, partly concealed by shrubbery, an old earth-work, and two dismounted old rusty 32-pound cannon, half buried in the sand. Cedar Key, and other islands, gave shelter to over 10,000 colored men, and deserters from the Confederate army during the war, under the care of the U.S. government.[6] About a quarter of a mile from this island, in the open but shallow water, a southern man, a few years ago, built a small house on piles, and some ten feet above the water, and lived in it during the summer. The house is still standing, and the roof was covered with great numbers of cormorants, a large sea bird. A pistol shot made a great many feathers fly.[7]

Cedar Key is merely a supply station for the west coast, and a red cedar and pine lumber center. They are constructing very durable buildings of concrete, composed of pounded oyster-shells, shell-lime, and a little sand. Large oyster-shell reefs are found along the coast. They keep no cows here, but use con-densed milk. Our landlord edits and publishes a weekly paper, keeps a drug store, doses the people, and feeds the traveler.

Jacksonville, 18th.—We left Cedar Key at 10 a.m., yesterday, and arrived here about dark. The railway for the first few miles, ran over lagoons and grass islands which spread out as far as we could see on both sides, presenting a diorama of low islands and water fields, the islands now and then containing a few pines, or palms, which are very pleasing to the eye. We passed, soon after, many trees and groves of the cabbage palm, which, with its straight, curious trunk, and its round, fan-shaped foliage at the top, brings the north-ern eye wonder and interest. After the first thirty miles the country is almost entirely covered with a thick growth of the pitch pine, and we passed several turpentine stills. Only for a few miles did we see any rolling land. We could see the apparently dead level far off through the tall pines, as the ground in most places contains little or no shrubbery save the Spanish bayonet.

We met occasionally several patches of cypress swamps, and in a few in-stances a dense growth of foliage full of white and yellow blossoms out of which rose tall trees covered with the long southern moss, which was swaying in the wind, and giving to the trees [a] weird and ghostly look.

We saw a few cattle along the neighborhood of the clearings, for there are some on the route, and a few villages, but they make no winter provision, and the cattle were poor and small. But the hogs! One of them would make a good addition to a menagerie in the north for an animated black pine slab.

Mr. Clay and self went through the meat market this morning; and that white folks will buy and eat such as the best beef we saw there, is beyond solution to us.

The weather here is warm as ordinary summer at the north, the flies are annoying, and a few mosquitoes are appearing. We have our tickets for 300 or more miles up the St. Johns river by steamer, and leave in the morning.[8]

BOATING IN FLORIDA

On Board the *Starlight,* St. Johns River, Fla., March 14.—We left Jacksonville this morning to go up the St. Johns river. Jacksonville is about the size of Adrian, with one main business street, along the river, and good brick buildings. The rest of the city is laid out in squares, with wide streets, well shaded with large water oaks. Very many of the front yards and gardens contain orange trees, many of them still holding oranges, while the blossoms are opening for a new crop. The orange crop is a peculiar one. The fruit ripens early in November, but will remain on the trees until the following May, and improve in quality most of the time.

It is a beautiful day over the river, warm sunshine, tempered with a hazy, dreamy atmosphere, like the warmest days of our northern Indian summer. We have just passed Mandarin, noted as the winter residence of Harriet Beecher Stowe, whose modest cottage is shaded by a cluster of magnificent old live oaks, and their huge bulk, draped in this wonderful grey moss, contrasts finely with the deep green of the magnolia and of the modest little orange trees; and the air is perfumed with the sweet odor of the orange blossoms.

While waiting at the dock at Tocai [Tocoi], we went out into a grove of water oaks, covered with southern moss. Its growth is wonderful. The limbs of the trees are literally covered with it, and it hangs down in long, waving masses, the branches being at times ten inches in diameter, and from four to ten feet in length, tapering to a point at the lower end; and then imagine a whole group or field of trees completely shrouded with this grey winding sheet, and you have a most wonderful sight.

Palatca [Palatka], 75 miles from Jacksonville, is a beautiful town, like a northern village, with a population of only 1,200; it has two very large, and one smaller hotel for northern winter visitors. The whole town is built by norther[n] capital. Col. Hart, a great orange grower, has a fine residence here. In his garden we saw blossoming in open air, various kinds of beautiful roses, and many varieties of fine flowers. In his front yard are large orange trees, full of ripe fruit, and the ground covered under them with dropped oranges. It is said he picked once from one of his trees, 4,500 oranges.[9]

The river about Palatca [Palatka] narrows to a half mile in width, and is very crooked. The shores are here heavily timbered, all in green leaves of various density of color, from the yellowish green of the live oak, to the dark varnished foliage of the magnolia, and the intermediate tint of the sweet gum;

and as we rounded point after point, bringing in view headland after head-land, in no place giving a vision of more than a few miles, with occasional clearings, with orange orchards, the scene was one of great beauty all the way, and the air was filled with the delicate perfume of the orange blossoms. Blue and white herons and other large birds are flying by, and in one tree not a hundred feet from the boat, six large eagles alighted. This afternoon the river becomes still narrower; on an average not over 100 yards, and we are sailing along low shores of timber and canebrake land, now covered by the very high water. The palmetto begins to appear again.

Just now we passed a small bank of earth, on which not three yards distant, was stretched a huge alligator about ten feet long, and we have had sight of several others. A few pistol shots sent this big fellow into the river with re-markable speed for an alligator.[10]

16th.—We remained over night at Sanford, on Lake Monroe, 200 miles up the river. This lake is about five miles across, and is a beautiful sheet of water. There are several landings on this lake and two or three large hotels. At San-ford we were transferred to a smaller steamer for the upper St. John.

As we enter the river from Lake Monroe, on each side are wide-spreading cane-brakes and reedy plains, covered in the back-ground with groves and isolated trees of the beautiful palmettos, with their straight bare branches. In the earlier years these trees have long leaves or spines thickly woven over and bristling from the trunk, and green ball-shaped tops standing against the sky above the horizon and stretching away in the landscape as far as you can see, presenting a scene of rare novelty and beauty. Alligators continue to make their appearance, and the water and air is alive with ducks, cranes and other large birds of various colors. As night overtook us, we tied up our little steamer to an oak and a palmetto; and the long moss from the trees brushed our upper deck. A huge owl lit on a limb a few feet from our stateroom win-dow, and gave us a most unmusical hooting near morning, demanding the cook's chickens.

17th.—This morning as we resumed our journey, we were saluted with the music of thousands of sweet songsters in the air and on the trees. Large alli-gators are basking in the sunshine, and the water fowl are all around us. To-day we are running again through the wide-spreading canebrakes and reed marshes, dotted occasionally with groves of the palm, which loom up in the distance like islands, and away beyond all is the green timber belt. We passed through a succession of small lakes on our way up, and the whole country seems to be under water, from the uncommon high water of the river. We reach the "depot" 300 miles from Jacksonville, at the end of our water route,

Fig. 2. An 1870s Florida curiosity shop filled with souvenirs made from alligators. (Florida State Archives. Used by permission.)

in the afternoon, and went aboard the horse, a mule car, for Titusville, on Indian river, eight miles distant. Indian river is a salt lagoon, running south along the coast about 200 miles. After a night's rest and a feast on the famous oranges of this region, we started on our return.

18th.—We are now on the move down the river, and intend to leave it at Tacoi [Tocoi], to go over, by rail 18 miles, to St. Augustine.

We have on board fifty "green turtles," weighing from 30 to 116 lbs., each, going to market, all alive.[11]

At Titusville we saw "pumpkins," good size, grown in the fields this winter; and we have on the boat cabbages full grown the same way. Flowers are blooming by the wayside, and we saw thistles of [the] most mammoth size in stalk and blossom. One I noticed was three inches in diameter in stalk, over eight feet high, and the blossoms over three inches across. The castor oil bean is a perpetual tree here, and we saw a horse tied to one of the trees at Enterprise. We have passed three large mounds, the work of the mound builders in Florida since we left Sanford. These mounds here are not very rich in relics.[12]

The banana trees show signs of last winter's frost, but are bearing fruit.[13]

FROM FAR FLORIDA

St. Augustine, Fla., March 23.—I am agreeably disappointed with this old town. We often read up a locality, and form our opinion quite contrary to fact. It is worth a trip to Florida to look upon this old Spanish fort, with its angles, embrasures, battlements, bastions and watchtowers, all surrounded by a moat forty feet wide and ten feet deep, now dry, all surrounded by outer defensive walls and embankments; the walls of the fort over twenty feet high, covering over an acre of ground, and all in a fair state of preservation, save that time has crumbled and seamed the corners and surface of the shell-stone of which it is built. The quaint old forms of an attempt at ornament in architecture—the damp old bomb proofs, with green mould a half inch thick on the walls—the huge old bolts to the prison rooms, the secret walled-up dungeon accidently discovered a few years since, in which was found the remains of two iron cages, with human bones in them, one of which was shown to belong to a female, with a ring on one of the finger bones—old dismounted Spanish cannon, others crushing down their rotten mountings, and many other interesting things, and we have before us one of the best preserved specimens of the forts of the middle ages, in existence.[14] The esplanade or parapet on the top around the whole extent of the fort, is some thirty feet wide, and the battlement around it some four feet high, and five or six feet thick. There is a large parade ground in the enclosure of the fort, the entrance to which was over a draw bridge, inside an outer fortified enclosure. The old pulleys used to raise and lower the bridge are still in the wall. This fort was built by the Spaniards with the enforced labor of the natives, and was commenced in 1620, but was not raised to its present magnitude until 1756, and it is not a little curious that the fort is to-day entirely in possession of some thirty or more Indians from the western plains, who are "prisoners." An Indian sentry meets you with a musket, and the whole fort, with an occasional looking-to by some officer who resides in the town, is in charge of these Indians.[15]

St. Augustine is on one of the coast lagoons, inside of Anastasia island. Outside the island the surf of the main ocean is now breaking, and there comes to us its roar, like the voice of many waters, as the equinoctial, which is now raging, rolls the huge waves upon the beach.

The old streets here are only some eighteen feet wide, and some of the old Spanish buildings remain, built of this "coquina," or fine shell-stone, ancient in style and marks of time, but the old fort and gate posts to the old town, and the old circular wells, are the great attractions. The old slave market building still stands in an open square. It is merely a raised platform of large size, covered with a heavy roof, which is supported by large square columns.

The people here live principally upon the winter patronage of the northern visitors. St. Augustine is completely protected from ocean storms by Anastasia island, which lies on the other side of the harbor, about a mile distant, and yet the U.S. government has built a stone sea-wall a mile in length, seven or eight feet high, and three feet thick.

There was no more propriety in doing this work here than there would be to build a sea wall along the river Raisin, at Adrian. One peculiarity here we find which we cannot account for. They do not consider a sweet potato fit to eat unless it cooks a "soggy" slimy watery mass of sweet pulp. The rich, mealy Jersey potato is considered fit only for negroes and cattle. There is no accounting for tastes.[16]

We have been over to the ocean shore, outside the islands, for shells, and visited the old lighthouse on Anastasia. The old walls around it pierced with loop holes for muskets for protection against Indians, are still standing, but the lighthouse is abandoned, as the sea is marching upon it, and one or two more hurricane storms and it will be the sport of the waves. The new lighthouse further in is 165 feet high, and has a powerful light.

Our journeying in Florida is ended; and we turn our faces homeward, more than ever in love with our own fair Michigan. Florida is a good place to spend a winter in, but for a permanent home, a month's travel here will strip off the flowery garment in which the land has been dressed to those who have never seen it, and show you a land devoid of almost everything which makes a desirable home, especially for men of small means. Florida raises fine oranges; and all the rest of her productions are worth but little more, in comparison with the productions of our own state, than the alligators that swarm in the swamps.

Were a good quarter of our beef to be hung up in the market of Jacksonville, the citizens would inquire what kind of animal it was. I write seriously;

they can raise garden truck, in some places, but transportation and commissions eat it all up before it gets to market. There is no feed fit for cattle; almost the whole state is pine sand land, and even oranges cannot be grown without imported fertilizers; and these are impairing the fruit. These remarks are general. That there are fine orange groves is true, but the finest are from the labor of twenty or thirty years.

The winters here are pleasant, but to a northern man the summers in the timber lands are the valley and shadow of fevers, and if not death, a loss of all the pleasure and energy of life.

The same labor, time and money that would secure an orange grove here, would in Michigan or any western state, secure a better home and income, together with health, and a society and means of education for children, worth more than all the groves of Florida.

If you seek a new home, let Florida be the last place you go to.[17]

FROM FLORIDA HOME

It was a beautiful day, the last week in March, that we entered the carriage of a "colored gentleman" who "lives on sick Yankees" during the winter months, in St. Augustine, on our way to the depot, homeward bound. We bade adieu to old Fort San Marco, whose ancient watchtower, and grey and time-worn walls, in plain sight as we entered the carriage, seemed to whisper

Men may come and men may go,
But I stand here forever.

We gave a parting look at the old fort, passed the ruined walls of some of the Spanish homes, all built of the same "coquina," or shell-rock, skirted the plaza, where stands a plastered monument, erected in 1812, and dedicated by an inscription in Spanish to the commemoration of the liberal constitution of Spain; passed the slave market, now used as a market for other commodities, and took our seats in the one car of the railroad, and moved off in an atmosphere full of the delicious perfumes of the blossoming orange groves.

The railway from Augustine to Tacoi [Tocoi] on the St. Johns river, was built by Wm. B. Astor for the accommodation of New Yorkers who have fine winter residences at St. Augustine, and he makes the great crowd of tourists pay for it by a charge of two dollars for fifteen miles ride but no one complains, for it is a great convenience.

At Magnolia on our way down the river, a couple of Nimrods displayed on the dock two large dead alligators they had shot near by. Many of the visitors are moving north, by "easy stages," stopping here and there, almost unwilling to leave the balmy air for the still uncertain weather of the north.

Florida as a winter resort, for pleasure, is perhaps unsurpassed by any locality in the United States, and we hear of benefit to invalids; but, with my present information, I am convinced that consumptives even had much better remain in the north in carefully prepared sanitariums and strict carefulness as to exposure to cold winds, &c.

Hotel fare ranges from $1.75 to $3.50 per day, but the law imposes a fine, or tax, of one hundred dollars for dying at a hotel; and fifty dollars in a boarding house. Of course none but liberal souled folks desire to die in Florida; but the public finances are liberally patronized in this way by the visitors nevertheless.

Our route was by rail from Jacksonville to Fernandina. The latter place is on one of the salt lagoons, an old town 250 years old, with ten or twelve hundred inhabitants. In the face of the fact that the yellow fever takes full possession of the place in the fall, tourists are informed that "it is unsurpassed in healthfulness." The steamboat ride up Cumberland Sound, about sixty miles to Brunswick, Ga., gives a pleasant variety to travel, and the numerous and extensive beds of "wild" oysters, at low tide run out into the sound like rough low rocky reefs, and the giant cranes, and other water birds, standing on them to secure some unwary oyster "on the shell" are the only despoilers of the beds. At Brunswick we strike again the immense pine woods, which cover so large a portion of the cotton states, and as night settled over us we were running by rail through these woods, frequently lit up by fires on either side, with an occasional glimpse of a negro cabin filled with ebon[y] faces of all ages, shining with merriment, and their white ivories flashing in the intense light of the "light wood" fire in the spacious fire place. At times we could look through the unchinked crevices between the logs, on the inmates, and so intense was the pine wood illumination within, and the darkness without, that the family looked like a group of old and young colored Shadracs [Shadrachs] in a fiery furnace, while we rejoiced to see them smiling and happy without so much as the smell of *fire,* at any rate on their scanty garments.

Morning found us in Macon, a well laid out, but, we judged, not a very active city at present.

Some very good land is passed between Macon and Atlanta, but the reddish yellow color of the soil gives it an odd appearance to a northerner.

Atlanta is a flourishing city, and seems to have fully recovered from the terrible scourging it received during the war. Soon after leaving Atlanta, we passed in sight of many long lines of earthworks, reminders of the terrible scenes of strife and carnage which were enacted all along the region during the war. Almost every mile of this section was gallantly defended and contested by Hood and his Confederate forces, but who was pushed back into and out of Atlanta by the invincible Sherman and his boys in blue. The fields are now smiling in the sunlight, and the farmer turns the soil for a crop of grain, where a few short years ago death and carnage reaped a fearful harvest, leaving no record but the storm-worn earthworks, and grass-lined rifle pits, and an occasional solitary chimney where once stood the mansion of an inveterate to whom the boys showed little respect. In one or two of the works near the railway, were trees growing several inches in diameter, all grown since the war. Thus kindly nature strives to cover the record of the strifes of her children.

We passed Chattanooga in the night time. This city is at the present time looked upon as one of the most promising cities in the south. Northern and foreign capital are erecting and running very large iron and steel works, and the great Southern railroad being built on a direct line from Cincinnati, leaves Nashville out in the cold, and makes Chattanooga the great center.

' Nashville and its environs, seen from the cupola of the state house, present as beautiful a circle and center of landscape and city as you often see. The land is gently rolling, with occasional higher spots, or hills, without trees, all around the city, with higher ranges of hills in the distance, the surrounding country dotted with farms and woodlands. On the outskirts of the city rise several hills upon which are still seen the earthwork remains of the several forts erected by the Union forces for the defense of Nashville. As I stood one day on the summit covered by Fort Negly and looked southwest and west, I could hardly realize that the beautiful rolling lands beyond the city were the battle grounds where the gallant Thomas went out against the boasting Hill, captured over four thousand prisoners in two days, and broke forever the back of the rebellion in Tennessee. All was now peaceful on the hills, and in the valleys. On one side a beautiful swell of land, overlooking the city, arose the grand edifice of the Vanderbilt University, instead of a fort; on the other-side [sic], the Fisk University, built by the earnings of the Jubilee singers for the normal instruction of colored teachers, by whom the ignorance of the colored race is to be conquered. In another direction is the immense structure of the Nashville cotton mills, in full operation, opening a new industry in the south; while in the center of the city, on a high elevation stands the noble state house, its foundations on a level with the roofs of the other buildings. The library in the state house is frequented by the professional students of the city, constantly. We saw there the full length portraits of General Thomas, and Senator Brownlow, other portraits of Lincoln, and Horace Greeley, with the governors of the state. I did not see that of Jeff. Davis.

With the exception of old earthwork that cannot be removed without more labor than the white men will put forth or pay for, and the grave yards, all mementoes or reminders of the war seem to be carefully removed out of sight as if the people wished the strife to be forgotten forever, and I did not hear an unkind word in eight southern states against the government or the north. The utmost good feeling is expressed and it is undeniable that the policy of the President has done more to bring about this result than all the acts of his predecessors. Lincoln is spoken of with reverence, and regret for his untimely death, and Davis seldom mentioned. There are signs of a disruption in political movements, but how soon it will come, is not certain. Were Hayes a candidate to-day, he would carry several southern states, by white votes, but what a new man might do, is very different.

From Nashville to Louisville is a strange country. The lands are rolling, and second to none in the south in beauty and fertility, most of the way. Through the mammoth cave region, all over the country there are sinks or depressions in the land, of no great depth, but evidently made by a subsidence of the earth, forming basins of greater or less magnitude, some of them holding the surface water, others dry and cultivated, and many of them having a center cavity through which the water is carried down to unknown regions. In other parts great springs burst out. In the village of Lebanon, thirty miles easterly from Nashville, we saw one rising in the public square with a volume of water equal to the summer flow of the Raisin. Of Louisville and Cincinnati, I need not write. We hailed with pleasure our own splendid state and country, and all things considered we saw not their equal.[18]

Adrian, April 4.—Messrs. F. R. Stebbins and Frank W. Clay returned from their trip this noon.[19]

3   1879 Indian River, Florida

Adrian, Dec. 18, 1878.—Ex-mayor W. H. Waldby accompanied by Mrs. Waldby, their daughter Bertha, and Miss Hortense Seaver, left this city on the 16th, for Jacksonville, Florida, and they are probably by this time rapidly nearing their destination in the land of orange groves and semi-tropical sunshine. The ladies will remain at Jacksonville during the winter. Mr. Waldby will return in a few weeks.[1]

Tecumseh, Jan. 8.—Mr. J. B. Swan, Mr. N. M. Sutton, and Miss Annie Sutton go to Florida the 21st.[2] Pleasure trip.[3]

Adrian, Jan. 16.—Florida Excursion.—The Florida excursion, organized by Messrs. Eberts & Hulett, starts for Florida on Tuesday next. Mr. Hulett was in town today making arrangements and seeing probable excursionists. The party will number about fifty and will be personally conducted by Messrs. E. & H. themselves.[4] The tickets for the round trip are put at the low price of $50. F. R. Stebbins, Esq., will be one of the party, and will gladly give any information in relation to the trip. Parties can take the morning train east to Toledo.[5]

Adrian, Jan. 20.—F. R. Stebbins, Esq., and Mrs. R. H. Whitney, of this city, will join the excursion to Florida, which starts tomorrow.[6]

Adrian, Jan. 21.—From Florida—Mrs. W. H. Waldby sends home the Jacksonville *Sun and Press* of the 14th inst. From it we hear that a tolerably healthy earthquake shook up all that region on Sunday night, the 12th. People were thrown out of bed, and things shaken up generally.[7]

We also learn from reports in this paper from various parts of Florida that the recent freeze had not seriously damaged the orange crop.[8]

Adrian, Jan. 21.—F. R. Stebbins, Esq., started for Florida this morning, and now that he has gone, we do not hesitate to print a little poem of his, which first saw the light in the *Florida New Yorker*, premising that the correct pronunciation of Augustine gives the emphasis on the first syllable:

A Southern Memory
Saint Augustine!
Dear old Saint Augustine!
Time-scared, yet beautiful!—thy face doth
seem,
In all my memories, a radiant beam
Of golden sunshine, guiding all life's dream!
Queen-robed Augustine!

Saint Augustine!
Quaint old Saint Augustine!
The blossom perfume of thy orange groves,
Sweet as the blessedness of youthful loves,
Seems calling me, where'er the wanderer roves
From thee, Saint Augustine!

Saint Augustine!
Wave-kissed Saint Augustine!
The north beach glitters with its wealth of shells,
Bathed in the beautiful blue ocean swells,
Which blend their music with the distant bells,
Of old Saint Augustine!

Saint Augustine!
Palm-crowned Saint Augustine!
The soft south winds still kiss San Marco's wall,
While in the frozen north I'm held in thrall
Longing for thee as the white snow-flakes fall,
Blue-skied Saint Augustine![9]

Adrian, Jan. 27.—The Florida excursionists were detained at Portsmouth, Ohio, by ice in the river, and probably did not reach their destination last evening, as was expected.[10]

Adrian, Jan. 30.—The Florida excursion party, which left the 21st, reached Jacksonville last night.[11]

AT SAVANNAH AND THE JOURNEY THITHER

Savannah, Ga., Jan. 23.—I did not intend to open my note book before our arrival on Indian river, in Southern Florida, but have thought a few lines from this locality will, perhaps, interest some of your readers. We were detained twenty-four hours at Portsmouth, on the Ohio river, on account of one of those immense ice flows [*sic*], which was heralded by telegram forty miles away, and when it reached Portsmouth was seven hours in passing, with the river full of ice, and running about four miles an hour. But the Mayor of Portsmouth took us through a very large steel manufactory there, where we looked into furnaces which register four thousand degrees of heat, and looked on the various manipulations of the ore until it comes out the finest steel. Not long after leaving Huntington, on the [West] Virginia side, the railway strikes the Kanawha river, and for forty miles we were whirled along its banks above foaming rapids and falls, with a wild confusion of immense rocks and mountain gorges on all sides.

This route is lined with coal mines, many of the entrances high up the hills; but we saw a few directly from the level of the railway, and we could look into their cavernous depths from the car window.

We took Richmond, in spite of the old earthworks which still remain, and laid over one day to explore it. Hollywood cemetery is the pride of the city, but the most impressive thing in it is the sod-covered grave of ex-President John Tyler, alone, in a small three-cornered lot that seemed to belong to no one, and without head-stone mark or enclosure, save the trees which grow on it. Verily, living Congressmen care little about the graves of dead Presidents,— and even proud old Virginia, who boasted herself "the mother of Presidents," lets one of her Presidential children sleep like a dog, in an unmarked grave. Such is Presidential fame. Of course, we took in the largest tobacco factory, and the plantation songs of the male and female operatives of all ages. These colored workmen and women and children get from three to six dollars a week wages. In the Capitol grounds were a great many tame squirrels, which would come at our call, and climb up our legs to receive nuts.

Six-hundred miles from Richmond brought us to Savannah, and here we have been spending two days, and enjoying the sights and beautiful weather. This morning I sought the open portico to read the morning paper. Yesterday we strolled along the wharves, where many foreign vessels are loading cotton bales. The rail of these large ships is twenty feet above the wharf, and the bales are drawn by steam power up an inclined plane some fifty feet long. A colored man, at the foot, fastens the tackle hooks to one end of the bales, then jumps on and has a merry ride up; jumping off just as the bale leaps over the rail, and swings over the hatchway. He then catches the returning tackle hooks, carries them to the dock, and repeats the ride. These cotton bales come from the plantation presses about four feet thick, and eight feet long. Before shipping they are compressed with powerful presses into eighteen inches thickness. We saw several presses at work, and they told us they could re-press 750 bales a day, and received fifty cents a bale pay. Of course, we have been to Bonaventure cemetery. Its chief attraction is in the long avenues of immense old live oaks, draped in the beautiful southern moss.

The weather is simply charming, the mercury ranging from 50° to 75°, at different hours in the day. The little negro children are rolling in the sand, the colored nurses out in the squares and parks with the white babies, and the beautiful camilias [sic] are in full blossom in the yards of the residences.

They have had no snow here this winter, but I can see signs of frost on the more tropical plants. Our party is a very pleasant one, and Mr. Hulett, who is with us, is ever busy to make our journey one of enjoyment. Everybody tries to please us, and a stranger went a half a mile yesterday to get me a specimen of the South Carolina super phosphate rock, because he heard me enquire for it.

We move on to-night, by steamer, to Jacksonville.[12]

FROM FLORIDA

Palatka, Feb. 1.—Our route from Savannah to Jacksonville ran down the Savannah river a few miles, and then we turned into one of the many inland channels which form the "inland route" of steamers. Just before leaving the river, we passed Fort Jackson, just opposite the sunken vessels and pile obstructions with which the Confederates completely filled the harbor. The rotten hulls of the vessels still rise above the sand-bars, which have formed around them, and the thousands of piles scattered in irregular positions, still remain, save where a channel has been cleared for navigation. Below Savannah we pass the great rice fields of this section, a region where few white men can stay in the summer and live, and where in the old days thousands of colored men and women slaves enriched the soil with their worn out bodies. So malarious is the air on this river that, even at Savannah, it is considered very hazardous to sleep on a vessel at the docks in the summer.

The morning found us somewhere off Brunswick, with broad, reedy marshes all around us, and the water full of ducks, and the balmy air making the outer deck pleasant without overcoats. After an hour's stop at Fernandina, and a pleasant stroll through the town, where the warm sun sent us into the shade for cooler air, we resumed our voyage. Not many miles from Fernandina our steamer turned into one of the channels to the ocean, where the passengers enjoyed an unexpected treat. The water was rolling in with gentle swells, porpoises were breaking water all around us; while as a wave came along, schools of dolphins would shoot out of them, throwing themselves entirely from the water, and then seemingly returning to ride in and shoot out of the next wave. They seemed to be of two or three hundred pounds weight each.

Occasionally a huge shark would surge upward, and turning on his side, show his wicked mouth and silver belly. The pretty little Mother Carey's chickens were flying about in little flocks, looking like the flashing of the silver-maple foliage, as, in their circuitous flight, they all, as one uniform action, turned the under side of their wings to us and the sun. As we entered the mouth of the St. John's river, the fun of the porpoises grew fast and furious. Hundreds of them were rolling upon their black backs, and pelicans and ducks without number were startled and aroused to flight by our advent.

Twenty-five miles up the St. Johns and we landed at Jacksonville, the first objective point to all Florida tourists. I saw but little change since last year, save a few new business places have been erected.

We found Mrs. W. H. Waldby and daughter, and Miss Seaver well located at the Windsor, and Mrs. Whitney secured rooms at the same hotel.

Mr. Sutton, of Tecumseh, and self came up to-day to Palatka, where we spend the Sabbath, and then move on to Indian river. Here we met Dr. House and Mr. Swan, of Tecumseh, who in company with Miss Anna Sutton, will make the Ochlawaha [Ocklawaha] trip next week.

I cannot see that the freeze of January 7th did much damage, though ice was formed as the mercury stood at 29° or 30°. Of course all the banana plants were killed to the roots, and the leaves on the lemon trees killed, and some of the young orange shoots show the sere leaf. In the gardens here, peas are two feet high, and beets, cabbages, lettuce, etc., are in good growth. Roses begin to open, and the plum-trees are in blossom. The oranges are in good order; and if the box I sent to B. & C. arrives safe, I trust the *Times* will have a chance to try them.

After we launch our boat on Indian river, no one but alligators, sharks and wild game will hear from us for two weeks.[13]

Adrian, Feb. 8.—As Mr. Stebbins stated in his letter printed yesterday, Mrs. R. H. Whitney is at the Windsor Hotel, Jacksonville, Fla. She has sent home the bill of fare for January 26. We notice that it includes new potatoes, new tomatoes and green corn.[14]

WINTERING IN FLORIDA

Titusville, Indian River, Florida, Feb. 6.—We are all mixed up in our mental almanac. We catch ourselves talking about "last winter," "this spring," and "this summer," and have to "take soundings" to be sure which term is right. At Jacksonville it was summer; we awoke at Palatka with the mercury at 32°, and had a fire all day; here the register marks 80°, and the sky is as blue and the air is as soft as summer.

We left Sanford, 200 miles above Jacksonville, on Tuesday morning, and were soon among the alligators and the wide spread marshes and palmetto groves along the tortuous channels of the upper St. John's river.

Just before noon the warm sun brought out the huge lizards, and the cry of "There's a 'gator," from the man in the pilot-house, brought us to the front with our rifles;—for I started for Florida with "malice prepense" against alligators, in my thought, and a good Winchester rifle in my hands. In less than an hour its deadly 44 calibre pellets sent three fine fellows to their rest, and furnished fifteen hundred pounds of meat for the buzzards. The first one raised his head in angry agony in the air, with his red mouth opened wide enough to take in a market basket, and lashed the ground with furious energy, with his tail, as he writhed in death throes, until he fell over into the river and sank.

The next one was lying on a little low sand bar, "squat" like an elongated toad, and I made a center shot on him, just back of the fore legs, and no doubt through his heart. He made two or three spasmodic efforts to move, and dropped his head, dead as a log. The third one was a big fellow, full ten feet long, lying on an abrupt bank, some four feet above the water.

The shaking of the boat disturbed the aim, and the ball struck his back bone, ploughing a large red furrough [sic] where it tore up his scaly hide. He was apparently completely paralyzed by the shot, and only developed a quivering spasm of life for a few moments, but finally rallied strength enough in his fore legs to pull his nether part along a few feet and slide down the bank into the water, where he rolled over, belly up, a departed saurian.

I really felt a little sorry for these monsters; and the wanton shooting of them is possibly inexcusable in a strict code of life, but they are such a concentrated combination of repulsive ugliness, without a single redeeming trait, that one can easily give way to the organ of destructiveness when he sees one, and has a good rifle in his hands; besides, what will become of the national bird of the cotton belt, and the pet scavenger of the south, the buzzard, if he doesn't have something to "scavenge" upon! and there are thousands of them on the St. John's that must be fed![15]

Titusville, like all Florida towns, is a small scattered settlement, in the sand and "palmetto scrub," but in front is the wide blue Indian river, a salt lagoon shut off from the ocean by a continuous strip of land, save a few inlets, for one hundred and fifty miles along the coast.

On this so-called river, southward, we propose to sail, and rough it a little, for the next two or three weeks, hunting and fishing. We have been looking over the sail boats, and intend to select one on which we can live, and go and come at our pleasure.

They have had a little frost here, but the banana plants are not killed.

The longer any one travels through the south, the more reason he will have to thank God for the culture and enterprise of the north.

We are in no hurry, and can take the slow-coach style of the country, with great resignation; but I cannot conceive a worse martyrdom than for a prompt, active business man to endure a year's business in the south. I once had occasion to show a little impatience with regard to a prolonged delay of some trunk checks. "Oh," said the agent, "it will be all right; everybody moves slow here. I was just so impatient when I first came here. I once attempted to hurry a colored man, who was hoeing in my garden as if he was digging his own grave. He stopped work, and resting his chin on the hoe-handle, drawled forth, 'Look-a-hea', Mister B., I once knowed a man to get hurt 'cas he was in a hurry! You jes' let me alone.'" And the whites are no better, and even northern men soon fall into the same lazy habit. Said another man when a remark was made about want of energy, "You northern fellows who come here to settle, flax around tremendously the first year;—the second year you don't work near so hard, and the third year you let the negro do the work." And this is the fact.[16]

We have been looking at a pine-apple garden. The plants are about two feet high, and set out eighteen inches apart, this close planting being necessary that each plant may receive support from its neighbor. The apples are not yet set. The pine-apple is propagated from suckers which sprout out of the main stalk, and they bear the second year after setting.

8th.—We had a fine thunder-storm this morning. The first rain of any account since we have been in Florida. We have engaged our boat, the *Ella*, for a three weeks' home on the river. It has a little cabin, enclosed on three sides, over the center-board, with good wide berths on either side, with mattresses, storage room off from it under the quarter deck; a fine roomy cock pit with seats; and we hope to get our stores aboard to-morrow, and be off; and as free rovers, we shall explore either shore, as we choose, 150 miles further south, some of the way in sight of the ocean; which we shall visit often, and all in the most interesting portions of southern Florida. We may get a chance to send out letters, meanwhile, good-bye.[17]

INDIAN RIVER, FLORIDA

Titusville, Fla., Feb. 10.—We have been detained here two days by a cold, rainy "norther," but this morning the storm broke, and after stowing our "things" aboard our little schooner, we are off, with a fair wind and new anticipations.

Fig. 3. Captain Charles R. and Mary Carlin. (Loxahatchee River Historical Society, Jupiter, Florida. Used by permission.)

Now comes in experience and skill in stowing our effects in the least possible space, out of the way, and yet easy of access; for we take aboard nothing that can be dispensed with. Our "cabin," in which three of us must sleep, and keep our valises, bags and guns, is eight by nine feet, and four feet high, with open sides above the deck, which we can close tight with canvas curtains, on cold or rainy days or nights. A small boat stove, and lockers under the seats in the cockpit, and storage room under the quarterdeck of our twenty-three feet craft completes the arrangements of our domicile for the next two or three weeks. We have hay mattresses on a raised frame, with sheets and blankets, which will afford us at least good camp-life rest at night, and reclining couch by day. Captain Carlin, a sober son of Erin, is recommended as a good cook and careful boatman, and the *Ella,* moves on like a staunch steed, ready for the race to Jupiter Inlet, 150 miles farther south.[18]

11th.—We anchored last night in shoal water at Faber's, a settler's station, having run only twelve miles, on account of a change of wind, and rather heavy sea, for the river at this point is four miles wide. We went ashore before dark and visited a so-called Indian mound. It was heavily timbered, and covered with bushes, and may be artificial, but I doubt it.[19] We slept well, and this morning set down to our *board* with good appetites for our coffee, ham, hominy, sweet potatoes, and bread and butter. Wind still ahead, but we go on. The river has narrowed to about three miles, and the shore seems to have a settler's clearing, with orange groves, about a mile or two apart.

2 p.m.—We have been ashore to visit the Dixon and Spratt orange groves, where they sold oranges for one dollar a bushel.[20] Here we saw the sugar cane growing, but found it very warm walking, and the cool breeze under our cabin roof much more pleasant.

The wind is still ahead, and we remain at anchor near a beach strewn with large and small "coquina" blocks, a shell rock which is worn into a thousand fanciful shapes by the action of the waves. Many flowers are appearing, and the spring foliage has started. Cabbages, peas, and tomatoes, are ready for the table. These shores are lined on both sides with beautiful palmetto trees of all sizes, the glossy magnolias, live oaks, and other trees, while vines, green and dry, cover the low growth in the hummock [*sic*] lands.

12th.—The wind changed during the night in our favor, and we move on with cool, delightful weather. Coots, and raft ducks, white herons, and white ibises are flying before us in large numbers, and some of them contribute to our stock of curiosities. I have preserved some of the plumage of one I shot to-day, a beautiful grey and black bird.[21] The weather is like the fairest summer day on our upper lakes.

About noon we put into the mouth of Banana river, a branch of the main water, at the base of the bluff directly in the face of one of those pre-historic shell mounds, which abound on this coast. The water had washed away a part of the mound, and left the heart of the mound vertically exposed, and the beach was a mass of the shells, and many pieces of broken pottery. The highest part of the bluff was twenty-five feet, almost perpendicular, a complete mass of shells, with streaks of layers of ashes, and other decayed matter. In digging into the bluff, I came across a few pieces of skull, and a yellow streak where the body had lain; but the bones had completely decayed. I took out pieces of pottery fifteen or twenty feet from the surface of the mound, in the face of the bluff, and the pottery was scattered through the whole mass, from top to bottom.[22] Soon after leaving Banana river, we passed two more high shell bluffs, which we intend to visit on our return.

5 p.m.—The breeze is dying out, and we come to anchor for the night. This has been a perfect day—the sun is setting in a clear sky, the air is soft and balmy, and the roar of old ocean, a few miles away across the strip of land east of us, comes to us like the "voice of many waters."

Fig. 4. An early twentieth-century view looking south toward the junction of the Banana and Indian rivers. The bluff and shell mound are on the left, and the south end of Merritt Island is on the right. (Author's collection)

13th.—The sun comes up in a clear, mellow sky, and the air is cool and invigorating, with a light fair wind. The song birds are making music on the shore, and one, with the sweetest tones possible, sings out as we stand with our guns ready, and in tune, as the ducks purr, "Shoot! shooting, shooting, shoot!" Those curious shaped waterworn coquina rocks again strew the shore, and the palmettos wave a graceful salute to the northern barbarians who have invaded these shores. After our well-relished breakfast we fall back on our couches and admire, as we sail the ever-varying beauty of the palms and pine of the low shores, on either hand.

We approach now the mouth of a little creek which puts in here, and while the skipper fills his water-cask, I examine another shell bluff, and procure more pieces of pottery, for this good fresh water made a favorite camping place for the old prehistorian.

Weather still delightful. After filling our water-keg and filterer, we sail on, and soon pass the mouth of the Sebastian river, 60 miles from Titusville.

12 m. [*sic*]—This is indeed dream life, sailing on in the delicious sunshine and soft air, sitting on deck or reclining on our couches, continually approaching some near object of interest and beauty, now we pass a grove of mangroves, now some new flight of birds, the jumping of the fishes, the drumming of the drum fish, and the rolling of the porpoises. These mangrove trees are a curi-

osity. Growing from the water they start up in a hundred small slim roots which unite some four or five feet above the water to form the body of the tree.

4 p.m.—I have invaded the culinary cockpit of the skipper, and made a corn cake for supper. All hands pronounced it a success. Evening gives us the close of another charming day. One by one the stars come out, with unusual brilliancy, and we notice the lower star in the handle of the dipper is below the horizon. Another boat passes us as we lie at anchor, and we see the owner cooking his supper over a fire burning apparently on the deck of his boat, but really on the bottom plate of an old stove.

14th.—The singing birds awake us to another beautiful day. The same blue sky with the rosy hue of morning just above the horizon—a bright silvery glare of light in the east, heralds the rising sun, while the loud roar of the ocean-surf booms grandly in the same direction. As the sun rises the rosy hue sinks into a purple zone near the land, and fades away as the sun comes forth, a deity indeed of another perfect day.

3 p.m.—For two days we have been sailing within sound of the ocean surf, and tantalizing visions of shells and sea beans, have excited our thoughts, and as we could endure it no longer, to-day we broke for the beach. A row in our yawl boat of about a mile in shallow water; a walk of a hundred rods through a fine palmetto grove, and the blue Atlantic in all its majesty was before us. The grand swells, ten feet high, were rolling in in quick succession, surging, curling, foaming and dashing in spray upon the wide sand beach, as far as the eye could reach, in both directions, on the coast, making the earth tremble with the concussions, and the ear tremble with their roar. But we came for "curiosities," and on we went down the beach, with our collecting bags. Like children, we were soon eagerly picking up the sea beans in liberal numbers, in size from an inch to two inches in diameter, many curious sponges, a few shells, and other "treasures." Full three miles down that beach before we began to think of the return. The day was warm, and with a peck of pickings in our bags, we found that three miles back a hard "Jordan" to travel, I believe. Would it never end? On, on, on, sand, sand, sand, and the only relief the grand rolling surf dashing at our feet. But all trouble ends at last, and we threw ourselves down for a rest at the end with great thankfulness for the repose, *and* our collection of sea beans, which we carry with care to our boat.[23]

There! dinner is over, and we do not feel as though we had walked six miles and pushed and rowed a boat two miles more, for we baked sea mullet, fried sea bass, sweet potatoes, coffee and bread, and oranges for dessert. Oh, we live like princes, and we don't envy kings.

15th.—We laid at anchor last night a mile from St. [Ft.] Capron, an abandoned government post, in the Seminole war.[24] Three houses, and a post-office in one of them, comprise the town. We send back letters from here with the cheerful prospect that they will be two or three weeks reaching home. Things move slow here, and the mail is no exception.[25]

ON INDIAN RIVER

February 15.—We picked, at Capron, some native lemons, for lemonade on board, hot days. Ducks, herons, pelicans, and occasionally the white ibis, are flying around; most of them at a safe distance; but once in a while one more venturesome falls a victim to our fire arms. Another beautiful day. We have just passed another abandoned station, Fort Pierce; now a wast[e] field, grown up with chapperal [sic].[26] For the first time we come in sight of a ridge of land that looks quite like hills, but not over fifty feet in height. The land seems to be more elevated as we approach south. We have just passed the St. Lucia [Lucie] river, apparently quite a stream, which takes its rise in the everglades. The volume of water is so great that Indian river, here three miles wide, is quite fresh.

2 p.m.—We are now passing the lower narrows, and the most interesting spot we have seen. The channel is about six rods wide, very crooked, and lined on both sides with a green wall of mangrove trees or bushes, which rest on the ten thousand bare roots, which shoot up out of the water and concentrate into the main trunks, and in many places these roots put out high up from the branches, and are growing down to the water. The whole system of the mangrove looks like a lot of trees that are never quite certain whether it is their duty to grow down or up; but with a dark green glossy foliage, they make a fine adornment for the shores. Here we are hemmed in on all sides with these mangroves, backed with rubber trees, palmettos, and various other varieties.

6 p.m.—Jupiter, at last! and we hail the sight of the immense brick lighthouse dock, in the mouth of Jupiter river, which puts in here. We were not a little surprised to find here a 400-ton Mississippi steamer, the *Bell[e] of Texas,* which certain parties are taking around the coast to run on the St. Johns river—a very hazardous feat. Such a boat was probably never before over the bar here, as the water is never over five feet at high tide, for the tide here is only about forty inches, but these flat-bottom steamers draw only four feet of water. The captain invited our party aboard to tea and good state rooms for the night.[27] We find here quite an unusual number of boats like our own; four or five anchored near us.

Fig. 5. Jupiter Lighthouse in the 1880s. (Florida State Archives. Used by permission.)

16th.—We vary our bill of fare this morning with fried "pompano," a very rare and fine fish, which actually jumped aboard our boat, after our arrival.

A fine young coconut palm, about fifteen feet high, is growing on shore, near by; and the seed-pod, about two feet long, is already formed, ready for blossoming.

To-day we have rested from our labors, and strolling on the ocean beach, listened with delight to one of the grandest sermons nature ever preaches—the thundering serf [*sic*] of the mighty ocean; and how anyone can hear such a sermon and not have God in his thoughts, is past comprehension; but the Loving Father is not seen without other light.

18th.—We are now in latitude about 26 degrees, 30 minutes, and only 75 miles from the island of San Salvador, the first land discovered by Columbus. Again we have been down on the beach, long miles. This time it was principally shells; and a peck or so was our spoils. We find, also, many curious-shaped sponges, of which we secured a fine collection. This whole coast, for four hundred miles, seems to be a fine sand beach, with an occasional cropping out of the shell rock.

19th.—Talk about fishing! You ought to have been with us! Yesterday, four of us caught three hundred pounds in two hours; surf fishing. To-day I went out, and in less than an hour caught over one hundred pounds. The method of fishing is to take a long strong line and large hook (I used my old cod line) with a heavy sinker, and coiling about seventy-five feet of line on the beach, for a free run out, grasping the line about four feet from the hook, whirling it and the sinker around your head to give it momentum, let it fly far out into the surf. You feel a bite, and begin to pull. He is a ten pound "crevalle!" and you soon find you have business on hand—an extra heavy wave, urged by the incoming tide, sweeps up over your feet, but you mind it not; that fish is "business," and the line slips in your hands; but he finds you are business also, and you grasp firmer the line, and pull harder, as the big fellow rolls and tumbles over and over as a surging wave strikes him and urges him ashore, and you soon have him flopping along the beach, and safe out of the water. Now, as he croaks like a hoarse raven, as you remove the hook, you can take a good look at him.

The crevalle is of the mackerel family, judging by the form of his tail; but the shoulders somewhat flattened, are stocky and heavy, and the full head rounds off short towards the mouth. You rebait your hook and repeat the whirl, and cast, in comes another; and so on as long as the tide runs in; for they bite only on the flood tide. I caught two of twelve pounds each, others of from four to nine pounds each, and a few blue fish. But you soon discover you are getting tired, and that every pore is streaming with perspiration, and you know not what to do with the greater amount of your catch, and you wind up your lines to go to dinner. We sometimes vary the sport in a troll with our sail boat, inside the bar.[28]

For seven days we have had sunny skies, at times a little too warm in the sun; but the hours pass all too quickly in our varied occupations.

We shall probably leave here tomorrow, on our return, but to visit new localities, up the side rivers, and other lagoons. I sent No. 1 of "Boating" on this river, this morning, by a boat starting up the river. It will be "of age" before it reaches you.

I laid in my berth this morning a long time listening to the drum fish. At times the sound was like a quick succession of blows on a heavy bass drum a half mile distant; at other times a steady roll like the largest steamboat whistle ten miles distant, and might well be taken for the distant whistle of the *Marine City,* and as I write I hear the distant drumming of this curious fish.[29]

AT JUPITER INLET

Feb. 19th.—Jupiter Inlet.—This morning was warm, with occasional rain, the first for a week, but we ran our boat across the river, to take a search for some wild lemons. We passed through a piece of tangled hammock, full of pawpaw [*sic*] trees, with the fruit already as large as black walnuts, a wild profusion of all sorts of climbers, and strange plants, some of them in blossom. But for a trail, cut out to a field beyond, we could not have passed through. We came out into a cleared field, cultivated by the lighthouse keeper, and found ourselves in an entrenched camp of the shell mound builders. On examination, I found two parallel ridges about eight or ten feet high, running back from large bluff ridge mounds, at right angles with the two, along the line of the river, near the inlet, for twenty rods and ten or fifteen feet; the two lines striking the shore line in the center, and the shore line cut through where the valley or passage-way between the two lines join; thus forming a narrow opening out to the river, and through which is a pathway now used to get through the almost perpendicular bluff mound facing the water. Following parallel lines back from the river, some forty rods, they turn off to the right and left, and enclose in an oval shape, this arable field of about two acres. The embankments, which seem to be principally oyster shells, in some places depressed, but all clearly defined. I did not follow around the whole field, on account of the bushes, but could see portions of the ridge all around the field. I found pieces of broken pottery in all parts of the mounds, and in the enclosed field. Some of them are plain, and some show the punch ornamentation. Further up Jupiter river are more shell mounds; in fact this whole country is covered with shells, in large mound masses, and in wide-spread fields. The mounds on or near Banana river are of an extinct species of small cockle shell-fish.[30]

After dinner another "norther" came down upon us, but, well sheltered in our little boat cabin, we can defy any cold you can send as far south as this.

20th.—It blew a gale all night, and blankets were comfortable; and I think the mercury would mark 50° this morning, but a warm breakfast, a fine sail up the river, and a clear sky, makes it all right, though the norther continues.

Pardon me for so much talk about the weather, but it is in the main so delightful, we do not feel like thinking; we only seek to enjoy. We think of the loved ones at home, and wish they could enjoy this trip with us; but though we have not heard a word from home for three weeks, we do not worry over it. How many tourists we find who spoil their whole trip by worrying about imaginary evils they could not help were they real.

We get our wood for cooking in a bag, the captain going ashore and cutting a bag full for our little cook stove. Our stove does wonders. Capt. Carlin bakes good bread, and does all kinds of cooking with it.

During our sail up the river to-day I shot a couple of pelicans, from the boat. One of them measured eight feet from tip to tip of wings. They are found here in great numbers. Tonight we are back to our anchorage, near the inlet. We varied our fare again today by boiled cabbage, from the bud or heart growth at the top of the palmetto. Raw, it is very tender, and tastes like a young chestnut. The tender edible part is about three inches in diameter and eight inches long, and formed in thick circular layers, from which comes the heavy stalk of the leaves. It is very tender, boiled; but its qualities, for relish, are rather negative, than otherwise.

Feb. 21st.—We took a sail this morning up Jupiter river, a stream which forms a junction with the Indian at this point, and landed for a stroll on the shores. Another high shell mound, thickly covered with small timber and bushes. These "air plants" found throughout Florida, are here in great numbers. The largest can be seen scattered on both dead and live trees, and is shaped very much like the pineapple plant, and puts forth a center stalk covered with a profusion of red and pink flowers. It seems to fasten to the bark of the tree, with roots, but for protection of position, and not for sustenance, for they thrive just as well if detached and hung up by a string. I found in the woods, also, another small kind, with a bulb like a small onion, and in rows or clusters, attached to the dry bark of dead trees, putting forth two lance-shaped leaves, green and glossy; this kind seeding on a central stalk, with one flower and seed-pod. There are other delicate fern-like varieties.

I have been out again examining the apparently fortified work of the shell mound-builders. With much labor, I pushed through the tangled brush and vines, one of which, by the way, I have no doubt is the original model of the wicked barbed wire which is used for fences, for it is exactly like it, and about as innocent an obstruction to push through. Once through these obstructions, I came out to a large open field, completely covered with the saw palmetto, a bush with many stalks and leaves, rising from a central root, from two to three feet, and falling outward in every direction, with the same fan-leaf of the real palmetto, but the sharp-edged stalks serrated like the sharp teeth of a fine saw; and it is no child's play to push through a thick field of it. I found the embankments did not encircle the back side of the field, and were much depressed in height, but clearly defined, and leaving a large opening out to a circular mound, a few rods out in an outer field, made of sand thrown up on the spot, and about ten feet high, sixty feet diameter at the base, and very symmetrical. It was evidently a burial mound, or a point of observation over the large low palmetto plains beyond.[31]

23d.—Up comes our anchor, and up goes our sail to a fair wind for a home-ward start. Farewell to Jupiter! Right royally have we enjoyed our week's so-journ here, in fishing, shooting, sailing and exploring the sea beach and the shell mounds. Sweet has been our sleep, with the rolling surf for our lullaby, and the music of the song birds for our morning call.

There is no place on the Florida coast so beautiful for a summer resort as Jupiter inlet, but few tourists visit it. Even sportsmen who come here, seldom come as far as Jupiter. A few gentlemen from the eastern states camp there every winter. The tall light-house recedes, the tall palmettoes fall below the vision, we turn into the tortuous narrow channel of the lower narrows, and Jupiter is lost to us.[32]

ORANGES, LEMONS, POTATOES, ETC.

February 24th.—We laid to yesterday, to procure an addition to our larder; for we have devoured provisions fearfully of late. Capt. Carlin managed to get a ham, some coffee and about a peck of potatoes: the potatoes costing the modest sum of one dollar for the peck.

From Lucie we sailed over to another inlet from the ocean, about fifty miles north of Jupiter. No large vessels can come into this river. I have no doubt one can wade over three-fourths the area of water. We have tried to get a few eggs of the settlers here, but in vain. Plenty of hens, but no eggs. Dogs soon die here, also northern horses and cattle.

25th.—Last night we tried to get back to the main river, but the wind failed us, and darkness overtook us in one of the wide side lagoons, by some islands, where we got aground, but the captain jumped overboard and pulled us off, and after finding water in which we could float, anchored for the night. I remarked to Sutton, "Early to bed and early to rise," and turned in to my little bed, but he being already "healthy, wealthy and wise," was bound to sit up and "have a fish." The idea of fishing in a puddle the captain had just been wading in, not ten rods distant! and after dark, too! But very soon I heard a splashing and thrashing in the water, and Sutton cried out, "I've got him!" and sure enough, he had hooked a big bass, but lost him. You may guess the fellow abed went into his pants in quick time, and coatless and hatless, was soon casting his line in the puddle. In less than five minutes he had a fifteen pounder channel or sea bass, which was safely landed in the small boat; and soon after Sutton caught another about the same size. We had several other bites, but lost them, for they pulled like a horse. Just as we were pulling in our lines, Sutton hooked a five foot shark, and we actually pulled him alongside the boat before he parted the line, and carried off the hook. But I tell you a fifteen pound sea bass is a gamy fellow!

While at anchor this morning, for breakfast, we were much interested in watching the pelicans fishing for their breakfast. Soaring a few feet above the water, with their long beaks pointed downward as they intently watched for fish, they would suddenly flash into the water, making the spray fly in every direction several feet high.

After breakfast, another head wind came up, and we sailed over to the site of old Fort Capron. Strolling on shore we found little remained of this old Seminole war station, save the ruins of the brick chimney, a lot of oleander bushes over twenty feet high, in blossom; and a lot of wild lemons, bearing, from which we selected a supply for lemonade. We saw here also two or three date palm trees. A squatter has located near here, and built a palmetto leaf thatched cottage, which seems to be very comfortable, on the top of an old pre-historic burial mound. The shore is strewn with small fragments of pre-historic pottery, of the most ancient type. In fact, some of it is washed out of a solid shell rock, which has been broken up by the waves, and I picked out of the rock with my jackknife, some pieces embedded firmly in with the shells.[33]

We had a grand chowder to-day out of the big bass. How Sutton did eat! and to tell the truth the "other fellow" kept him good company! We rise every morning about sunrise, wash on the deck, sometimes in fresh, and sometimes in salt water; throw up our cabin curtains for a free circulation of the soft air, while the skipper heats up his little stove and gets breakfast, to which we do ample justice, while the birds on shore carol to us their sweet songs, and the sharks and porpoises display themselves in the water, and the little silver mullets are jumping three feet or more out of the water all around us, the pelicans are fishing for their breakfast, and the ducks, and coots and cormorants are passing constantly, engaged in some laudable work. The wind changed this morning, and we moved off finely for the upper narrows. We saw two men digging up a barrel of something which was buried under the sand. Capt. Carlin says it is whiskey. Can it be there are "moonshiners" here?[34] A dozen miles' sail brought us to the upper narrows, made by a series of beautiful palmetto and mangrove islands. We ran ashore on one of the islands, and while the captain went ashore for wood, Mr. Sutton and self took the yawl-boat and pulled out into the river a few rods, for a little fishing. Sutton soon hooked a shark, some three and a half feet long, and we had to gaff him into the boat to save the hook, and then he disputed possession so vigorously I had to watch my chance and thrust my jack-knife into his throat, severing the blood-vessel, and that soon quieted him. Soon after, I hooked a bass, and we brought him into the boat with the gaff. He was judged to weigh twenty-five pounds. He was, by measure, three feet long, and twenty inches girt around the shoulders. A lot of large cat-fish were made no account of. We had no delay in having a glorious dinner of a part of that bass.

This has been another perfect day. We can ask no change.

Feb. 26.—This morning we went ashore on one of the nesting islands of the pelicans. It is too early for laying, but the old nests are there, by hundreds; and hundreds of pelicans were in the vicinity. The trees on the island of about two acres of land, have all been killed by the roosting of the birds. The nests were made of sticks and reeds, and were built principally on the ground, and raised about eight or ten inches, and about a foot and a half at the base, in size. A few sentinel birds had made their nests in some branches of the dead mangrove trees. The river in this vicinity is noted for the green turtle fisheries. The turtles are caught in nets and put in pens made in the stockade style, by driving poles in the mud, in shallow water, till ready for shipment.[35]

We hailed Turkey creek, where there is an orange grove, the last on the river going south, with pleasure, for we had been out of oranges a week, and were rejoiced with a new supply, from the trees.

Feb. 27.—Weather-bound again, by a strong norther; and as we swung at anchor near two very large shell mounds on the east of the river, this morning, our little boat danced merrily, but the captain wired up his one piece of stove pipe, and we managed to have a good hot meal, just the same. Every north wind, we imagine snow storms in the north, while we stroll around in our shirt sleeves; but we have heard nothing outside the Indian river country for a month. And so, while the norther blows, we ride our boat at anchor in a sheltered cove, while we stroll on shore, dig in the shell mounds, or sleep, as we choose.

Feb. 28th.—Well, we are out of potatoes. Did you ever get out of potatoes? and did your wife tell you to send some home for dinner? and when you forgot the potatoes, and was met at noon with the inquiry as to where they were, and you replied, "bless me! I forgot them!" how quick came the reply, "then we can't have any dinner!" And what is dinner without potatoes, either in your home, or with wanderers on Indian river? But *you* can get them in a dozen places within a half a mile; not so with *us;* but Capt. Carlin says he knows of but one place for twenty miles where there is a hope of getting them, and that is at a colored man's place about five miles away, across the river, and the white caps rolling high between. But we must have potatoes, and up comes the anchor, and up goes a reefed sail, and we move out of our sheltered harbor into the howling wind. We had some lofty tumbling, and Sutton would persist in sitting on the upper side of the boat, and wishing he was ashore, but we passed over safely, and came to anchor in shallow water by Peter Wright's, and Carlin went ashore. Blessed be P. Wright, may his shadow and potatoes never be less! for ere long we saw the Capt. coming down to the shore with a bag on his back. Now perhaps you don't care a fig what was in the bag, but had you been one of us ravenous fellows, and realized that this was our only chance for potatoes for four days, you would have shouted, when you saw the bag containing a bushel of the finest sweet potatoes, fresh from the sand.[36]

March 1st.—Laid at anchor last night in the wind, without shelter, save our cabin, but managed to sleep pretty well. This morning the wind abated a little, and we worked up to the large shell mound, at the mouth of Banana river, of which I spoke in a former letter.

The air is cool and bracing in this "norther," and we are perfectly comfortable without any extra clothing.

Banana river, up which we propose to return, is another salt lagoon, branching off from Indian, nearer the ocean, with Merritt's island, twenty-eight miles long, between the two rivers. This island is a few feet high, and underlaid with shell rock, which crops out in many places in the bank, forming a natural wall. We have made only eleven miles to-day, against the head wind, and we come to anchor to-night under the lee of a low island, which breaks off the waves.

March 2.—We remain at anchor until afternoon, and go ashore for a stroll inland. We pushed our way through a dense growth of reed grass eight feet high, and came out to dry land, and a little clearing in the hammock, on the edge of a widespread saw palmetto plain. Here was a small board cottage a few orange trees, bearing some fine fruit, a few neglected flower shrubs, but all deserted and desolate. It was the same old story we hear so many times in Florida. A start with great anticipations, then sickness, perhaps death, or a flood, such as they had in this section and on the St. John's river last fall, which covers the place with water; and then desertion, or ruinous sale to speculators. It was a sad sight. In a little shed with only a roof shelter, was the rusty *debris* of a home outfit. On the ground, among many other things, was a lady's hand-satchel, the leather rotten and the frame all rust, which seemed to speak of an almost sudden flight, even for dear life.[37]

Sailing up and down the river, we often see a little clearing and a cabin, and we ask Capt. Carlin, "Who lives there?" "No one, sir," is the frequent reply, and the same story of discouragement and abandonment under the awakening from the delusion of a flowery home and orange groves and wealth in Florida; and I think there are ten failures to one success, both on this and St. John's river. God pity the northern women and children who are doomed to a home in almost any new location in Florida; for they must bid farewell to almost everything that constitutes a home in the north. And to any man who dreams of settling here, I would say come and investigate through all seasons of the year, before you think of moving.

March 3.—We went ashore, this morning, at Wilson and Burnham's grove— one of the best, and yields about 75,000 oranges a year, for which they get, on the ground, about $1.50 per hundred.[38] And these people have, if they have any idea of a comfortable home, condemned themselves and families to twenty or more years worse than northern imprisonment, isolated from all the refinements and advantages of society and homes. This is about five miles from Cape Canaveral. We have had windy weather, and one rainy day, but this morning the warm sun comes out again, at times rather too warm. Just now I thought it a little mixed to be driven to the shade the third of March, and pulling off my coat, thought to brave it out; but had to give it up, and seek shelter from the sun in the shade of our little cabin, where, with a free circulation of air, it was just right.

The northern connection of Banana with Indian river is a third of a mile wide, bordered with marsh land, and is very shallow. Our boat draws only about eight or ten inches of water, but we get out of the channel and aground at times, in the middle of the river, and Capt. Carlin jumps over and "boosts" her into the channel. At one place where the abrupt bend gave us a head wind, the captain waded in the deepest part of the water and pushed the boat a mile or more. These are splendid waters, usually, for timid sailors, for you can wade in three-fourths of the river.

March 4th.—We awake this morning at anchor off Titusville, and have just eaten our last meal on board; and begin to pull out our "things" to go ashore. We part with the *Ella* with regret, as well as pleasure. For over three weeks she has carried us safely and comfortably, through smooth waters and rough waters, with fair winds, and adverse wind, and we had become almost at-tached to our little cabin, with its hay mattresses; for it has been our home, and our little boat stove, that has cooked our corn cakes, and bread, and po-tatoes, and meats, our coffee so capitally—even the little copper hooped water cask, and the storm battered filters, which gave us pure water, and the pine board that served us so well for a table for many a meal, which we eat with such keen relish; and not least our faithful Capt. Charles R. Carlin, who has tried so well to please us; to all, good bye. Around the winter fires of future Februarys in the far north, two thousand miles away, we shall remember these pleasant summer days, and blue skies, and balmy airs of February, 1879, on Indian river.

As we go ashore, with our yawl-boat piled with bags of "curiosities," and baggage and guns, the same warm sun shines out of the blue sky, and the gentle ripple of the broad river in a western breeze answers back to us, "Good bye."

I do not know if I have interested any of your readers in these homely sketches; I have tried only to give a concise sketch of our trip, believing that next to the personal enjoyment of travel is the perusal of unpretentious narrative of the experience of the travelers.

We move for St. Augustine to-morrow.[39]

FACTS FROM FLORIDA

St. Augustine, March 13.—We left Titusville on the 6th, and after an eight-miles ride on a wooden raft, by mule power, came out to Salt lake, the St. Johns river connection, to find the little steamer a mile from shore on account of low water; some two feet lower than last winter, and over ten feet lower than the marks on the trees which show the high water of the great storm of last September. This storm, of which very little was said in the Florida papers, was a very remarkable one. It rained in torrents, with high wind, for nearly forty-eight hours, and the rainfall was simply immense; for it raised the water over hundreds of square miles of the widespread marsh and lake region of the upper St. Johns and Indian river country, and the everglades, ten feet above the usual high line. Almost the whole of southern Florida was inundated; all the wharves on both rivers several feet under water, or carried away, many houses and stores at the landings had two or three feet of water in them, and the groves and other fields covered with water. Thousands of cattle perished, and nothing has so discouraged the settlers since the great freeze in 1835, when the mercury was only 7° above zero and killed nearly all the orange and other fruit trees in the state.

We had to pole out to the stream on a large scow lighter. On our way out the alligators were showing their heads on the water, and I could not resist the temptation to a shot, my ball went through his head, and our captain had one of his hands pick the victim up and hoist him on the scow. It was a small "gator," only between four and five feet long.

Although in the aggregate the alligator is not a handsome reptile, in detail he is quite symmetrical, and its soft velvety skin, with its well arranged sectional marks, well formed claw feet, and delicate fin edge of his tail go far to improve our estimate of him on close inspection, and the young ones are often carried north for pets. At lake Jessup, a few miles above Palatka, we visited some very large sulphur springs. These waters were so strongly impregnated with the lower regions that the air was odorous of sulphur. At this point, called Clifton Springs, there is a landing-dock and a well-filled store with all kinds of goods for the interior settlements. We met here a man with a light ox-cart and oxen, who said he had come sixty miles for a stock of family stores. He had been twelve days on the way, hunting all the way, and brought in a load of venison, for which he received enough to buy his goods to take back.

On the steamer, down the river, we fell in with an excursion party from Georgia, and were invited to join them, and take advantage of a special night train from Tocoi to St. Augustine, instead of stopping over Sunday at Palatka. The train was on hand at Tocoi, and a moonlight ride brought us in here at midnight.

St. Augustine is the place of all others for a quiet sojourn in Florida. The hotels are full, and we spend our time in strolling among the old ruins, curiosity stores, sailing, wandering on the beaches, and other excursions. Yesterday we went in a little steamer to Matanzas, eighteen miles down the lagoon. Matanzas is noted as being the place where the Spanish Governor, over three hundred years ago, murdered in cold blood over two hundred shipwrecked Frenchmen, because they were "heretics," and for another old curious coquina fort, of which there is no history, but supposed to be two or three hundred years old. The foundations have settled, and there are great rents in the walls from top to bottom. It is an upright oblong square some thirty feet high, with a lower section of about half that height, and the tops of both sections are covered with a dense growth of bushes. The lower section was no doubt intended as a platform on which mounted cannon commanded the inlet from the ocean.[40]

"Blue-skied Saint Augustine" has proved worthy the name during the month, there having been but two or three stormy days, and nothing can be more pleasant in the way of pastime, than a sojourn here during a part of the winter months, but as for a resident home in Florida, increased observation only confirms my last winter's experience, that this state is the most undesirable place in the United States. The soil around St. Augustine is to all appearance as good as in any part of Florida, and yet, for one hundred and fifty years, the early settlers did not raise enough provisions to save them from actual starvation, if the regular supply ships from Spain failed them; and I doubt if the result would be much different to-day if all outside supply were cut off; at least they would be confined to a very poor living. But they have oranges? oh yes; very sweet oranges; and very odorous is the perfume of the orange blossoms; but it is a very significant fact that nearly every orange grove, except such as are held by wealthy northern men as luxuries, is for sale. In fact, everything is for sale, as a rule; for experience has taken the romance out of "homes in Florida." Of course there are exceptions; and others being here and cannot sell, are braving it out, and will whistle strong for their situation.

We hear little of the summer experiences of a summer sojourn in Florida. St. Augustine is probably as desirable a summer residence as any here, but they had forty deaths here, last summer, of which the papers did not speak. It was the result of some malignant fever; the residents declare it was a malarial fever. But it killed just the same.

We leave for Jacksonville to-day, and shall work towards home by easy stages. Very pleasant has been our sojourn; but we turn homeward with pleasure. For a permanent residence, there is no place like home; and that home [is] in the north.[41]

Adrian, March 27.—F. R. Stebbins, Esq., has returned from his Florida trip. His journeying up and down Indian river has given him an appearance of the dusky warrior. We are pleased to welcome him home [t]hough we shall miss his excellent ar[t]icles written for the *Times* during his travels.[42]

Adrian, March 28.—Indian river oranges, to be appreciated, should be tasted. Beals & Colvin have just received by express a few direct from the grove.[43]

4   1880 Our Florida Letter

Adrian, Feb. 3.—F. R. Stebbins, Esq., starts for Florida this afternoon.[1]

Tecumseh, Feb. 5.—Mr. N. M. Sutton started last Tuesday on his Florida trip. He expects to take very nearly the same route as he did last winter, but will give more attention to hunting. He proposes to shoot some bear and deer before his return. F. R. Stebbins, of Adrian, goes with him, and they expect to be gone about two months. We presume the readers of the *Herald* would like to hear from him occasionally.[2]

Adrian, Feb. 19.—An interesting letter from our indefatigable traveler, F.R.S., has been received and will appear soon.[3]

THE SNOWY SOUTH

Montgomery, Ala., Feb. 5th.—Leaving Adrian with a slight covering of snow on the ground, we found more at Cincinnati, and six or eight inches at Louisville, and the same depth all the way to Nashville. This was the 'snowy south' with a vengeance; and we queried if we might not go skating by the time we reached Florida. But before we reached Montgomery the snow disappeared, and we took courage. To-day, through the courtesy of J. Ben Gus, a former resident of Adrian, we have been riding around the city, which claims a population of 20,000, and is the central depot of a very large cotton trade. At this place, near the close of the war, and the national troops were on their way to take possession of this city, the people gathered all the cotton in the city into one of the outside cotton yards and warehouses and burned it, with one exception. A widow, with two boys, determined to save her only surplus means, and piling her cotton directly against her dwelling, awaited the advent of the "Yanks," who must spare her cotton or burn her house with it. Of course her cotton was saved, and became the only capital she could furnish to set her sons up in business. The foolish people who burned their cotton, felt peculiarly sheepish as they looked at its ashes and learned that not a bale of it if private property would have been molested.

We strolled through the halls of the capitol where for a time the Congress of the leaders of the Confederate government met and spouted their high-sounding words of treason, and from the cupola had a fine view of the city and level surrounding country. We also looked in to an artificial ice factory, where by chemical action in the passage of ether through a prepared enclosure by means of a pipe, cases of water are frozen in about nine hours. The blocks of ice are slipped from the cases and transported to all parts of the country. The manufacturers realize about one cent per pound.

The manufacture of cotton seed oil is carried on here on an extensive scale. This mill, which like nearly all the manufacturing enterprises of the south is carried on by northern capital and skill, works up 3,000 bushels of seed a day, and we were shown over 40,000 bags of seed in store. The manager showed us the entire process. First the cleaning from the seed the particles of cotton which remain when the seed comes from the gin, and a sheet of fine fibre cotton some three feet wide and nearly an inch thick runs constantly from the machine. This cotton is sent to the batting factories. The seed then runs into another machine, which hulls it, leaving only the "meat;" this running into a boiler, which separates the hull from the inner portion, the hulls passing to the furnace room, and furnishes the principal fuel used to generate the steam for power. The clean seed then passes to the crusher, then is ground, put in thin canvass [sic] bags, and subjected to immense hydraulic pressure to press out the oil. This oil, they say, furnishes the material for most of the "olive oil" used in America, being sent first to Italy for the transformation. It is also said to be used by large hotels in place of lard for cooking.

Titusville, Feb. 13th.—We arrived at Jacksonville on the 7th, and after securing our stores for our cruise on Indian river, came directly on to this point. The weather all the way had been rainy and chilly, but yesterday the sun came out so warm we were glad to get in the shade, and this morning the weather is all we can desire. We find our skipper all ready for a four weeks' cruise. We see corn here tasseled out and the ears silked out, but oh such corn! Tube roses are blooming in the open garden and we have ripe tomatoes on the table. The oranges are as good as ever, and the finest two cents a piece. The banana fruit is maturing, and there having been no frost, the tall plants with their huge leaves are looking finely. If the wind serves, we shall explore the lagoon north of here before we go down to Jupiter inlet.[4]

OUR FLORIDA LETTER

On board the *Ella,* Feb. 12.—Capt. Carlin reported the *Ella* ready for sailing this morning, and after stowing away sundry provisions, guns, blankets, and other bedding, we hoisted sail to a fine wind, and steered for a few days' exploration of the north end of the river, some fifteen miles above Titusville.

The weather is all that we could desire; mercury about 79°, and a soft southerly breeze, which made sailing, as we reclined on our couches with our side cabin curtains raised, most enjoyable. This part of the river is about six miles wide, and a fine sheet of water, fringed with palmetto and pine groves.

About two p.m. we reached the head of the river, anchored in the mouth of Turnbul [Turnbull] creek, a fresh stream, which drains wide extensive marshes at this point, dotted with occasional palmetto hammocks, adding a fine feature to the lowlands of the swamps.

We sailed without wood for our little stove, and the captain and myself took the small boat, and made for a little palmetto grove a half mile away, our course being through a crooked bayou, fringed with tall reedy grass. I saw the dead stalks of some summer weed which were three inches in diameter near the root, and ten feet high. On our way I brought down our first duck, with my Parker, and soon after a small alligator showed his nose above the water, and I completely demolished it with my Winchester rifle. He turned up on the water, apparently dead; and we rowed over to him, and Capt. Carlin reached to take him by the fore leg which was raised, but no sooner was he touched than he gave a flop and went to the bottom to die some more before he let folks handle him. We found a beautiful dry grove in which were many red cedars mixed with the palms, and tall slim trees of small size, I think a species of boxwood, but called here "cracked wood," I think from the fact that the smooth bark is just about the color of the skin of the cadaverous Florida "cracker." At 4 p.m. we partook of our first meal on our boat, and had the first cup of clear good coffee since we left home.

The day closes with a clear sunset, and we go to our couches well pleased with our first day on the river.

13th.—A fair morning, with a light breeze still from the south, and we sit in our shirt sleeves while breakfast is preparing. The ducks are feeding in the marsh pools, and various birds of large and small sizes pass and repass. Mr. Sutton tries to hit an alligator, at long range, which just shows the top of his head above water, and is difficult to hit at any long distance.

Breakfast disposed of, we all take the small boat and explore the creek up into the country all the way for several miles through reedy marshes, and past palmetto groves, and live oaks completely covered with beautiful festoons of the grey southern moss. We brought back lots of ducks, and Sutton hit a couple of "gators," but they escaped by sinking.

After dinner, with a fair wind, we made sail for the celebrated "Dummit[t]'s" orange grove on the east side of the river, nine miles distant, and anchored in the bay for the night.

14th.—We anchored half a mile from the shore, to avoid mosquitoes which infest this shore, but no sooner did darkness come than a perfect swarm of the fiercest fellows come down upon us, and actually drove us to our nettings for protection. How they did sing around! but they could not get us, and we slept in peace. In the morning they were all gone. After breakfast we took the small boat, and visited the orange grove, two miles away on a lagoon, and situated on a fine piece of hummock [sic] land fringed at the water edge with palmettos. This was once occupied by the Spaniards, and after them there grew up a large grove of wild oranges. These trees were grafted some thirty years ago, by Capt. Dummit[t], who discovered the grove when in service in the Seminole war. He also added new trees, until now there are 2,500 old bearing trees, many of them ten inches in diameter, and twenty-five or thirty feet high; and they pick from this grove on an average, 250,000 oranges, and the ground is now covered with thousands of wind-dropped fruit, which cannot be shipped. These oranges are very fine, and we carried away a supply for our boat, for which the keeper would not take pay. Picking also some limes for lemonade, we took our way back to the *Ella,* and moved for the other shore to prepare for our trip down to Jupiter Inlet, where we went last winter.[5]

I shall endeavor to avoid sameness in my letters of last winter, and shall not repeat many things of interest reported at that time, but your readers must excuse at times unavoidable departures from this rule. But I hope to visit new localities, and confine my letters largely to them.[6]

SCENES AND INCIDENTS

On Board the Boat *Ella,* Feb. 15.—We had heavy rain last night. It has been regular summer weather for two days, the mercury ranging from 78° to 85°, but with this rain came, very acceptably, cooler air. We laid at anchor last night off Titusville, and the wind being fair we turned our prow southward this morning. We had one reef in our sail, and before we had been on our course a half hour a furious gale set in from the north, and no shelter for ten miles, and we could not beat back with our flat bottom boat and a small boat in tow, and we were obliged to "come to" in the wind, and roll in the gale, and a sea that would not disgrace Lake Huron, until the Captain lowered the "gaff," or top spar to the sail, to within ten feet of the deck, and the outer end as low as the main boom; thus forming a small bag of sail, low down, and we came on our course and drove before the gale to Fabers, where we came to anchor in shallow water. The *Ella* behaved splendidly, and we took no water over the ledge around the cockpit, and only a few waves broke over the storm deck; but the small boat would at times make for us on the top of a wave, but did not come on board. We went ashore at Fabers and dined with Irvin and his intelligent lady.

The wind abated about 4 p.m. and securing a new stock of eggs and oranges we moved down four miles and anchored for the night off Spratt's grove. This grove is peculiar; the trees growing in the midst of a palmetto forest, the palms being thinned out about half to make room for the orange trees, which were loaded with fine fruit, and hundreds rotting on the ground, some of them nearly four inches in diameter. The oranges here are so juicy we cannot cut one open with a sharp knife without the juice running from it, and they are very sweet. We dispose of a half dozen a day.[7]

16th.—This morning we up anchor and sailed three miles before breakfast, down to Williams' grove. Mr. Sutton and self rowed ashore and found the proprietor and his lady very willing to show us everything; the lady her flowers, guava jelly, citron preserves, etc.; the man his growing citrons, a yellow fruit hanging on a low shrub-like tree. This fruit is the same that is made into the dried citron of commerce, and these were some nine inches long and six or seven in diameter. We also saw the flowering guava, the tropical paw-paw [sic], also tamarind trees. We secured some of the seed of a beautiful flowering shrub now in blossom, called the ponceana [sic].[8] This coast for several miles is called Rockledge, from the cropping out of the bank the coquina, or shell rock.

From Spratts we crossed the river over to Merrit[t]'s island, about two miles distant, and visited the home of one Dr. W. Westfield [Wittfeld], whose grounds run over to Banana river, and are on quite an elevation for this country. Here they say they never, or at least hardly—well, no matter—have any frost, and we found vegetation in full leaf—ripe guavas, pawpaws [sic], lima beans, full grown cabbages, and other garden vegetables of various kinds. The doctor was cutting his sugar cane to send to the mill for syrup.[9] There is a fine old burial mound near the house, and his garden was the camp ground of the ancients, and is full of fragments of pottery.[10] From here we sailed to where we are now tied up, at the mouth of Banana river, and the foot of Merrit's island, under the bluff of the large prehistoric shell mound of which I wrote last year. The base of this mound is over forty rods wide, and it is thirty feet elevation, in the central part, composed of the clean shells of a now extinct species of cockle shell fish. How long ago this section was inhabited, one can surmise by this pile of shells from their daily food, and from the fact that I find here also pieces of pottery fully incorporated with the underlying shell rock.

Last night after dark we succeeded in netting a small mullet, the favorite food of other fishes. I soon had a piece on my hook, and swinging out some fifty feet of line from the shore, ere long I had a bite and landed our first sea bass, which weighed fourteen pounds. We find swarms of beautifully striped butterflies here, so tame they came around us like flies. While at anchor here a man appeared who had rolled a large cask, end over end, from some wreck on the clean shore, a mile distant, and through bushes and saw palmetto obstructions. Toward night we moved about two miles to where an old man from New Jersey is trying to improve the land, and if any spot on the earth is good missionary ground for improvement, it is the particular spot on which this man has located, for it is nearly all white sand covered with pine and saw palmetto. We found the old man out in a strip of land a rod or two wide, from which he has grubbed the huge snake-like roots of the dwarf palmetto which fill the ground. His name is Haddock, and as he raised from his stooping posture as he worked, with difficulty and supported his attenuated form which carried the weight of seventy or eighty years, on the top of his hoe handle, he presented a curious picture—a mess of sundried skin drawn over bones of medium structure, around which a lot of rags, surmounted by an old short cape on his shoulders, all held on by straps and strings, his head covered by an old coarse palmetto hat, and unable even with the aid of the hoe to stand erect, he presented as sad a specimen of humanity in connection with his surroundings, as one often looks upon. His eyes seemed to struggle for a little life only when he asked if we knew "his brother in Detroit." We left him in the field, and looked into his cabin, on our return. It had one room some ten or twelve feet across, and contained a rude bedstead with netting, a table which was packed with a bushel of bottles of all kinds and sizes, a stool, and various cooking utensils, a cook stove, some side pork hanging on the beams above, and the rest of the room filled with tools and implements of various kinds, and everything, stove, pans, bedstead and netting, all one color from smoke. He is attempting to build a new house, of coquina, palmetto roots and plaster. I looked at it, the walls being partly up, with an eye to description, but soon gave it up with the remark "it cannot be described!" and it cannot, except by picture illustration. The ground plan had no form known to science and it had four chimneys in a room not over twelve feet across, with three fire places. One of them on the outside of the house. He has also been digging a crooked canal some ten rods long to bring the river to an artificial pool back of the house, and no nearer than the river now is, and must have moved, with a great rude wheelbarrow, a thousand cubic yards of sand, and piled much of it up around his new house, but a few feet from it. And here this poor old man lives alone, and God only knows what must be his aspirations, thoughts, and memories of past years, as he toils on, and must ere long die alone. We left his place saddened and humbled before God, when we thought of our own blessings of families and friends, with thankful hearts remembering who hath made us to differ from this man, who seems to have abandoned all hope when he entered into this barren sand bank in Florida, to die unattended, and only remembered as we remember the shell mound builders by the strong work he will leave behind him.[11]

We moved on again three miles, and anchored close to the shore, behind a point which gave us shelter from a strong wind. We soon had our lines set and Sutton caught a seventeen pound bass. I caught only a large cat-fish, which a possum carried off during the night. This morning I was up at sunrise and at it again, and soon landed an eighteen pounder; and not long after Sutton pulled in one which weighed seventeen and a half pounds, and we roped them and kept them alive in the water until, we sailed, about 9 o'clock, to the west shore, four miles, to Peter Wright's place to get a supply of sweet potatoes to take to Jupiter. We gave Mrs. W. a seventeen pound bass. Here we found pine apples commencing to fruit. We have not been troubled by mosquitoes so far since we left Titusville.

We had rain again last night, but to-day is fair, with mercury 78°, and a fine breeze. A little warm strolling on shore, but just right reposing with free circulation in our boat shelter cabin. We lie here to-night at anchor, and move on in the morning.[12]

SAILING ON SUMMER SEAS

Feb. 19th.—We are now navigating the river on our way to Jupiter very lei-surely, and after leaving Peter Wright's, and seeing the last of his spouse clean-ing the big bass with a hatchet, we sailed over to the east shore, to a point easy of access to the ocean.[13] The mercury this morning 76°, through the day 80°, with a fine breeze. On our way over we hailed a boat passing up and sent out my last letter, to Titusville, 65 miles north. On the east shore at this point the land between Indian river and the ocean is only about forty rods wide, and ten feet high. The settlers of this region have commenced to cut through the sand, by which they hope to get a new outlet to the ocean.

The same grand surf as always was breaking along shore as far as we could see, in each direction. After laying in a new stack of wood we sailed back to the east shore, farther down, and anchored in the mouth of Sebastian river for the night.

Feb. 20.—We are pushing on for the first narrows this morning. These nar-rows are caused by the number of mangrove islands in this part of the river. We caught but one bass at Sebastian, for our breakfast; and two fine sharks for a breakfast for the buzzards. We didn't come down here exactly to feast buzzards and other birds, but they find a good living in our wake all the same.

Our next point was Indian river inlet. We tied up here for the night, and a fishing in the surf the next day. The foliage is in very fine color, and the weather like a pleasant June in the north. A great many pelicans resort to this locality, and are constantly lying around, and congregating on a sand bar some five hundred yards off. Eagles, fish hawks, man-of-war birds, and a dozen other kinds are around us. The boilers of some old steamer's wreck are rising above the water a few rods from shore, outside the inlet, and the wreck of a government steamer sunk during the Seminole war is seen inside.

Feb. 21.—Rained during the night, but all fair this morning; and after the most important duty, breakfast; we go for surf fishing. We caught in a short time sixteen fine sea bass, from five to ten pounds each. Pretty soon I felt a heavy bite, and pulling in found I had hold of a monster of some kind. At first I supposed it a shark; and finding I could hold my own with him, and my strong tackle holding, I gradually pulled him ashore, the surf occasionally giving him a tumble shoreward, which you may be sure I quickly took advantage of in pulling in; and at last by hard pulling I had him on the sand beach. It was a large "Sting-ray," too heavy for our balances, but was judged to weigh over forty-five pounds. His body was flat; in shape a little out of square, with his head and tail at opposite points or angles of the square, and two feet four inches across one way, and two feet the other, and the tail or "whip," two feet eight inches long besides. The body about seven inches thick, white on the under side and dark on the upper. About a third of the distance from the body, in the whip, which was about two inches in diameter at the body, and tapered down to one fourth of an inch, was a very hard and sharp sting, covered with sharp barbs, the sting being about four inches long. I hope to be able to cure the whip and bring it home. Before dark we moved over to St. Lucie, and anchored for the night.

During the night Mr. Sutton caught a four-foot shark, on a set hook from the boat. We expected mail at Lucie, but got none, and were obliged to move on without any hope of getting any for three weeks more. The last news from home being the *Times* of the 6th of February.

We entered the lower narrows about noon; and the passage under a clear sky and a fair "balmy breeze" was one of rare beauty.

The green glossy mangroves coming down to the water's edge, now and then a palmetto, and a rubber tree, and vines and flowers, our narrow channels winding all points of the compass, now and then opening out into a miniature lake with jutting mangrove points, and cozy little coves and bays, all silent, save the occasional rustle of the palmetto leaves, and the distant roar of the surf on the ocean shore. And thus for nine miles we glided along this changing, charming scene of beauty, until we rounded the point into Jupiter river and came to anchor near the light house, just as the great lantern began to flash out its bright light over the ocean. During the last three miles of this trip the river all around us was alive with "pompano" jumping sideways from the water, and skipping along as one would skip a flat stone. Two of them struck the sides of our small boat with thuds which threatened to split the sides, and we heard several strike the bottom of our large boat.

Our one coconut tree at Jupiter has grown finely since last year, and the little coconuts are now set and as large as small apples. We are now anchored in a little cove formed by a sand bar close to the inlet from the sea, and are paying due attention to surf fishing, but a few rods distant.

The 23d we caught in three hours seventy five lbs of crevalle, of from three to ten pounds weight. The 24th, before breakfast, I caught near our boat, twenty-three pounds of blue fish, and crevalle, and ladyfish. The bluefish went directly into the frying pan.

Feb. 25th.—I could only register a ten pound crevalle this morning, as we had but a few minutes of right tide, but about 4 p.m. the tide was right, and Mr. Sutton and self caught twenty blue fish and crevalle, all weighing eighty pounds.

Feb. 26th.—I caught my largest crevalle this morning, and the largest anyone has caught. It weighed fifteen pounds. I caught also four blue fish three and four pounds each. Occasionally we get hold of some big fish which tears loose. I had a forty pound bass [al]most in shore yesterday, but he escaped. I think this will give you a fair sample of our fishing experience so far.[14] The birds near our boat are very tame. One poor large grey sea gull is our pet, because he has a broken leg, and we feed him. He alights on the beach close by, day after day. As I write he sits not thirty feet distant, watching our culinary operations; and crows and buzzards furnish as much amusement by their antics and petty fights over some dead fish not six rods distant. Of course we do not shoot them.

We shall probably move up Jupiter river to-morrow, what we shall find there time will disclose.

We have our four-pound pine-apple which Cap. Carlin picked from his garden a little before it was ripe. It will be in good order for dessert in a day or two.

Six large ocean steamers have passed here, about two miles out, in two days. We suppose they are the Havana and New Orleans boats.

The weather has been fine for nearly a week—plenty warm—ranging 80° or a little more during the day, at times 85°.

The sharks here at Jupiter so far have broken all our tackle.[15]

MORE FISHING AND BOATING

Feb. 27.—We are still at Jupiter inlet, and have a full week of unsurpassed weather, except it has been a little too warm. We moved our anchorage to-day up to the light-house landing, and had our boat and crew, and a lot of crevalle and blue fish, the largest weighing fifteen pounds, photographed by the assistant light-keeper.[16]

We have had fine feasting here on the blue fish, fresh from the blue waters of the ocean. We tried for the large sharks which infest the inlet. We had large hooks with chains attached, and lines almost as large as a clothes line, but they rolled up in our lines and bit them apart and went off with the hooks and chains. But we shall rig new ones.

Feb. 28.—Just before sundown yesterday we took the small boat and went up to Jupiter river and shot three pelicans, as they flew over us. We have skinned two of them, and shall try and preserve them for mounting. We took another long stroll on the ocean beach to-day, after shells. The mercury has been as high as 85°.

Feb. 29.—About ten o'clock, the wind being fair, and we can go through the lower narrows with no other, we turned our prow into the Indian river, for another charming sail through this beautiful part of these waters.

Although we look a little rough in our cruising rig, and do not use rose water, we are rather luxurious in one of our habits. Like the ancient orientals, we take our meals seated on our couches, our table being a board running across the centerboard, and over the foot of each couch, so that after our meals, which we enjoy with a keen relish, we have only to fall back upon our couches and take our siesta to our heart's content.

March 1.— We anchored last night in the river, near the mouth of St. Lucie river, which is twenty-five miles south of the Lucie post office, and tried for bass, but caught only two sharks nearly four feet long each. Before noon to-day we sailed for the east shore, and visited "Old Cuba," a noted settler in this section. He is a funny old fellow from the island of Cuba. We were cordially welcomed by the "Indian-tanned," dried up little old man, whose merry black eye twinkled, as with a shrug of his shoulders, and queer grimace of the mouth, he invited us to his rude seats by his palmetto-thatched cottage, as he expressed it, to "talkee talk, and makee lie," a very good comment upon the usual bragging talk of his tourist visitors.·

"Old Cuba" invited us into his banana grove and showed us, he said, 5,000 plants, nearing, or nearly large enough to bear. Some of these plants were twelve or fifteen feet high, and six inches thick at the butt. The banana is propagated from suckers, or sprouts near the roots, the same as the pine-apple. We saw here corn ready to boil, but poor stuff. He had also two kinds of paw paw [sic], and many garden vegetables. We invested in a few dozen bananas, a part of which were green, and now hang in our stays, for future use when ripened. Fine large fruit at one cent each.[17]

Capt. Carlin said he must do some clothes washing here, and Mr. Sutton and self took the small boat and started for a trail over to the ocean, about a mile down the river. We missed the trail, but we went over to the ocean through the worst lot of saw palmettos I think even Florida can produce, in many places well tied together by strong vines, on which we were forced to use our knives. I found a large hole sawed through my heavy pants, when we got through, as clean as if done with a knife. We made new collections of shells, and returned on the trail without difficulty. We enjoy these ocean beach strolls so much we improve every opportunity. I am much surprised at the perfect clearness of the atmosphere here. A point of land ten miles away looks just as green as one three miles away, in the entire absence of the blue smoky haze we almost always see in the north.

March 2.—We anchored off Lucie P.O. last night. We came twenty-five miles away from Lucie river, to which point we return to-day, just to get our mail, and hear from home, having heard nothing later than the 7th of February. We were well pleased to find a number of copies of the *Times* up to the 14th, which is the latest date we have heard from any part of the outside world. Before we started on our return to Lucie river to-day, Capt. Carlin reported a large alligator up the coast half a mile, where he had been to find bait, and Mr. Sutton and myself took our Winchester rifles and went for him. Ere long we saw his black head rising just above the water enough for him that he could see out. We walked up to within about fifteen rods and both fired at the same time. The thrashing he made in the water soon told us we had hit him, and of course in the head, a vital part. The water was, where he laid, only about two or three feet deep, and at times his tail would go up four feet in the air, then his black head would rise, both lashing the water into foam; then he would roll on his back, four huge legs sticking up, and he finally ceased to struggle, except at intervals. Capt. Carlin came up with the small boat, and we hitched a strong rope to his tail and towed him ashore, where it took three of us to pull him on the almost level beach. We had both put our balls into his head. I put my rule to him, and he measured ten feet long, and he carried an ugly set of teeth, well worn. I think one would enjoy a picture of us as we were hacking away at his hide to secure some specimens as trophies. We intended to secure his teeth.[18]

A little below Lucie we went ashore where a man keeps "a store," to get some flour. We found a woman and two bright looking children. The woman was from Detroit, and wished she was back there. The store was located on the old Seminole war post, Fort Pierce, and was kept in a shanty ten feet square, thatched on top and sides with palmetto leaves, and with no floor, and the place filled with an odd assortment of boots, shoes, flour, buttons, butter, tobacco, a bed, etc., etc. We asked if the roof did not leak? "A little in one place, but we put the bed there and save the goods." was the reply.[19]

March 4.—Leaving the carcass of our alligator for the birds, we started back for Lucie river. A few miles down we went ashore at a deserted plantation and picked a pail full of fine French lemons, and laid to for the night by a grand stretch of palmetto hammock along the shore. The next morning the wind being dead ahead for Lucie, we ran over to the east shore, four miles, to where we could get easy access to the ocean again. A Portuguese settler has located here this winter, and we found a good trail, only eighty rods to the beach, where we had another grand stroll on the wide sands. This morning Sutton and myself took the small boat and rowed out a mile for a fish. Sutton rowed. Sutton likes to row, and I like to see him row. It always did please me to see another man row. It is so comforting to see a fellow buckle to it, especially against a head wind, while you sit in the stern and admire his skill, and then the rower is so glad to have some one appreciate his nautical proficiency. I take great credit for unselfishness when I consent to let another row; it so improves the muscles, and expands the chest. It is a great privilege to be allowed to row—and then how proudly the rower can show the blisters on his hand for days after! I always did admire rowing blisters on the hands; that is, on an-other fellow's hands! and so I let Sutton row; for we must not be selfish in this great world of benevolent opportunities. I almost forgot to say we didn't catch any fish. We move now for Lucie river.[20]

DOWN IN FLORIDA

March 8.—At the close of my last letter we were just starting for St. Lucie river, twenty-five miles back,—south. The wind being contrary, we sailed over to the east shore, some twenty miles down the river, to visit a life-saving sta-tion, and the ocean, and bag more shells. We found the station in charge of an invalid old man, over seventy years old, all alone, and seldom visited by any of the boats going up and down with stores. He said he had been sick, and had no medicine, no meat but fat pork, and no vegetables. A tourist had given him some alligator meat which helped him. He no doubt had the scurvy. We gave him some lemons, and moved on for St. Lucie river.[21] This is a fresh water river, and enters the Indian 115 miles from Titusville. For about ten miles it is half a mile wide, above that twenty more miles, from ten to forty rods wide, and deep water. It has a north and south branch, and each one is thirty or more miles long. The country all through this section is low and largely flooded in the rainy season, especially in September and October. We tarried but two days up the Lucie, it was so very warm, away from the ocean breeze which we get on the Indian. We managed to "bag" an eight-foot alligator, a sixteen-pound cock turkey of most beautiful plumage, a coon, a fox squirrel, a white heron, a white egret, and a rattlesnake, the first one we have seen in Florida. This bringing in alligators, after we shot them, is sometimes exciting work. We put a ball through the head, and by all the common laws of life, the fellow ought to be dead, and after some active thrashing he turns up and appears to be dead. But don't you be too sure, for he makes things lively sometimes when we least expect it. This one Mr. Sutton shot from the shore, and put a ball through the top of his head, and he turned up for removal. We went out with the small boat to pick him up. I put a gaff into the wound to his head, thinking to tow him ashore with that. In an instant he rolled and pitched and broke the gaff, then settled quiet again. We then pried up his tail with an oar, and slipped a noose in the boat's tow line over it, added a half hitch, and laid to the oars. After hard work, we started him, and towed him up to the large boat. Attempting to secure him with another rope, he took another surge, rolled himself up in the tow line and threw nearly the whole of his body over the bow of the boat, and we had to put another ball through his head before we could quiet him. After leaving Lucie we anchored for the night near the mouth. In the morning we secured another turkey and an alligator only three inches short of twelve feet long. We towed him ashore without any trouble; we put two more balls through his head to prevent surprises, and found him a very old one, showing marks of many a fight.

Did you ever try to skin the armor plated back of an old alligator? No? Then don't you try, unless you wish a good job to let out. I took a piece some fifteen to eighteen inches off the broadest part of his back, all covered with the ridges of bony plates. At times, as I entered the knife, he would squirm and paw with his huge legs, which I avoided with some dexterity; but I was bound to have that particular piece of hide, and though it took me nearly an hour to secure and clear it from the flesh, which grew close to it, I have it hung out to dry. I also skinned one of his legs with the claws on, which I hope to be able to cure and bring home.

March 8th.—We arrived back at Lucie post-office yesterday, and welcomed letters from home, and the *Times* up to Feb. 20. Weather still fair. No rain for two weeks. From Lucie we ran to the east shore again, to another life saving station, and another run on the ocean beach.[22] After our return to the *Ella*, which was anchored in the channel of one of these side lagoons, while dinner was cooking, I baited a hook and threw [it] out with about fifty feet of line. I soon had a bite, and found I had a heavy one. With no little exertion and careful playing, I drew him alongside, and Sutton gaffed him into the boat. He measured three feet, six and one-half inches. We put the twenty-four pound balances to him, and he settled it to the bottom before his tail was clear from the boat. We then cut him in two pieces, and weighed them, and he scored just thirty pounds.

March 9th.—We came to anchor last night off Pelican island, the noted breeding place of these birds. Thousands of pelicans covered the bare ground and the few dead mangroves, and when we approached to land, they flew, and the air was black with their numbers all around our heads. We found only a few dozen young ones left. They were nearly grown, unable to fly, but waddled off to the water. We caught one with our hands but did not harm him. The full grown pelican measures from seven to eight feet from tip to tip of wings, and the head and bill from fifteen to eighteen inches long.

In the morning we secured a few more pelicans for skinning, and moved on to Wilson's orange grove, on the Banana lagoon, with Merritt's island on our left, and five miles from cape Canaveral. Merritt's island we made out to be nearly thirty-five miles long, and from two rods to four miles wide. Lord Sykes a few years ago tried to buy this island for a park, but could not get a title.[23]

After a day at Wilson's to prepare the skins of our pelicans, the next morning we moved on up the river six miles and struck another trail, of about a half mile over to the sea, and went over for our eighth and last visit in this section, to the ocean. In these visits we have averaged a visit in every twenty miles for one hundred and sixty miles of the Florida coast.

Titusville, March 13.—We arrived here last night and finished our cruise on Indian river. While we were at anchor five miles out for dinner, we had our last fishing. Mr. Sutton caught a twenty pounds, and a twelve pounds bass, and I had the fortune to haul in another of thirty pounds, which we presented to the landlord of our hotel. We were just thirty days on the river in the *Ella*, and think we have explored this grand lagoon of 100 miles in length, and some of its tributaries pretty well. The interest of this trip is unsurpassed and we come back to civilization with eminent satisfaction with our enjoyment of it. The only possible fault we can find is the extreme warm weather. We slept many nights on the boat with no bed covering but the sheet, until near morning.

And now some reader may ask, what does all this amount to? Living a month cramped up on a small boat, hunting, fishing, and killing and skinning alligators and pelicans. To the worn down business man, the professional man, student, or any one suffering from the many causes of the ailments of our

Fig. 6. Pelicans nesting on Pelican Island. (*St. Nicholas,* September 1899)

northern winters, it amounts to a renewed bodily strength, and longer life; a
relish for plain food unknown at home, and an appropriation of the food by
the system not experienced amid the luxuries of home life. To the victim
of catarrhal affliction, who buys and uses his handkerchiefs by the dozen,
through the northern winter, a dispensing of eleven of them, and a free
breathing without the use of the one. To the rheumatic, the absence of his
pains;—to the victim of headache and dyspepsia, a clear head, and hearty
meal, without evil result;—to the sufferer from colds and ordinary coughs, no
colds, and no coughing, and with all, a glorious converse with nature in forest,
field, sky, and water; foliage and flowers; living in the open air like the sweet
song birds who awaken you in the early morning. Again, with all the enjoyment of this open air semi-savage life, one becomes better fitted in body and
mind to appreciate and enjoy the many privileges God has bestowed upon us
in the refinements and comforts of congregated civilization in our homes and
home society. I would not always be a savage, and for a steady business stand
astride a twelve foot alligator stripping his mailed hide from his back, jumping occasionally to avoid a blow from his tail or his strong clawtipped legs, in
his dying struggles; but I would not miss *one* such experience for the best

opera. It gives vent I think to the savage instinct which most men have bottled up in their nature in spite of their refinement, and leaves one's mind calmer and better fitted for the highest plane of action in social life.[24]

LETTER FROM FLORIDA

[N. M. Sutton]

Titusville, March 14.—Dear ones at home:—It is now six weeks since I left home, and I often looked back and wondered if you were all well. I could only hope you were as I could not get letters from you in this out of the way isolated country. We returned here last Friday evening, after a thirty days trip on the river, all of which time I have enjoyed the best of health. I went to the office and they reported all our mail sent to St. Lucie, ninety miles below. I was a good deal disappointed in not getting some mail, but in the course of an hour the mail from the north came in, bringing a letter from Anna and mother. I was glad to hear from home but sorry to hear of mother's illness. But as you report convalescence, I presume there would not be any use my hurrying home on that account.

We have had a very pleasant trip, going over the same ground we did last year and much more, as we have traversed the Indian and Banana rivers from one end to the other and stopping at all the places of interest, as well as going quite a way up the St. Lucie river. On the latter, we went principally in search of deer, turkeys, alligators, etc., all of which we saw and captured except the deer. We only went out after deer one day or a part of a day, but it was so hot I was entirely used up and resolved not to try it again. I sat down to rest and it was so hot I found it cooler to be on the move. I said to myself, if this is winter, what shall the summer be? Where I was hunting was on a very level pine plane [sic] with occasional bunches of palmetto scrub, and I thought what a poor place to hunt deer where they can see you a mile and still you could not see them ten rods. And it was but a few minutes before three nice deer jumped out of a bunch of palmetto scrub not more than fifteen rods off that I had partially passed. They made a speedy retreat, and I gave them a farewell shot with my Winchester and in a moment they were gone. Mr. Stebbins remained at the boat and the Captain took a different direction. He started one deer and shot a nice turkey, a rattlesnake and a squirrel, and on my return I shot a coon and lugged him home or to the boat, as I did not know of the Captain getting the turkey and I knew we were in want of some fresh meat. But when I found we had a turkey I threw the coon in the river for the 'gators. On my return to the boat I came down on the other side of a swamp that I could not cross until I got to the river. As I approached the river I discovered an alligator's head out of water; I let him have and he turned up his toes, but he soon righted up again. I called for the small boat, and after firing several more shots we got a line around him and towed him to the large boat. He measured nine feet. It seems as if some of the 'gators are as hard to kill as the Kill Karney cats. They will twist and squirm after their head has been off an hour.

From here we went up the river a few miles and camped or cast anchor for the night, as we were at home on the boat night and day. It was in a shoal place and seemed to be headquarters of all the frogs on the St. Lucie river. I think they must have been having a revival, as they kept up a continuous croaking. And the musquitoes [*sic*] too were very numerous, and seemed quite determined to get inside our sand-fly nettings and get a taste of northern blood; and they succeeded pretty well as quite a number found their way inside and annoyed us some. The air was much warmer than on the Indian river. Mercury 90° in the day time and 85° at night. The thermometer varies much less here than it does at home. It has been blowing for nearly two weeks from the south and the temperature is nearly the same as it is in the West Indies, as the gulf stream runs very near the coast, in many places from two to three miles. I was talking with a gentleman from Ohio last evening about 9 o'clock. He said it seemed like frost the air was so cool. We had quite a high wind all day from the south. I told him we would look at the thermometer and found it stood at 80°. We concluded we would miss the frost. After getting through with St. Lucie we came down and anchored near the mouth. While the Captain was getting dinner, Mr. Stebbins and I went on shore for wood, and in a little clearing, I discovered a nice turkey; I returned for my gun, but he was gone on my return. I determined to try for one in the morning, so I got up before the sun, a rather unusual occurrence, and I stayed in the bushes a spell and heard them about, but the bushes were so thick I could not get about much. At last a nice one flew up in a tree and I soon dropped it. I was in the bushes after my turkey when they set up a brisk firing down at the large boat. I soon heard a splash and a cry for the small boat. I found myself surrounded by a thicket, chinked with three cornered cactus. I finally made out to get out and found the Captain had put a ball into the head of a twelve foot 'gator. He showed the marks of some fierce battles. One jaw had been torn off in the front so that he had lost some of his teeth, and one hind leg had been bitten badly. He was estimated by the natives to be forty or fifty years old. We cut off the jaws of all we kill to save the teeth. We also killed one ten feet long near St. Lucie post office, and had quite a time getting him, as he did not give up very easy. The one we killed near St. Lucie river we three could not pull on shore, so we got him in the shoal water and cut off his head and some scales from his back, and as we left the buzzards were looking him over preparing to make an attack. We have caught lots of small sharks three or four feet long and some longer, but did not get any large ones at Jupiter. We got hold of one that took the boat about lively, but it broke the line and took the hook. We have caught bass that weighed 30 pounds, and many that weighed from 12 to 25 pounds. The last day we fished was on the river opposite here, in the afternoon before we came in. Mr. Stebbins caught one that weighed 30 pounds, and I one that weighed 12 and one 20 lbs. They are a gamey fish to pull in. I lost my hook trying to pull in a large one. We visited Pelican Island on our way up, and it was a sight indeed. I should think there was five or six acres in it, and most of the trees dead. It was just night when we got there. We anchored and went on the island. There were thousands of pelicans on the trees and ground and we could have shot lots of them had we chose[n] to. We looked over the island for eggs and young ones. We found no perfect eggs but quite a few young ones toddling about like goslings, so we could pick them up.[25] In the morning we shot four and next day put up three of them. We also put up two at Jubilee, and I got a beautiful specimen of white pelican, so I now have four to bring home. I think I can set up quite a pelican rookery. The specimens are all different. It is a desolate country for any one to live in, but many of the people seem quite contented. Many live in houses sided and roofed with nothing but palmetto leaves. Some have floors and some have not. They live on hog and hominy, fish and venison, and don't seem to care what the rest of the world is doing. There are only two or three nice orange groves on the Indian and Banana rivers, but lots of ordinary ones. There are some fine banana groves and some day they may come to account. It seems healthy in the winter, but I guess there is a good market for quinine in the summer. It is Sunday to-day, and as there was no church, I thought I might as well write a little. There is a little church building here, but they give three reasons for not having church to-day. They do not know where the key is, and there is no minister, and the hogs sleep under the church so the flees [sic] are so thick in the church the minister can't stick to his text. The last one that preached there picked two hundred and fifty off him after church.[26] The town is very quiet to-day. Last night fifteen or twenty negroes, with the aid of whiskey, gave the people a serenade for three or four hours at midnight. The mercury is 84° at 2 p.m., so you see how little the temperature varies. It is 10° cooler than it was last year, so it is not near as pleasant for those that wish to hunt in the woods. The night before we came in I slept all night with the curtains up and nothing but a sheet over me.

The orange trees down the river are mostly in bloom. We manage to get all the oranges we want to eat, and hope to get a box in Jacksonville to send home. We leave here Tuesday morning and may stop at Sanford and at Palatka, and go up the Oclawaha [Ocklawaha], then over to St. Augustine for a few days, and try and get home before the middle of April. You can read

Mr. Stebbins' letters and see how we are getting along. I will write often and keep you posted as to our whereabouts. It seems nice to have a little rest before going over to the St. Johns.[27]

Adrian, April 5.—We are happy to announce the safe return to his home and friends of F. R. Stebbins after an absence of just two months in Florida. The quantity and variety of curiosities he gathered and brought home with him indicate that he was not idle.[28]

Tecumseh, April 8.—Mr. N. M. Sutton returned from his extended Florida trip last Saturday, having been gone from home over two months. He bought an excursion ticket to Jacksonville and return, the route chose[n] being to Cincinnati and Louisville, Thomasville, Ga., and Jacksonville. After a day at the latter place he took the boat up the St. Johns and proceeded at once to Enterprise, which is located near the head of navigation. He then proceeded by a horse railroad seven miles long across to Titusville on the Indian river, and spent thirty days upon that river in a sail boat. At the south end of the Indian river he went west across the country to the St. Lucie river, where the best hunting grounds are found. A graphic discription [sic] of his hunting experience on St. Lucie is given in last week's Herald.

Retracing his steps he proceeded north again via the Indian and Banana rivers, visiting Pelican Island on the way; then across to the St. Johns and down that river to Tocoi, thence fourteen miles over to St. Augustine. Here he remained eleven days, and made a study of that quaint old town. Thence he returned to Jacksonville and from there home by the same rail route he went down upon. Mr. F. R. Stebbins of Adrian accompanied him during the entire trip, and both gentlemen were highly pleased with their journey. Down on the Indian River in March the thermometer averaged about 90° every day. On the way home through Southern Georgia and Alabama he passed thousands of acres of growing cotton and corn, which are now finely started.[29]

Tecumseh, April 15.—N. M. Sutton has on exhibition at his store a coconut just gathered from the tree, and a lot of West India shells which he brought from Florida with him.[30]

5 1881 On the Bounding Billows

Adrian, Jan. 8.—Mrs. Howell writes from Jacksonville, Fla., that the morning before New Year's the mercury was nineteen degrees below zero, all the oranges in that neighborhood being frozen solid.[1]

Adrian, Jan. 10.—Messrs F. R. Stebbins and A. H. Wood[2] leave this afternoon for a trip in the south. *En route* they will be joined by Hon. J. B. Chaffee[3] and brother.[4] Cincinnati, Chattanooga, Atlanta, Fernandina, and Indian river, will be points visited, and perhaps Cuba and Mexico. A pleasant journey to our friends.[5]

Adrian, Jan. 10.—Nineteen degrees *below* zero at Jacksonville, Fla., seemed like a pretty cool story, but if Mrs. Howell said it we were bound to believe it. Mr. Howell told us the story, but now, on again looking his letter over, he finds it to read "above" instead of "below," which is better, as well as warmer.[6]

Adrian, Jan. 24.—A note from F. R. Stebbins, Saturday, announced his arrival in Jacksonville, where he and Mr. Wood were making preparations for a trip to Indian river.[7]

SEEING FLORIDA

Jacksonville, Jan. 15.—Our route this year was from Cincinnati over the new Cincinnati Southern railroad to Chattanooga, 335 miles, by daylight. We found good sleighing all through Kentucky, with six or eight inches of snow, and freezing weather. The snow disappeared near the middle of Tennessee.

One hundred miles from Cincinnati we came upon the canyon of the Kentucky river, which is cut by the river through the sandstone ledge three hundred feet deep, and extending up and down the river as far as we could see, and our track ran for some distance directly on the edge of the chasm, where we looked down to the water from our seats. This gorge we crossed on an iron bridge with lattice work iron piers two hundred and eighty-six feet high. A building on a small interval by the water looked almost like a children's play house.

The view up and down the river from the bridge is a grand one. Chattanooga is one of the most prosperous towns in the south built up largely by large iron manufacturing interests. As we moved on in the morning, a fine view of Lookout Mountain brought to mind the great and stirring incidents of the war, which clustered so thickly around this locality.

We stopped over one train at Atlanta, now a growing and prosperous city of nearly forty thousand inhabitants. Northern enterprise has taken it from its ruins, and even instilled into the southern element here a life which makes Atlanta seem like a northern town.

We met here Mr. Noah Fowler, once an Adrian boy, who showed us around the city. We passed Ben Hill's residence, and ex-Gov. Bullock's. Atlanta is the home of both the U.S. Senators and two members of Congress. We met also Volney Spalding, our old friend of many years ago at Palmyra.

We see here very little show of the scourging Atlanta received. All has been rebuilt much better than before. Our attention was called to a hole through the hollow base of an iron gas post, made by a piece of shell as it exploded and took off the leg of a colored man standing by. The mercury went to below zero, with heavy fall of snow during the cold snap. We saw along the route three Georgia cotton fields yet unpicked, the hands being busy in securing it. This is unusually late for picking, but rainy and freezing weather has prevented it earlier.

Signs of the freeze in northern Florida are seen here. All the banana plants are killed, and the leaves of the orange trees are falling, but the owners hope the trees are not killed. Two hundred miles up the St. John's river the cold was barely below freezing, and did much less damage. There does not seem to be any great rush of travel here yet. I think the tide is yet to come.

We find Senator Jerome B. Chaffee here, and Mr. Wood. Senator Chaffee and myself go up the river with him next week. Mrs. Howell is enjoying the climate, and finds her health much improved.

Enterprizse [Enterprise], Jan. 19th.—We left Jacksonville on the 17th. During our stop there we improved an opportunity to go down to the mouth of the St. John's, twenty-five miles. The ride by water was of no particular interest. While strolling on the beach watching a large porpoise, a gentleman came along with a long-range rifle, and invited our party to take a shot at the fish as he occasionally rolled up his back a quarter of a mile away. Shooting porpoise on the wing that distance is no very certain work, it being entirely uncertain to guess within three rods the spot he will break water, and then only show his back three seconds. Your correspondent tried a shot, and all who watched the strike of the ball, declared the fish was hit. He floundered a little and disappeared. It was, of course, largely a chance shot, that distance.[8]

Porpoise. Caught on Florida Coast.

Fig. 7. Hunters posing with their porpoise prey in an early twentieth-century post-card. (Author's collection)

After visiting Palatka we took boat for this place, over 200 miles by river and 100 by straight line from Jacksonville. The oranges in this locality were not injured, the freeze being only four degrees, and only an hour or so in time. This forenoon our party went out for black bass, and Senator Chaffee and Alf. Wood caught all the bass, six in number, and the rest only catfish.

We expect to go on to-morrow for Titusville, on Indian River, 75 miles farther on.

The mercury to-day on the north side of the house is 75°, and the sun was so hot I had to take off my coat and fish in my "shirt-sleeves." Strawberries are in blossom and peas and radishes are on the table.

The hotel here has a fine orange grove free for the eating of the guests, at all times. The proprietor says they use for the guests, about sixty thousand during the season.

A welcome sight of the *Times* greeted us at Palatka, and I think I shall get another at Sanford to-morrow.[9]

Titusville, Feb. 2.—Mr. Stebbins, a gentleman from Michigan, shot a porpoise with his rifle while passing through Banana creek on Monday afternoon. The animal sunk to the bottom, but was noosed and hauled aboard. It measured about 7 feet, and was estimated to weigh over 300 pounds.[10]

ON THE BOUNDING BILLOWS

Titusville, Feb. 1st.—Leaving Enterprise on the steamer *We-ki-wa*, we made the landing at Salt Lake, where we took land conveyance for this place, in due time.

Our transfer from the steamer was a novel one. The wagons come alongside the boat, and we stepped from the steamer's lower deck into the wagons. The boat was aground in twenty (20) inches of water.

A pleasant ride of seven miles, part of the way over a hard sandy road, through a pine forest, and part through swamps with the water over the wheel hubs, brought us in two hours to the Titus house.

Our landlord, Col. Titus, is a man with a history. A filibuster under Walker, he was captured in Nicaraugua [Nicaragua], but managed to some way save his life. Afterwards he led a life of adventure in Kansas, and along the frontier. He, with a party skirted the whole coast of Lake Superior in open Mackinac boats. He saw Prof. Houghton's boat capsized, and helped bring ashore his body. Was with Fremont in California, and with the army in Mexico. Crippled with rheumatism he drifted into Florida, and says he could not live anywhere else.[11] While at Enterprize [Enterprise] I visited a shell mound of large dimensions, composed almost entirely of conical snail shells. They are carting these shells on to the orange groves, in large quantities.[12] After a few days' stop at Titusville we chartered a sail boat with a good shelter cabin, for a week's trip around Merrit[t]'s Island, and set sail with a fair northern wind. The weather was threatening, though everybody promised us a clearing up, but we had not sailed ten miles before a furious norther set in, and with all sail lowered to a "pocket" we ran before the gale forty-five miles in a little over six hours, and rounded the lower end of the island into a sheltered bay just at dark, and anchored, while the norther howled, with showers and mist. We could only go on shore between the rains. I went over to a burial mound where some parties had been digging. They have thrown out a lot of bones and large, long conch shells. On the shell mound is a gum-elembo, a tree that cannot stand frost, and it is green and flourishing. At this point the wild morning glories are in blossom, and show no signs of frost. The old hermit Haddock, of whom I wrote last year, was only a mile from our anchorage. He is dead. "Old Cuba" the Cuban patriot refugee has also finished his career. He was found drowned near his banana plantation, with his boat capsized.

We were detained four days by the "norther" at the foot of Merritt's Island. It would not avail to fret; we do not swear; and so we took it as easy as possible.

We had plenty of provisions, good appetites, and with a box of those delicious Indian River oranges, we managed to pass the time between the eating and digging in the shell mound. The greatest trial we had to endure was the knowledge that all around our boat was plenty of these big sea bass, and owing to the cold storm we could not get a single mullet for bait, and we baited ourselves with oranges.

We found the oranges at Jacksonville all off flavor, probably from two causes. They were picked too early, before they were good, or were from some locality where they were chilled enough to injure them in flavor. On the lower part of the river, for a hundred miles up from Jacksonville, the oranges were all frozen in the cold snap, and worthless; but higher up [they were] only chilled and are in the market. On Indian River the oranges are uninjured. The orange everywhere in Florida does not attain its full perfection in richness before February.

A tramp on the lower end of Merritt's Island near our anchorage showed that frost does not visit this locality, in the growing of large tropical paw-paw [sic] trees, which cannot survive frost. The young fruit was just forming. We saw there also a curious tree called the wild fig, a member of the rubber family. Its peculiarity is in never depending upon its own trunk for support, but is always found clasping in sneaky contortions some other tree. One I saw here was over eight inches in diameter, but wound around the trunk of a palmetto in coil and twist with a shape to make a curiosity hunter groan in spirit that he could not appropriate it for his collection. I groaned spiritually, as I left it standing, never expecting to see it again; but the norther still continuing the next day I could not be content until I had secured it. A half mile run across the rough channel, and with axe and saw we secured the specimen, and with no little labor we got it into the boat, and without shipping much water got safely back to our large boat and hoisted it on to the fore deck with rope and pulley. I shall have it sent home from here, when it arrives, if it ever does. I think it will pay for the trouble and expense, as a specimen of the two trees. It will weigh over 200 pounds.

Just after our four o'clock dinner on the fourth day of our detention, the wind abated a little and we hoisted sail to beat up against the wind. We made only about a mile when the wind howled down again, and we were forced to run into a sheltered cove near the island, where we laid at anchor all night and the next day and night, the north gale still blowing. During the day we went ashore on Merritt's Island, where there was a clearing. We found some cabbages growing and weeds and flowers in blossom. We procured from a settler some fine pieces of sandal wood, which grows here, built a fine bonfire, and replenished our larder with some ducks. In the morning Mr. Wood caught an eighteen pounder channel bass, which graces our breakfast table; part of it, I mean, for even with our splendid appetites we could not finish him at one meal. Limes are raised here in great perfection. During the night the gale abated, and after breakfast we started to beat against a light wind still from the north. It takes a large amount of questioning of the people here to obtain information about things here. A prevailing mute soberness, tinged oft with sadness is a noticeable trait. It seems a sort of animal wariness, lest in an unguarded moment some enemy shall "gobble" them up.[13] Ralph Waldo Emerson would find here his idea of evidence of "good breeding" in perfection. But let him not shout too fast or too loudly, for he will find the alligators very reserved, also; and a close investigation will show him that both alligators and Florida "crackers" have more numerous "breeding" than *good*. Give me the good hearty, rosy laugh of the north, and Emerson may revel to his heart's content in the sallow, sad-eyed reserve of the southern natives, and the supercilious leterary [*sic*], aristocrat of the "hub." A great many fools pass for wise men, by "reserve." Give me rather the jovial fellow who will even tell you all about his family and his cousins and his aunts, for I never see the silent man but I think of treason, stratagem and spoils, in his eye.[14]

The sixth day the weather abated and we beat against it twenty miles. The next day the wind was very light, and still ahead, but we moved on slowly into the creek which connects the two lagoons, the last three miles actually sailing through the crooked channel by the light of Venus, towards which we moved. The brilliancy of the stars here is remarkable. Venus shed a brilliancy over the water like a moon in its first quarter, and we could not have sailed after dark without her light.

We anchored for the night about midnight through the creek, and after a grand breakfast, with a good appetite, on warm corn cake, Beals and Colvin's ham and butter, we were becalmed, but took to the poles and moved on. The norther having despoiled us of anticipated sport, we despaired of the usual excitement on these waters, but about ten o'clock a huge porpoise broke water about six rods distant, and I sent, as he rose, a Winchester ball "plumb" through his body, about a foot aft his forward fin. The water was only about thirty inches deep, and he made it fly lively, and the blood spurted from the wound. As he moved away at full speed, bubbles on the water marked his course, so we could follow him with the small boat. We knew he was our meat, for it was evident the ball had gone through his lungs, but we were anxious to reach port and we rowed up to him. He tried to swim away from us, but I got another ball into his head, and he turned up a dead porpoise. We looped a rope around him, towed him back to the large boat, then hauled him into the row boat and brought him in to Titusville. He was judged to weigh three hundred or more pounds, and was nearly seven feet long. I intend to have the jaws preserved and sent home.

Thus ended our nine days' trip, and although the long norther spoilt much of our plan, as we sailed across the river to this port six miles, with a fair wind and a glorious sunshine and balmy air, we all voted we had "a good time," after all. We start for St. Augustine to-morrow.[15]

Adrian, Feb. 8.—There seems to be no lack of Florida oranges, notwithstanding the fact that they were all killed by the frost.[16]

SEA BEANS AND AN EPITAPH

St. Augustine, Feb. 7th.—We left Titusville on the 1st, with a promise of fair weather, in a day of sunshine and soft air, making the seven miles journey in open wagons, without overcoats, and had a pleasant day on the boat. Just at dark we passed a small raft of cedar logs, in the middle of lake Harney, on which without shelter of any kind were three men and one woman. They begged to be towed down, but our captain refused. The odd rainy weather which lasted all the next day had just set in, and I do not think the rafters had a pleasant picnic that voyage. It was still gloomy weather, on the second day, between Sanford and Palatka, but there was much to admire on the wild shores. The many swamp maples were all aflame in the warm red of the newly starting foliage, and contrasting with the deep rich green of other trees, overshadowed by the huge trunks and wide-spreading branches of the cypress and live oaks draped in profusion with the long grey moss, made a charming picture in spite of wind and rain.

At Palatka I found a man from Jackson in the business of preparing skins of the birds of Florida, of which he keeps a large stock mounted, and ready for mounting, for supplying persons and museums.

At St. Augustine, for four days, we have been simply killing time around a coal stove, reading the papers, and watching the clock for breakfast, dinner and supper, while the norther still blows chilly, with the mercury ranging from 45° to 58°. Several times a day, it is true, we make a break, and with buttoned overcoats, walk through the plaza, read the names of "our dead" on the confederate soldiers' monument, or still more desperate, face the wind on the sea wall, and shiver at the sight of a ship-load of Maine ice unloading at the wharf.

Varying the amusement, I stroll through the curiosity stores, peering into every nook and cavern to see if back of the multitudinous forms of sea bean, alligators' teeth, fish scale, and snake-rattle jewelry, perchance I may discover something of real rarity. Some one may ask what I mean by "snake-rattle jewelry." It is the "rattle" of huge rattlesnakes mounted on breast pins, and worn by "ladies!" For the good name of gentle woman, I believe such taste is of rare occurrence among northern visitors.[17] During my researches I chanced upon and secured a very fine specimen of a tooth of the fossil mammoth

Fig. 8. Confederate monument in the St.
Augustine Plaza. (*Harper's New Monthly
Magazine,* December 1874)

shark, from one of the phosphate beds near Charleston, S.C. I have also a very
fine small specimen, I found in the snail-shell mound at Enterprise.

Sea beans, once a great curiosity, have become so common that only the
rare specimens excite remarks.[18] In this line your correspondent wears on his
chain probably the finest specimen in Florida, certainly all the curiosity shops
in Augustine cannot show one to compare with it, in kind and size and
beauty. These beans have to be polished to bring out their beauty, and they

are as hard as ivory. But the champion polisher, a colored man of Jacksonville is dead.

The old process was by hand, and very slow. This Peter Morrison invented some machine which did the work well and quickly. What it was we could not find out, for when we called upon him last winter, he took our beans for future delivery, and would not let us enter his work shop.

Last summer, in snake and ornamental grass time, Peter took his knife, and pail of "forty rod," and went into the marsh for grass. Alas! a venomous snake disputed possession, and Peter was "petered out." I owed him one for being kept out of his sanctum, and am going to write his epitaph—

Kind friends who view this sandy bed,
Here Peter Morrison lies dead,
Killed by an angry copperhead.
On cutting grasses he was bent;
The snake bit him, and down he went.
He drank the whiskey in his pail,
But all he took did not avail.
The question is not settled quite,
"Did whiskey kill him, or the bite?"
Yet drop a tear on Peter's bier,
He'll no more polish sea-beans here.

But Peter has escaped the coldest winter the "oldest inhabitant" ever saw in Florida. I have been in the state four weeks and have not seen over four days one wished to be out without a light overcoat.

You have no doubt seen an account of a plan to drain Lake Okeechobee and the large section of wet lands in southern Florida. I was shown a private letter from the leader of the enterprise in which he said he was promised unequivocally aid to an amount sufficient to accomplish the work. I think the lands belong to Florida as "swamp lands," and the state gives a large amount of them to the company. I think the design is to clear out the old canals now choked up from the Matanzas lagoon here down Halifax river to Mosquito lagoon, over to Indian river, up the St. Lucie and through the swamp to Okeechobee, thence down the Calooseehatchie [Caloosahatchee] to the Gulf of Mexico, a water communication directly across the state, and redeeming a million or more acres of now worthless wet land. The great freeze this winter in this section has given great interest to more southern portions of the state beyond the frost line. This scheme is of national importance, if it succeeds, in opening a large amount of the country to easy access where all tropical fruits and plants can be raised in our own country, and unlike all the now dry sections of Florida, these reclaimed swamps will give really rich soil.[19]

Slowly but surely the old coquina walls in Augustine of the old Spaniards are passing away before the march of improvement by "Yankee" invaders. The old Spanish mansions were built of this shell rock, on the street line, quite plain, square or oblong in shape; or, if with any architectural ornamentation, it was on the side opposite the street; making the back side of the home the front side; the sometimes arched and pillared porticoes facing the gardens in the rear of the house, the street side containing a narrow hanging balcony for witnessing street parades. Starting from the front walls of the street side of the houses shell rock walks from eight to ten feet ran around the whole lot, making a comfortably fortified enclosure, and broken only by necessary arched top gateways closed by heavy plank doors with huge iron hinges and fastenings. These walls are year by year taken down. Some of the old arched ways still remain, but the old wooden gates or doors have disappeared, and are replaced by those of modern times. One can in a few places, looking through the shrubbery on the garden side, catch glimpses of rude, arched and pillared porticoes, the outside of the portico on a line with the outer wall, making the open space under a part of the upper story of the house. What visions of senoras and senoritas do these old alcoves bring up? For Augustine in the olden time was a fragment of Spain, in manners and customs, transplanted in the new world. Two hundred years ago; from the balconies flashed back from bright eyes of Spanish beauties the ardent fiery glances of the spurred and booted cavaliers as they galloped by with clanking sword scabbard keeping time to the pattering hoofs of the steeds on the coquina pavement where wheeled vehicles were not permitted. But England came, and Spain faded away. England departed, and Spain again took possession, only to give way to the manifest destiny of the universal Yankee nation. New laws, new customs, new inhabitants, until only a few almost ruins of old Augustine, in the old fort and a few buildings of the old Dons, now usually inhabited by negroes, remain.[20]

The descendants of the fiery old Hernandez keep boarding houses for the Yankees, and of other ancient houses make curious palmetto braid work, or mount sea beans for winter visitors, whose home land in the north was a howling wilderness when these Spanish ancestors rode at the head of gay and brilliant cavalcades through the streets, emblazoned in golden stars and orders of the proudest nobility of old Spain.

As I finish this letter, on the 8th, a southwest wind is bringing warmer weather, and our windows and doors open for the air, and our overcoats hang on the rack, we all hope to remain there.[21]

Adrian, Feb. 26.—Mr. F. R. Stebbins is home from his Florida excursion, the trip having yielded the usual amount of enjoyment. Mr. Wood will tarry in Dixie some time, returning by way of New Orleans.[22]

Adrian, March 29.—In front of the store of F. R. Stebbins is a very singular and unique tree growth. About four feet of the trunk of a palmetto tree is completely encircled with the huge trunk of a wild fig, or india rubber tree. The specimen is a treasure from Mr. Stebbins' Florida explorations.[23]

Adrian, April 18.—An eight foot alligator shot by ex-Senator Chaffee in St. Johns river, Florida, has been stuffed by J. W. Helme, Jr. Another reptile nine and a half feet long, shot by A. H. Wood in the same place, is in the course of preparation.[24]

Adrian, May 20.—Arthur Howell brought home from Florida, four young alligators. Two he gave away; one to Miss Hallie Chittenden to open and shout [sic] the gate for her; another to Ed. Stephenson, to be trained for a future member of the common council, and two will be kept for domestics about the house.[25]

Adrian, May 21.—A huge alligator, that fell before the unerring aim of our townsman, A. H. Wood, during his trip in Florida, last winter, has been stuffed, and now occupies a high shelf in the clothing store.[26]

Adrian, May 30, 1883.—One of the most interesting objects in the museum of the Scientific society is the alligator shot by Senator Jerome Chaffee in Florida.[27]

6   1882 Among the Mangroves

Adrian, Jan. 13.—Mr. F. R. Stebbins left yesterday for Florida. We hope to hear from him during his absence.[1]

Titusville, Jan. 25.—We were the recipient of a call from Mr. F. R. Stebbins of Adrian, Mich., on Monday morning. Mr. S. comes nearly every winter to Florida to escape the biting cold of the winters north.[2]

Titusville, Feb. 1.—Mr. Stebbins and Mr. Carlin have gone on a two weeks' trip to the Banana.[3]

ON SUMMER SEAS

Banana Creek, Jan. 26.—We had been detained three days at Titusville by a furious gale from the east, with rain, but the storm broke last night, and by 10 a.m. to-day we had our "things" and stores aboard the *Ella,* and struck out for the mouth of this strait, a channel about nine miles long, connecting the Indian and Banana lagoons, above Merritt's island. Five miles sailing brought us to the "creek" and we are now sailing on it. Flocks of ducks are constantly rising before us, with an occasional pelican and heron. On both sides are wide-spreading savannahs of low, reedy lands, dotted with many palm trees, and far and near they raise their green, round tops against the sky. These palms, with an occasional cluster of hammock growth of various trees, all green in foliage, form very picturesque scenery as the eye sweeps around the low horizon.

There has been no frost to harm anything this winter here, and every thing is in its best winter dress of green.

27th, noon.—We have just dissected our first alligator. Yesterday p.m., when about half way through the strait we stuck off into a side bay three miles to "Pepper's haul over," where we sailed to within fifty rods of the ocean, and we had a long stroll on the wide, hard sand beach, and after a four o'clock dinner, moved out into the bay and anchored for the night. After breakfast we up anchor and had to beat against a head wind on our course. About an hour ago we saw a large alligator in the distance swimming across the creek, and Mr. Chas. W. Gunn, of Grand Rapids, my associate on this voyage, tried his long range rifle on him.[4] The third shot hit in the head, and we soon had a rope to him, from the small boat, and towed him ashore. He was the most beautifully marked "gator" I ever saw. All of his scales finely mottled and streaked in black and grey and white, like the shell of a sea turtle. He measured ten feet eight inches long. Securing some pieces of the hide, and the jaws, for the teeth, and satisfying ourselves that he had been stealing ducks for his meals, we left him for the buzzards.

Just as I finished the above we saw a sail coming, which proved to be Mr. Wilson, from Wilson's grove, with a boat load of oranges for market. He rounded to and sold us fifty splendid oranges for a cent apiece.

28th.—Yesterday afternoon we sailed to the head of Banana lagoon and anchored near a trail over to the ocean, a half mile distant. We had another long stroll on the beach, where we secured a few shells and sea beans, in our collecting bags. Having netted some mullet for bait, on our return, we soon caught a fifteen pound sea bass, out of which we had a fine feast this morning, and a capital chowder for dinner. We came to anchor to-night some five miles from Canaveral light, across the land. On our way to-day we visited a deserted orange grove, called De Soto. Formerly there was an expensive mansion here, built by a Mr. Paterson of Toronto, who had it furnished and conducted in the English style.[5] The mansion burned, the man died, and the heirs let the place go to ruin. We took a few fine lemons for lemonade. A Mr. Reed, from Boston, is making his headquarters there for a season.[6]

The weather since we started has been all that could be desired, as pleasant as the best summer weather in the north.

30th.—We have laid at anchor to-day off Hogan's, a place on the east shore of the lagoon, the place I visited three years ago when it was a deserted spot. There is now a new house and clearing, and a pine apple field of twenty-five hundred plants.[7] A good trail of a mile or more brought us again on the ocean beach, and one of more interest than any we have yet visited.

The beach was strewn for miles with many varieties of shells, sea weeds, countless numbers of sea cucumbers, anemones, sea spiders, etc. I found here in great numbers the dead shells of a small variety of anemone I have never seen before. They are very fragile, but I hope to get some of them home unbroken.

My collecting bag was heavy on our return, but Capt. Carlin carried it back to the boat, and I did the grunting for him.

The first tornado I ever saw in Florida, struck us just after our dinner on board. We saw the black cloud, covering the northern horizon, coming down on us, in time to make everything snug; raised our shelter canvas over the cockpit, gave the anchor fifty feet of cable, and rode out the fierce wind and waves of an hour's duration, dry and safe.

Not half a mile from our anchorage is a small island where congregates a large flock of those splendid white pelicans. We are plotting against two or three of them for specimens, but while one can shoot grey pelicans in plenty, these rare white ones are very wary, and we are not sure of success.

Why is it when you wish very much to obtain possession of a certain thing, it is so often so hard to secure? Or is it because it is so hard to obtain that we so much desire it? We can, if we wish, get a dozen grey pelicans with a little effort, but we don't want them; we desire white pelicans. But white pelicans are as shy as deer; and though we tried to ambush them, we failed.

And then we took our surf lines and went over to the ocean for a fish. In an hour's time we had on the sand five sea bass, in all some seventy pounds weight, the largest 25 pounds. We brought back for our use what we could, and gave the rest back to the sea. Mr. Gunn had taken with him his gun, and on our arrival at our river landing a fine large otter was swimming a few rods away. A charge of double B shot turned him up. He is four feet from tip of nose to end of tail.

Jan. 31.—A little rain last night, but clear again this morning. I tell you we do not envy any hotel loungers. We have the best corn and wheat cakes, coffee, ham, fish, hominy, chowder, etc. you ever tasted, and day and night the pure, soft air, which of itself is almost meat and drink.

Feb. 1st.—We left Hogan's this morning with a fair wind, and anchored near Merritt's island about noon for a visit to a Mr. Allen from Minnesota, who settled here for his health a few years ago. Unable to find sweet potatoes in Titusville, we were promised some at Allen's. We spent an hour in trying to find the trail to his house, but thick hammock and tall saw grass marsh blocked our way, and we gave up the effort and went on to the next settler.[8] He had no potatoes. On we went to the clearing of a German. He had no potatoes to sell, but would give us a pailful; and we dug them and were happy. We secured here a piece of Cassava root. It tastes raw, like a Spanish chestnut, cooked, looks like a sweet potato, but tasteless. The Cassava is cultivated, and is a long tender tuber-shaped root.

2d.—Laid at anchor last night off Dr. Wetfelt's [Wittfeld], an old German resident, and who is an enthusiast on the habits and varieties of butterflies.

With the assistance of his daughter, he has collected many varieties, and during a chase last evening he related to us many interesting facts about butterflies and birds. He trains at call the forest birds to visit his premises for food. He related a fact, established by repeated observation, respecting the cardinal bird, that the young after they are fully fledged, are ranged in a row, and fed from the bill of the male bird. Even hominy strewn on the beach was taken up by the male bird and placed in the bill of the young birds, long after they were fully able to pick up their own hominy.[9] After breakfast we crossed over to the ocean. We are out of fish, and shall try the surf for bass.

Feb. 3.—Still at rest in this quiet bay. The sandy beach here is lined with the queer horse shoe crab, some of them two inches across the shell. Many of them have barnacles on their shells, and growing on one I saw a live oyster. After breakfast we went surf fishing over on the ocean. We had caught all the bass we needed, and I was about to pull in my line, when a huge shark took the hook fast. Now came the issue of who should "come in;" but the shark soon compromised by rolling up on my line above the wire, and cutting the line, coolly taking away my best hook and lead.

I wound up my line, thankful that I had it left, and went down the beach for sea beans and shells. Mr. Gunn just now shot a couple of mallard ducks, and Carlin is laying in stock of wood for our cook stove.

Feb. 4.—"Rocked in the cradle of the deep;" that is, about 25 inches deep, the soundings of this anchorage last night, in a strong southwester, which made the *Ella* dance pretty lively, but we slept well. About daylight the captain took an observation, and said: "We must get out of this, for it is going to blow." We thought it was blowing then, but we up anchor and tore through the white caps to the Merritt island shore, where we found anchorage in too shoal water for any heavy sea, and none too soon; for the wind increased to a heavy gale, and has been howling all day. We went ashore on the island and visited a couple of settlers, a mile or so distant, on the Indian river side. Dug some more sweet potatoes, saw a fine pineapple field, and beautiful roses blooming in the open air, and were back to our boat for dinner.

This afternoon two of us went ashore with our guns. One discharge of both barrels of my Parker brought down seven ducks.

Leaving Banana lagoon at the south end of Merritt's island, we sailed out into Indian lagoon and rounded into a bay on the east, where the old hermit Haddock lived and died, of whom I wrote in past winters. The place is deserted and the half finished house desolate. Here we took another trail a mile long through a saw palmetto plain, over to the ocean again.

Fig. 9. Rockledge as shown in an 1885 Florida souvenir picture book. (New York, Adolph Wittemann, publisher. Author's collection)

Titusville, Feb. 8.—We have finished our cruise of two weeks on the Banana lagoon, and are back to this point, before we go down to Jupiter, on purpose to get news from home, having heard no later than the 12th January. For two weeks we heard not a word of the world's doings away from our boat, and we deem a forty-five mile sail to get news from home, a pleasant pastime, as we are in no hurry. On our way up yesterday we landed a few minutes at Rockledge, about twenty miles below this, and the most beautiful spot on the lagoon. The shore is shell rock with deep water, and the water front land for two hundred feet wide is a beautiful level palmetto grove, all clear from underbrush, making a most charming shaded spot, a quarter of a mile stretch. Back of this the hotel and store and a few houses, all flanked by fine orange groves, a charming picture of tropical beauty.

We were very glad to get letters from home here, and the *Times* up to Jan. 18.

We start for Jupiter and perhaps farther to-morrow.[10]

WINTERING ON THE INDIAN LAGOON

On Board the *Ella,* Off St. Lucie, Feb. 16.—After mailing my notes of our trip on Banana lagoon, we replenished stores and started southward on the Indian lagoon.

We had to beat against head winds, and one day had to lay to, the wind was so strong. Went on shore and dug in a large mound but discovered nothing. The 10th we went over to the ocean again at two different places during the day. We anchored for the night near life-saving station No. 1.

These life-saving stations on the coast of Florida are of very little importance or efficiency. They have comfortable houses of large dimensions, boat houses, and good boats, but there is no force that could begin to move one of the boats out of the houses, and they could be of no possible use to save life from a wreck. Should any one come ashore near the station, they would be cared for at the house. The boat house of No. 1 was blown down two years ago, and has never been rebuilt. The boats are covered with some of the boards from the ruins.

In the morning we went ashore, where an old man has located and lives all alone, and a more perfect picture for an illustrated Robinson Crusoe could not be sketched.[11] A little way from a low oyster shell beach, is a cottage, thatched on both sides and roof with closely laid palmetto leaves. An old man, tolerably erect, and of good stature, with long grey hair, and a long white beard, and with the weird dreamy look of a hermit, invited us into the hut. A couple of cottage chair frames, the seats some kind of dried skin, a rude bedstead in the corner, and a rude rough board table, composed the furniture. A square rough coquina stone altar in the middle of the room served for a place to do his cooking, over an open fire on top, and no place for the escape of smoke but the two doors always open. The walls were hung with utensils, skins, etc., and the floor with a heavy manitee [sic] net, the skull of the manitee [sic], a wild cat, and other like works of nature. He cultivates a small piece of land, cleared except of the large live oaks which are only killed. He gave us some of the largest oysters I ever saw. I bought a finely marked tiger cat skin of him, and we moved on, and anchored for the night not far from the large barge of the U.S. coast and river survey force, Maj. Boyd in command.[12]

The major insisted that we come aboard and dine with him, a partial acquaintance having been commenced on the steamer on our way up the St. Johns river. We found him in very comfortable quarters. The *Steadfast,* although of necessity a scowhull for the shallow water here, is large, commodiously fitted up with several state rooms, dining room, kitchen and other rooms.[13]

The next morning, we took Maj. Boyd in our row boat, and we went with him through a series of side lagoons, over to a trail he had out to the ocean, where his work was in progress.

While the other parties went to the woods, I went a long, three miles down the shore. When a fellow has tramped two full hours away and is just as tired as he can be, how much sport is there in the contemplation of the fact that he has to do it all over again to get back. Nothing can save one from despair, ordinarily, but in my case, my course was on the higher level plateau of the beach, where we find the sea breeze, and the course back was over a lower line where we find the shells; but with a heavy bag of treasures growing heavier with every step with new shells, you may rest assured the starting point was reached with no feigned thankfulness. We parted with Major Boyd and his associates next day with regret, for we found them true gentlemen.

Last night we tied up to the mangroves at Indian river inlet. The most interesting things we found there were the carcasses of five large black fish, ten to fourteen feet long each, thrown upon the beach, and swarms of sand flies.

St. Lucie P.O.—We have just been to the post-office here, and found letters and the *Times,* up to February 1. This is the last office on the lagoon, and ninety miles from Titusville. We go from here to two or three more crossings to the ocean, and then to Jupiter, 45 miles.

Capt. Carlin signals for dinner, and I close this for the mail here.[14]

AMONG THE MANGROVES

Lake Worth, Feb. 21.—After sending out my last letter from St. Lucie, we sailed eighteen miles, and across to the east shore and into a bay skirted by mangroves, where we anchored, and taking the row boat we made for an opening in the shore where the foliage met over a narrow channel, running into the mangrove swamp. Through this we pushed and pulled the boat, part of the way cutting with an axe a course through the closely overhanging branches and limbs and snags in the water; at other times lying down and pushing under. We were in the heart of a dense mangrove forest, and the scenery was new and strange. At one time we heard not far off the agonized bleating of a deer, no doubt falling a victim to the deadly panther. We pushed on a half mile out into an open water fifty feet wide for quite a distance, which ended in a narrow sand beach within ten rods of the ocean over a sand ridge.

Now it happened that an alligator laid on that beach, just where we wanted to land; and I could not do anything else but bring my Winchester to bear upon him, and after I fired, that 'gator, whose brains were not very numerous, or he would not have disputed our landing as he did, hadn't brains enough left to speak of. He gave two or three flounderings and turned up dead as ever a 'gator was. He was only six feet long. On our route back, not having to chop our way, I could take more time to note the peculiar features of the mangrove swamp. The trees were not over forty feet tall, but started in an impenetrable thicket of roots that some six to eight feet above ground concentrate into a sort of body, that generally branched off into a tangled top, with thick, glossy, rich green leaves. The tangle of roots and branches is so impenetrable to anything of any size, that a settler here once saw a bear caught in it in trying to escape, and the man worked in and killed it. The mangrove, not satisfied with its hundred other roots in the air, puts forth a hundred more sprouts from the branches, and sends them down, straight stems, to take root. Some of these stem roots are ten feet long, in clusters and single stems.

We have not been very seriously annoyed with insects except once on the Banana, a little red bug, so small one cannot see it, without sharp eyes, struck us, and its bite is more serious than a mosquito bite; and at Indian River inlet, the sand flies were very numerous, night and morning. They are like the little black gnat of the north. You can hardly imagine a more intense annoyance than a swarm of these sand flies. They fill your eyes, and nose and ears, and cover every spot of exposed flesh, and the poor victim of a tourist can only thrash around in despair, and cry out, "Why are we tormented before our time?" But these flies do not last long after the sun is up.

Sunday last we tied up to the low bank, in the lower narrows, at a place used for a camping ground by the Indians, every [*sic*] since the discovery of the country; it being the only dry spot for several miles. It is in a thick grove of fine palmettoes, while on all sides around, the river is enclosed, seemingly, such is the crookedness of the stream, and the shores are fringed with the dense, green, glossy foliage, of the mangroves hanging over to the water's edge. We remained here the night, and then moved on for Jupiter. Passing through the narrows, we shot an alligator, eight feet long. Gunn and myself both hit him in the head, and killed him instantly. We save the lives of a great many ducks, every 'gator we kill. We have a great love for the ducks, and we shoot the ducks to save them from the mouths of the alligators, and we shoot the alligators to keep them from killing the ducks. Thus we kill two birds with one stone. Do you say the alligators are not birds? Please tell me then why do they lay eggs? for they build a raised nest in the marsh and deposit the eggs in it for the sun to hatch.

Speaking of birds, we have here a great variety, largely water birds; we have the grey and white pelicans, white egrets, large white heron, the small white heron, the small white ibis with black tipped wings, the large white ibis, the wood ibis, great blue heron, small blue heron, cranes, gannets, man-of-war hawks, cormorants, buzzards, eagles, hawks, half a dozen kinds of ducks, gulls, crows, &c., &c. The roseate spoonbill and red flamingo, once plenty, are rare now. There are various other kinds of native birds, and many songsters on land. There is one water bird, a kind of gull called the shear-water, from its bill and method of killing its food. Its bill is long like a pair of shears, only the lower half is nearly two inches longer than the upper. It shoots into a school of small fish and eats them in pieces at once.

We arrived at Jupiter inlet on the 21st, at 3 p.m., thirty hours from the Indian camp ground, and only 15 miles. For five miles we had to tow the boat against wind and tide, and for a quarter of a mile we pulled the boat from stake to stake with a long rope, and the rest of the way beating against wind and tide. Of course we tied up over night. We had determined to improve the first fair wind and sea and go down to Lake Worth.

This is another lagoon south of Indian river, about twenty miles long and about two miles wide, with an inlet from the ocean, twelve miles from Jupiter, and our course was outside on the ocean that distance. We anchored for the night at Jupiter, and about daylight Capt. Carlin aroused us from our sleep with "If we are going to Lake Worth now is the time of tide to cross the bar. Shall we go?" And we said "go." In less than thirty minutes we were on our course, and with the ebb tide passed out into the blue water in fine style. Now I can never decide whether this gulf water is blue, or green, but it is beautiful. We moved down the coast with a light wind and sea, with a light ground swell, and only a little ripple of wavelets. An ocean steamer passed us only about a mile away. The wind was so light we made coffee and had a good lunch on our way, and did not enter Lake Worth until nearly noon. We entered the lake near the north end, and thro' a very crooked and shoal passage. In passing over a long stretch of water, about two feet deep, and clear as crystal, we passed close by over fifty large sharks from six to ten feet in length. We nearly ran on to a saw fish that must have been over fifteen feet long. Just before we came in another large steamer passed not a quarter of a mile away.

We are now moving towards the lower end of the lake and propose to take it all in before we go back to Jupiter. We can see fine coconut trees on shore, and here and there a settler's house.

The weather continues warm, a little too warm in the sun, but always delightful in the shade. Our pores keep well open when we exercise on our tramps on shore and on the ocean beach. We have visited the ocean beach sixteen times, and walked it nearly thirty miles, in all.[15]

MARCH IN FLORIDA

Jupiter Inlet, March 4.—I closed my last letter just after we entered Lake Worth. That day we sailed down a few miles and tied up to the rude wharf of the oldest settler who remains here. During the war a settlement was started here by some men from some of the southern states, as a refuge from the confederate army, with some of their slaves. They succeeded admirably in getting beyond conscription service, but they also got beyond any base of supplies, and before they could raise anything they nearly starved, and had to abandon the settlement. Mr. Charles Moore, a resident of twenty years in Florida, came to this place about ten years ago. He found a few coconut trees, and has now over twenty bearing trees.[16]

The coconut tree bears in about eight years from the nut, which is planted, and at that time is a foot in diameter at the ground. These trees are now bearing, and do so continually the year round, new blossom stems putting out every month, and have on them now in clusters, ripe nuts, and other grades of growth, back to the blossom. Each stage of maturity has its own stem on which hangs the fruit, and always starting from and remaining near the base of the massive stems of the leaves at their junction with the body of the tree. Each blossom stem sets a large number of nuts, but they seldom mature here over six or eight nuts to a stem. On Mr. Moore's place are over eighteen hundred bearing banana plants, and coming on, some three hundred coconut trees. There is on his place an oleander hedge some forty rods in length, about fifteen feet high, and in full bloom. There are in front of his house three or four hibiscus plants in full bloom, eight feet high, and the regal blossoms, some five inches across, present a beautiful sight. Large quantities of tomatoes are raised here, and are ready for market by Jan. 1st. All tropical fruits can be grown here. Mr. Moore would take no pay for a bunch of bananas and a pail of tomatoes. He picks his tomatoes green, and they ripen on the way to market.

After breakfast we gathered some curious prickly pods containing a large drab bean. We left Mr. Moore picking tomatoes in the field the 23d day of February, and moved off down the lake with a fair wind.

Our next stop was at Mr. Pierce's, who has been here ten years, and came from Illinois. I partook of the hospitality of this family three days, while the rest of our crew went into the woods and swamps, five miles, for a hunt. I found the Pierce place on an island. Tomatoes are his principal crop, though he has a fine lot of cabbages well under way, also a lot of coconut trees growing nicely, some of them bearing nicely, and I found Chicago and N.Y. papers on his table only two weeks old. Mrs. Pierce did all she could to make my stay pleasant, and her little seven years old daughter, Lillie, guided me around and told me the names of trees and plants.[17]

I gather from the people here, that all the coast below Lake Worth is entirely unsettled until you reach Miami, fifty miles. At that point commences a line of scattered settlers, on the main land and on the keys. These settlers are chiefly a class of people called "conchs," I suppose because they eat largely the shell fish of that name. These people are a distinct and peculiar people; born wreckers; and a report of a ship ashore will gather them to the spot as quick as the dead carcass calls the buzzards; and yet they are said to be honest and religious. One of their peculiar customs is to have their children in turn ask the blessing at the table. These folks are said to be descendants of the tories of the revolution, who fled to the Bahamas after the war. It is certain that they came to the Florida coast from those islands. They might be an interesting people for some one to investigate.[18]

We sailed from Pierce island, two miles, to a narrow crossing to the ocean, where I secured on the beach a bag of those curious finger and vase sponges. At 11 a.m. the 27th of February, we turned our bow northward, and henceforth, save a side excursion up Lucie river, our course will be slowly homeward.

The lower end of Lake Worth, the most southern point of our tour, is in latitude 26°30′ and abreast the southern end of lake Okeechokee [Okeechobee], which is only thirty miles distant. The everglades come up to within five miles of us at the south end of Lake Worth.

I wish to remark if there is a man, woman or child in the north who has a comfortable home, and is ever discontented and dissatisfied with home, let any of them live in Florida a while, and if it does not cure them, they have a worse home than can often be found in the north. In this lower Florida many of the settlers are from fifty to a hundred miles from any store of supplies, and sometimes are obliged to go without ordinary supplies for weeks together. I was once in an intelligent, worthy family, where they had no butter, sugar, potatoes, no meat but salt pork, except occasionally venison or ducks. Of course no milk but the condensed can be obtained. The water here is always as warm as summer river water north, and no ice. It is a peculiar fact that the water from the deepest well is no colder than surface water, and gets colder by being drawn and set in the air in the shade. In these remote places there are no school houses or churches, and really worthy people forget sometimes even the day of the week and month, and some pay no attention to such a matter. On Lake Worth the people are particularly isolated, having to go outside on the ocean twelve miles, and with their small vessels, are often deprived of that channel for some time by adverse wind and wave, and then it is a hundred miles to supply stores. But there is a good set of men here, and with their tropical advantages for early vegetables, they will in time change the lack of transportation and supplies, and they are already talking of a church and school house. The population of this section is seventy-five, and more are coming. In a few years the coconut exportation from Lake Worth will be very large.

On our way up the lake we stopped at Dimmick's [Dimick's], a Michigan man.[19] He has twelve hundred coconut trees well started. We laid in five bunches of bananas at Moore's, three or four hundred bananas for one dollar, and moved on for the north end of the lake. Mr. Moore had Irish potatoes as large as hen's eggs from planting the first of January. We anchored for the night at the upper end of the lake near the inlet, and next morning found the sea too heavy for our little boat. We changed anchorage and went to gathering conches, which we find all around us in shoal water, where we can wade with our pants rolled up, and we determined to turn "conches," and have a conch chowder for dinner. While we were at our meal with a good relish for our new dish, a settler came along in a row boat, and we hailed him and invited him to chowder, and we, after dinner, went ashore with him to his cabin.

His name was Rogers, he was a South Carolinian; and he had been here alone a year and a half. His hut was made by placing small joists together from the ground like the roof of a house, and thatched with palmetto leaves, all open at one gable. All his goods were stored here, and all his bunk; his cooking was all done outside over an open fire. He seemed hopeful of the future, was in an orange grove, and on an island near by had a banana field. He said he raised bunches of the dwarf kind that would weigh a hundred pounds. He received good returns for his fruit when the New York market was not glutted with foreign fruit. When it was, the sale merely paid freight.

We had a taste of uncertain navigation in getting away from Lake Worth. We had been detained two days by adverse wind and heavy sea, but the third day with a passable wind not quite contrary, and apparently not a very heavy sea, we decided to go; and after crossing the bar safely, we ran out a mile into the gulf stream water, with a fair wind, our boat riding the heavy swells nobly; but when we turned on our course, with wind and wave striking us quartering on our bows, we pounded so we could make very little progress, and we decided it was "no go" that day, and we went back to anchorage and made another conch chowder. Next morning early we tried to go out again, but found the sea too heavy for our flat bottom boat. As our fresh water was getting low we sailed over to the west shore of the lake to replenish. There are no wells or fresh streams near here, and Capt. Carlin went ashore and dug a hole in the sand but a few feet from salt water and found good sweet water. We have to wade ashore, having left our row boat at Jupiter, on account of our sea voyage. But we get our boat within ten rods or less of the shore, in fifteen inches of water, and hard sand bottom.

Mr. Gunn, who is an amateur bird collector, goes into the woods for birds; we must pass the time some way until the sea "goes down" and so we gather some more conch shells. The water is warm in the lagoon, and capital bathing. While waiting we were joined by two boats with Mr. Reed, from Boston, and Mr. Williams, from Taunton, Mass. While we were lieing [*sic*] here a large open English boat, called a "ship launch," washed ashore on the beach, with oars all in. We could not make out the name on the stern.

On the fifth day of our detention, old Neptune graciously said, "You may go," and we waited not on the order of our going, and a gentle wind and easy ocean swell, gave us a beautiful sail to Jupiter. We made the run to Jupiter in about three hours, but we found the tide running out the narrow entrance so strong we could not enter with the light wind, and we came to anchor outside, and rocked on the swells a couple of hours, then sailed off and on for two hours more, until the tide turned. All around us sharks were taking exercise by throwing themselves out of the water, at times ten feet high, whirling in the air, their white bellies glistening in the sun like silver, and making the water fly finely when they fell. We have just anchored near the light house, and save the detention in getting away, were well pleased that we visited Lake Worth. The latest papers we have seen were from New York, dated Feb. 11th.[20]

FAREWELL TO JUPITER

On Board the *Ella,* March 6th.—With an east wind and a flowing tide we left our anchorage near the light house this morning at Jupiter, and turned into the Indian lagoon for a return through the narrows. The beautiful, clear, opaline blue tide water of the gulf stream had already backed up the coffee colored waters of the Loosahatchie [Loxahatchee], which forms a junction here with the lagoon, and we could see every fish near us, and every sand ripple on the bottom. We soon lost sight of the inlet, and bade it farewell, probably forever.

We were much amused over an article we saw here in one of our popular monthlies, at the light house. The writer pretends to give a narrative of a trip on Indian river, and gives several thrilling descriptions of personal adventures. He did come here; and had the same boatman and boat we have. Our captain declares that every instance of peculiar interest, such as the breaking loose of the boat in the night, the collision with another boat, the catching of the big shark, and the adventure with the young pelican, is a pure and simple fabrication. One would like to see the belt made from the skin of the imaginary shark. I think I can say I have always confined myself in these letters to strictly truthful narrative. I could easily invent very thrilling experiences.[21] We passed through the lower narrows in fine style; moving in four days over ground that took us nearly two days in going down. Just before we arrived at the mouth of the St. Lucie river, we had the captain put Mr. Gunn and myself ashore, and we went over to the ocean and walked up the beach two miles to another trail, where the *Ella* picked us up. I may have tired the reader in my letters by my frequent repetition of our visits to the ocean, but my excuse is that my twenty-six visits to, and some forty or more miles strolling on the beaches, during this trip, have afforded to me the greatest interest and enjoyment of the tour. About three p.m., we passed into the wide mouth of the St. Lucie, and with a strong wind directly aft, we went tearing up the river, the white foam surging from our bows in fine style. We are glad to have a change to fresh water; and can now bring out our soap.

March seventh.—We anchored last night ten miles up the St. Lucie, near where we find a party from Cazenovia, N.Y., in camp in a dry, open pine grove, and near where a party of Seminole Indians were camped a short time since. The Indians evidently had only two sheltered tent habitations, and left the poles standing. The main part of the encampment had slept in the open air, on beds of a few saw palmetto leaves, each brave having a bed to himself, always his head against the trunk of one of the tall pines, and no covering but his blanket and the sky. This morning we started out for a stroll before breakfast. In about two hours we caught seven black bass and sea bass, the largest black bass five pounds; the largest sea bass sixteen pounds; forty-seven pounds in all. We are somewhat surprised to find the salt water sea bass in this perfectly fresh water.

We tried both kinds of bass for breakfast, and fresh caught and hot from the frying pan, you may believe they were both good. After a long tramp in the pine woods, we hoisted sail and ran down towards the mouth of the river, and anchored near a grand palmetto, and other dense tropical growth, hammock. Just before dark at this point we succeeded in adding wild turkey to our provision supply.

March eighth.—I had a long walk this morning in a trail over to a settler's house on the Indian river side of the bank, cut by the settler to have access to a cultivated field near our anchorage. At the house the women were setting the breakfast table on the open portico. The growth of tree, vine and shrubbery, was a tropical tangle. There were the large live oaks with wide-spreading branches, with scant foliage, but the bare limbs covered here and there with air plants, the blossom buds on the flower stem all red and ready to open in large red flowers; all around an interminable tangle of smaller growth, the foliage so dense overhead the sun never enters; all this tied together with all kinds of vines and creepers, some of them like barbed wire, in thorns. All through this, and climbing to the top of the thicket, were woven in a climbing cactus, which starts from the ground a fist thick leaf two feet long and two or three inches wide, the edges well set with sharp thorns; and from this leaf starts another just like it, and so on in a succession of links it runs out ten or fifteen feet, of the same size the whole length.

We were under way soon after breakfast, and at ten o'clock rounded St. Lucie point, and into Indian river, our course once more towards the north; one hundred and fourteen miles yet distant from Titusville, and three hundred and fifty from Jacksonville.

Arriving at Lucie post-office we were delighted to find letters from home as late as the 19th of February, and a lot of *Times* up to the 17th of February . . .

March ninth.—We wished to make a run of a dozen miles this morning to a certain ibis hunting ground, and though it was blowing hard the wind was fair for our course, and with double-reefed sail we started. The wind increased so we had to lower the gaff and spill half the wind out of the sail, and then we drove before the wind to our anchorage.

We had a second shower, for over four weeks, to-day. The mercury ranging for six weeks, save a very few days, about 80, but with always a refreshing breeze.

In the afternoon we had a fine run to Pelican island.

March tenth.—I shall not repeat my description of Pelican island in former years, but when we landed yesterday we found for the first time the birds were nesting.

All over the drier parts of the island the nests were scattered in almost countless numbers, chiefly on the ground, but a few on the dead limbs of some old mangrove trees; and we saw illustrated the entire growth of these birds from the chick just pecking his bill through the shell; the little fellow just ushered into this world of fish and tourists; the larger growth with only arms for wings, all covered with a white furry down, up to the full grown bird nearly ready to fly. And a more truly developed exhibition of ungainly action was never seen. Some of the larger birds would waddle out of the nest, rolling over perhaps once or twice in the effort; others remain and snap their long bills with an angry cry as they thrust them at us; a little way off the old ones were standing around on the ground and in the shallow water, and flying so near us we might reach them with a fishpole, and in numbers certainly into the thousands. Many nests contained newly laid eggs, seldom more than three in a nest. We did not shoot down any of the birds. After sundown we had an interesting visit from one of the young full-grown pelicans, which came swimming out to examine our strange craft. Capt. Carlin met the distinguished guest with the row boat and brought him alongside. He was a big fellow, as large as a full-grown goose. After a reasonable interview, we invited him to leave, but he would not go. We pushed him overboard, but he then tried to get aboard the large boat, and did get on top of the rudder, not over three feet from our cockpit seats. We pushed him off, but he clambered back again, and struck his foot long bill at us with an angry scream and snap and with his long bill he kept us at least two feet distant, and we let him remain, and he held the fort until this morning, when he was found actually on board, on deck; we pushed him off again, and he swam away.[22] Just before dark we had seen countless numbers of white herons, ibises, egrets, and man-of-war birds, settling on a mangrove island not very far away, and as it is very difficult to approach these birds in daylight, we determined to try them after dark. We left our affectionate pelican in charge of *Ella* and rowed and pushed and waded up to the island, but we could not clearly see even the white birds by only starlight, we could hear their cawing in the trees, and as we frightened them to a rise banged away all our barrels where we thought they ought to be. We picked up a white ibis, two egrets, and a fine man-of-war, or "frigate bird," which measures seven feet from tip to tip of wings. I shall try and bring home his skin.

As we were about to leave the island, in the darkness, a white egret actually tried to alight on Mr. Gunn's head, for a roost; and Gunn came very nearly catching him by the legs. We hurried our departure; for the idea that brave hunters like ourselves were to be turned into bird roosts, was not agreeable. We shall choose daylight for our hunting after this.

On our way up we visited the "agricultural college" of Florida. It consists of a solitary coquina building, forty miles below Titusville. The building is about sixty feet square, and two stories; very plainly built, and was never occupied, and never will be for its original purpose. It is said to be a standing monument of a corrupt job some ten years since, costing about ten thousand dollars, but absorbing the fifty odd thousand of the Florida agricultural fund. But this coquina rock is very porous, hence the absorption.[23]

March twelfth.—Our course on these waters is ended. For forty-six days we have been on our wanderings on the *Ella,* the general incidents being duly recorded in my letters, and sailed about six hundred miles. We have been virtually in the open air night and day, for our little shelter cabin is enclosed only on top and three sides, and we almost always kept the side windows open night and day. My grey suit, a fair color when we started, is a dingy yellow now from the sunlight, and many a small rent, and an ominous fraying at the knees, tells of many a battle with saw palmettos and thorny vines and shrubs, and I lay it aside for my "best suit" cheerfully. Henceforth we are the patrons of hotels, steamboats, and railroads. To-morrow we pack our collections and curiosities and ship them home by freight. I have nothing wonderful, and yet some things to me curious. I have "a few more beans," "sea beans," and I intend to distribute them through the houses of Lenawee to such as desire them. We look forward with pleasure towards home, for home is dearer than all the world beside.

Fig. 10. A personable pelican. (*St. Nicholas,* July 1889)

To readers of my letters this winter let me say, if they have noticed a lack of description of the country and places, please remember I have written up this section fully for two winters previous, and could not go on to repeat former descriptions. If I have interested the readers of the *Times,* my ambition is satisfied.[24]

Adrian, March 21.—Just after mailing his letter to the *Times,* mentioned elsewhere, Mr. F. R. Stebbins realized a faint conception of the horrors of a forest fire. The palmettos and dry grass around Titusville, Fla., where he was stopping, took fire, and for half an hour it looked as though the place was doomed to destruction. Luckily, however, no building burned, and no great damage was done.[25]

Adrian, March 24.—Mr. F. R. Stebbins returned from his trip to Florida last evening.[26]

7   1883 Life on the Lagoons

Manchester, Jan. 18.—L. D. Watkins leaves for Adrian on Monday morning, where he will be joined by F. R. Stebbins of Adrian, and Mr. Sutton of Tecumseh, and proceed to the land of flowers and oranges. They go equipped for observing and preserving curious and valuable relics, and such as they may find on land, river or sea. They have chartered a sailing craft, in which they purpose taking a cruise through Indian river and perhaps around the coast to Key West. We have the promise of a letter or two for publication.[1]

Manchester, Feb. 1.—L. D. Watkins did not go south as he intended.[2]

Titusville, Feb. 1.— Messrs. Stebbins and Sutton gave us a short call yesterday afternoon. They came on the *Osceola* yesterday and expect to start down the river in a day or so on a pleasure trip. Mr. Carlin will carry them with the sloop *Ella*.[3]

Adrian, Feb. 7.—The *Florida Star,* published at Titusville, Fla., on the 1st, acknowledges a call from Messrs. Stebbins and Sutton. By the way, we note by the same paper, that on that day the thermometer stood at 66 degrees at noon.[4]

NOTES FROM FLORIDA

Mosquito Lagoon, February 2.—After resting two days at Titusville, procuring stores and fitting out our boat generally, this morning, at 10 a.m., we hoisted sail, and steered for the little canal leading to Mosquito lagoon, which was built by the United States government during the Seminole war, connecting Indian river with the other water, and is about a fourth of a mile long, twelve to twenty feet wide, and cut a large part of the way through the hard coquina, or shell rock, in some places eight or ten feet high. The rock is, in many places, worn out underneath, forming a very romantic passage-way for our boat. Mosquito lagoon, like Indian river, is very shoal, and Capt. Carlin had to go overboard and "boost" the boat over the shoals to get into the three or four feet deep water.

We are now running before a nice breeze, bound for Mosquito inlet, which connects this water with the ocean. This lagoon lies north of Indian river, along the coast, and this is my first visit to its water.

February 3.—We anchored last night opposite a hotel at "Oak Hill," near the north end of Mosquito lagoon. Here we find a great number of beautiful mangrove islands; beyond them we enter another long stretch of water called "Hillsboro River," and beyond that another section called "Halifax River," all forming really one lagoon, about sixty miles long, with a fine inlet from the ocean, nearly midway between the two ends. This morning, after our breakfast on warm corn cake, baked sweet potatoes, Adrian creamery butter, Beals & Colvin's ham, and capital coffee, we moved on past the islands, through a very crooked channel hidden in a broad expanse of very shallow water. After making our way through the channel, we made a fine run for "Turtle Mound," a prehistoric shell mound over fifty feet high in the center, and covering about two acres of ground. We can see it a long distance, and it looks like quite a hill. It is composed mostly of oyster shells.[5] The ocean shore was only about forty rods distant, and we went over, Mr. Sutton in his shirt sleeves; and while I am writing, under the cabin, he is outside, in the same rig, trying to hit a coon on shore with his Winchester rifle. A grand surf of a half-dozen breaking swells, ten feet high, was thundering along the coast as far as we could see. Large white herons are seen along the shore of the lagoon, at a safe distance, but Sutton dropped a fine duck just now as it flew by. The sail this afternoon is one of unsurpassed beauty; as I write, looking out from our open cabin, aft, on both sides we glide along past low wooded shores of a dense mass of deep green foliage, like a trimmed hedge, now within a few yards distance, and now they recede to a half mile; every now and then water ways open away to new islands, and headlands, while in the distance, astern, we leave behind green islands and headlands; and before, new and changing scenery of similar description, is ever coming into view. A constantly changing beauty of land and water, I believe unsurpassed in the world.

We close the day at anchorage near New Smyrna, an old settlement, where over a hundred years ago one Turnbull started a colony of Minoricans [Minorcans], to cultivate indigo, but the scheme failed, and the colony was broken up. The place consists now of a few houses and a small hotel for hunters and fishers.[6]

We visited Mosquito inlet, where a fish factory for extracting the oil from fishes, and preparing the scraps and bones for fertilizers, has just been erected.[7] While fishing for bass in the inlet, Mr. Sutton hooked a large shark, and succeeded in hauling him into the very shoal water on the flat beach, when the hook pulled out. But N. M. did not mean to lose that shark. He dropped his line, and seized the monster by his tail; then the shark doubled on him with open jaws, wide enough to swallow a small dog. Then the fisherman let go as quick as he could conveniently, for he did not like the looks of that open countenance, armed with triple rows of very sharp teeth. Then the shark would straighten out, and Sutton seize him again by the tail, and give him another pull on the beach, dropping his tail as he again moved on the enemy with that wicked mouth over seven inches across, until well nigh exhausted, the man had conquered, and had the big fish high and dry on the beach. But the truth must be told that at one time, when Sutton's feet slipped, the floundering was so promiscuous, it was hard to tell which was Sutton, and which was shark. The shark was six feet four inches long, and would weigh over a hundred pounds.

To-day we are moving southward again, and stopping at Titusville for mail, shall move on down towards Jupiter.

6th.—Last night we laid at anchor in Mosquito lagoon, about half a mile from shore, in shoal water. The weather is as warm as midsummer in the north. This lagoon is well named, for we have had plenty of mosquitoes. Low shores with palmettoes along the shore flats, and pines in the back country; a few settlers' houses are seen on both sides of the water.

7th.—We passed the canal and came out into the Indian before night, and anchored in front of a fine orange grove, where on going ashore we found the owner, Mr. Perry, from the city of New York, who is also the owner of the celebrated Durmont [Dummitt] grove, a mile farther on. He gave us half a bushel of oranges, for which he would take no pay.

This is the grove purchased two years since by the Duke Costellucci [Castellucia] with so much parade, where his wife, a German girl of New York, with money for a poor Italian duke, was made a "duchess," and they essayed to play the *role* of nobility in an orange grove in Florida, almost entirely isolated from every part of the world. The natives here soon found the "duchess" ought to put the "t" into the title, and made sport of her coarse "style."[8] The grove was sold to Mr. Perry this year, who is spending the winter here with his family, and is a very frank and hospitable gentleman.

The people here are very proficient on the conch shell, as a musical instrument. Last night I was awakened by the sound of a shell blown from a boat coming in. As the pure mellow tones died away on the perfectly still air, from the shore another performer took up the strain, and sent it back like an echo, which was answered back again, by the first performer, with variations, all as pure and beautiful as the mellow notes of the French horn. Ere long, between the music of the shells, the colored women on the shore struck in with a wild

chanting of voice melody, of similar tone to the conchs, which added a peculiar weirdness to the concert; and as I look out upon the still night, and the
palm-lined shore lighted by a brilliancy of star-light seldom seen in the north,
I could easily imagine myself on the coast of Africa, and listening to some
incantation of the pagan natives.[9] We arrived at Titusville at 3 p.m., and are
off for Banana Lagoon as soon as we can lay in a supply of fresh water.[10]

Adrian, March 3.—Read the letter of F. R. Stebbins, in this issue. With our
thermometer but little above freezing, during the 24 hours, it is refreshing to
read of one which does not go below 70°.[11]

LIFE ON THE LAGOONS

Banana Lagoon, Feb. 9.—We came through Banana creek yesterday, with the
same beautiful weather we have had since we started aboard the *Ella,* mercury
from 70° to 78°, and a fine sea breeze. Laid at anchor in a broad shallow water
bay, at the north end of this lagoon. Of course, we are on our old cruising
grounds now. This morning, after breakfast, we started on a trail over to the
ocean, we had heard reports of whales ashore, somewhere above or below
Canaveral light, and we proposed to find out about it.[12] After a very warm
tramp of about a mile through the palmetto and oak scrub, on a pretty well
defined trail, or path, we came out on the ocean beach, and found that, as we
were in search of stranded whales, we had struck a bonanza the first time.
Along the shore, at a distance of three miles, laid the decaying carcasses of ten
whales, swashing in the surf, or thrown back up on the beach, in an advanced
state of decomposition. The tide was going out, and in about an hour the
monsters laid out of water. Some of them still retained their general form,
others were more decomposed, and many of the bones were strewn along the
beach, and sections of the vertebra, ribs, bones, &c., which were eight feet
long, eighteen inches broad, and would weigh several hundred pounds each.
Some of the sections of the vertebra were a full foot in diameter. What a mine
was here for the scientific society. A car load of these specimens could be
collected on this beach, but we were four miles from even our little boat, and
to carry some of these largest bones was impossible. Yet we were bound to
have some of them, and we went at work at first at the teeth, which we found
intact in two of the largest whales, and we performed a very neat piece of
dental work in extracting forty-five teeth, from four to five inches long, and
in an odorous atmosphere such as you may imagine arises from decomposing
whales, each forty-five feet in length. Words cannot describe it; but the fumes
of the Stggian [*sic*] pit could not have driven us away without those teeth. We
rested satisfied a little way off from the carcasses, when we had the ivories safe

in our collecting bag. And now comes in our work. Thus far our task had been play, with the odors thrown in; but we decided to bring away some of the bones. Of course we could not take the largest, but Capt. Carlin hung two large pieces of vertebra on a pole and carried them on his shoulders, and we started on the back track of three miles up the beach, and another mile over the trail. I think we shall all remember that tramp, for I tell you to my personal knowledge, two of those ribs and that bag of large teeth part of the way, were heavy before reaching our boat, but the oldest of the party must be permitted to boast that he took the lead, and came out ahead, and as fresh as any one. It was a big job for us, but the bones are now in our small boat, which we tow along with us, and we hope to get them home. We are satisfied though with one whaling expedition, if we have to "tote" bones like these four miles, with the mercury at eighty, and a clear sunshine.[13]

10th.—We tied up to the rude wharf at Burnham & Wilson's orange grove, on the east side of the lagoon, a little before sunset last night. When within half a mile of the shore we became agreeably aware of the difference in an odor from forty foot whales, three weeks dead, and a newly blossoming orange grove of eight hundred trees. The air was full of the delicate perfume of the blossoms. The odor of the orange blossoms is as agreeable as that of the tube rose, and very much like it.

Burnham & Wilson's grove is about five miles from Cape Canaveral, on a rich piece of sand, and grows sugar cane, pine apples, bananas, etc., as well as oranges. It is twenty-eight miles from Titusville, the nearest point of communication with neighbors of any number, and of shipment of products; but the water way helps out, as time is of little consequence here. What is not done to-day can be done to-morrow, or next week, just as well. We laid at this dock over night. Large flocks of ducks were feeding all around us within ten rods of our boat, and seemed almost like tame birds. We have found the ducks very tame everywhere. Hundreds of them feed near the shore right opposite the houses of Titusville.

12th.—A fair wind brought us to anchorage at the foot of Merritt's island, where we laid over night, and "bagged" a ten pound crevalle, an eighteen pound sea bass, and an unfortunate raccoon. Next day we run down the shore a few miles, and made another visit to the ocean, across a nearly level plain, about two miles through a thick low growth of oak and saw-palmetto scrub, the bottom dry white sand. We sat a long time on the beach, in a delightful sea breeze, and listened to a grand sermon from the thundering surf. Near night we saw a heavy storm coming up, and we up anchor and made for shelter in Turkey creek, some ten miles away, across the lagoon, which we made safely, through the white caps. This morning all is fair again, but rather warm for comfort. Our bones lie bleaching on the shore at Turkey creek—whale's bones, I mean—as they were cumbersome in our small boat, to await our return from further south. The specimens are clean, but have not yet acquired the perfume of roses. We hope by our return they will be improved. After rowing up this creek about three miles, we started on our way. Up Turkey creek we saw two more wrecks of rose-hued dreams of flowery homes in Florida—deserted plantations.

13th.—Laid at anchor last night in the mouth of Sebastian river, and move on to-day for Pelican island. A couple of miles from Sebastian, we called on a settler, a Mr. New, an old friend of Adrian college, and some of its officers, and well known to others of our citizens. He has a very pretty location, under the shadow of a fine group of palmettoes, and about half an acre set out with pine-apple plants. He keeps also a little stock of goods, and is starting another house. He says he is delighted with the place, and is fixed for life. The lagoon in front of him is some three miles wide, and he gets the ocean breeze over a narrow strip of land between the lagoon and the sea.[14] A little after noon we reached Pelican island, the breeding place of these birds. I have in former years described all this, and only repeat that hundreds of the birds were there, old and young. Mr. Sutton took some views of groups, which we think, if they develop well, will prove interesting. He brought with him a small camera for views.[15]

14th.—We laid-to last night at the mouth of a side channel, which runs up to a life saving station, and this morning took the small boat and went over, calling, on our way, on the old hermit, Estes, of whom I wrote last year. He is crippled with disease, and hobbles around on crutches, and spends most of his time keeping up a smoke in a huge pan in the center of his hut to drive off the mosquitoes, which are thicker than usual this winter.

We are now under way for St. Lucie, where we expect letters and papers from home, having heard nothing for three weeks, and nothing from any part of the outside world since Feb. 2d. We are having a very pleasant time, although we think the weather a little too warm. For fourteen days thus far on our boat we have not had ten minutes rain in the daytime, and only two or three light showers at night. The mercury has hardly varied five degrees, standing day and night from seventy-five to eighty. Everything on the shore is green, and like midsummer growth in the north. Arrived at St. Lucie, and found the *Times* up to Feb. 1st. We find no orange groves further south than sixty miles below Titusville; below that point is the home of the banana and pine apple. We shall go over to Indian river inlet to-morrow, and then disappear from all mail facilities for two weeks longer.[16]

SURF AND SEA

On Board, February 16.—Yesterday we sailed over to Indian river inlet for a little fishing. The inlet is about three miles from Lucie P.O., and we found a wonderful change there since last year. A new inlet has been formed by the washing out of a sandbar and plain some twenty rods wide, a hundred rods long, and an average height of about eight feet. We used to hunt over this beach for curiosities, and fish from it in the surf, and moor our boat near it, on the lagoon side. This beach and piece of land is all gone, and the sea waves and tides are breaking over its whole extent. Similar changes are in many places recorded along this coast. We visit places where not many years ago the sea rolled in through an inlet into the lagoon. Any heavy storm is liable to close the present inlets, and open new ones. We had several hours fishing near the inlet with fair success. We had out both bass lines, and shark lines, and caught a number of bass, crevalle, and grey snappers, from five to ten pounds in weight each. I had a large shark on my bass line, but the hook pulled out. Sutton had one on his shark line, but the hook broke; then one took his bass line and made things lively for a time. We finally worked him up near the boat, but could do nothing with him until I put a thirty-eight calibre pistol ball through his head, and he turned up. We lifted him into the boat, and found him five feet in length. We had on our bill of fare to-day, snapper, bass, and drum fish. We might have added crevalle, shark, mullet, and cat fish; but we can't be expected to eat everything in any one day.

17th.—Last night we rested in a quiet bay opposite the entrance to the old inlet creek through the mangrove swamp, we explored last year. This morning we pushed into the creek a hundred rods, but found the water so low it was impossible to get through. Went back to the *Ella,* and moved on to another crossing to the sea. In the afternoon we resorted to a novel and interesting shelter from a heavy squall, which came down upon us. Instead of making for the windward shore for shelter, we sailed directly to the shore exposed to the full strength of the wind coming over five miles of open water, two miles wide. We soon entered perfectly quiet water, over which the wind swept without raising a wave three inches high, and in large sections was actually glassy smooth, as if in a perfect calm. Such a water, in such an exposure in a high wind was indeed a curiosity. I found the water three feet deep, but completely filled with a growing water grass to within a few inches of the surface, and so compact that although we could sail through it no waves were raised by the high wind.

18th.—We had a high wind through part of the night, but our grass bed kept the water perfectly still, and our boat rested as quietly as if on shore above the water. Our two bushels of oranges, put aboard ten days' since, are nearly gone. The orange culture here is, no doubt, largely on the increase; but a comparison of figures of values in agricultural products of Florida, and even Lenawee county alone, is suggestive of thought for such as are inclined to be captivated with flowery visions of easy wealth in orange culture. From figures put forth by a document issued by the Florida Bureau of Immigration, I find the total value of the orange crop in this state, in 1880, was a little short of $675,000. With the exception of one or two cotton counties in the north part of the state, the orange crop must be seventy-five per cent of the whole exported agricultural products of Florida. Making allowance for the increase since 1880, a very liberal estimate of the surplus of the entire agricultural productions in the whole orange section of the state, and $2,000,000 would be a reasonable total. How much short of this is the exported surplus of our own county? These documents here are very liberal in estimate about what "can be done," but comparison as to what *is* done does not look favorable for a change from Lenawee county to Florida. From observations during six winters I have visited here, my first impressions are only strengthened. Only as a matter of health, should any man who prizes good society and social advantages, ever think of coming to Florida for a home. For any man, woman or child who has any aspirations, or love for a refined and comfortable home, had better leave hope behind when they come here to live. We ran into the "Old Cuba" place to get some bananas, and found there beans and radishes, full grown, and new Irish potatoes, large enough to eat. It rained last night, and a little this morning, but soon cleared off into the usual perfect weather, with mercury 76° to 80°.

From a trail to the ocean, near the Cuba plantation, we walked down the sea beach three miles, to the life saving station, where Carlin met us with the boat. On our way a strolling panther jumped over the sand ridge into bushes. Near the station the peculiar concrete lime rock breaks out into a bluff some twenty feet high, and worn into caves and spouting holes, that must make a grand sight in an easterly ocean storm.

19th.—From the station we ran directly for the mouth of the St. Lucie river, some five miles away, passing the coast survey vessel, moored at this point this winter. Last night we anchored ten miles up the Lucie. I caught, this morning, a sea bass and a black bass, and we had both kinds for breakfast. While I write, these early song birds are singing on the shore. Nowhere in Florida have I ever found as fine singers as on the St. Lucie. The song of the cardinal or red bird is very fine. Perched on some tall bush or a palmetto, on a still morning, we hear his clear voice with tone like a silver bell, ring out, "Sweet, sweet, you sweet! meet you, meet you, meet you! hello! hello! hello!" In some parts the mocking birds are plenty; and one so fortunate as to hear a choice singer in his native pine grove, will never forget it. His song cannot be described better than to say it combines all the notes of the most beautiful song birds, with charming original variations. For the first time in two weeks this morning there was a change of wind. It has been blowing steadily from the southeast every day, now it comes from the north, and as it was a favorable wind to get through the lower narrows, after Capt. Carlin had "done up his dishes" we hoisted sail for Jupiter. On our way out of the Lucie river we had a little excitement in a race with a forty-foot two masted yacht run by a fancy New Yorker. Owing to a short bend in the river we had to beat against the wind about a mile. The other boat had one tack the start of us, but Carlin put the *Ella* after him. We had it about equal as we were both on the last port tack before we could take a fair wind, the other boat ahead. Capt. Carlin suddenly took a starboard tack, and shot across a point into a fair wind on our course. I took the tiller, and the captain raised the jib, and we went booming before the wind, leaving the crack boat far behind before she got ready to tack. A fine run through the lower narrows brought us to Jupiter Inlet early in the evening.

21st.—We have been at Jupiter two days, and cannot start on our return until the norther ceases. This north wind brought cooler weather, which is agreeable. This afternoon, when the tide turned to come in, we went to the south beach for a little fishing. I caught five kinds, crevalle, grouper, snapper, lady fish and a cat fish. One of the snappers went into our frying pan, and we have just dined royally on him. The government is building a fine new two-stories house for the light-house keeper, and a dozen men are at work. Men and materials were all brought from New Orleans, on a N.Y. steamer, from which the lumber was rafted in through the inlet.[17] It is very curious to watch the income of the tide into the river. The Jupiter river water is the amber colored swamp water; the gulf-stream water a beautiful opaline light blue. The incoming tide of gulf water meets the river water with a distinct line of color, and gradually pushes back the yellow water up a mile or two, with scarcely any commingling at the point of contact. As I write, the blue water has just

Fig. 11. The Jupiter Lighthouse keeper's house under construction in 1883. (Florida State Archives. Used by permission.)

pushed back the yellow past our boat at anchor above the inlet, and is rushing inland at a speed of four miles an hour.

22d.—This morning the wind came in from the east, which gave us a chance to go back through the narrows, and we improved it, and reached Peck's lake by supper time.

23d.—Laid at Peck's lake last night, and, after breakfast, walked up the ocean beach three miles for exercise. We found quite a number of tourists at Jupiter. Mr. White and brother,[18] from Port Huron; Mr. Reed, and Com. Welch and lady, from Boston; another party from Connecticut; another from Pennsylvania; and others from other sections.

We are having a fine run with a fair wind to-day, and hope to reach St. Lucie where we expect mail from home. Although we are many miles away, and it will be weeks before we reach it, we feel a satisfaction in the fact that our course hereafter is towards home. We reached St. Lucie for anchorage for the night, and shall move on towards Titusville in the morning. Mercury ranges about 79°. At St. Lucie we found the *Times* up to February 10th.

25th.—After a visit to old Estes' place, to take a picture of his palmetto thatched cottage, we moved out into the main channel, and run before a strong wind, rounding into the mouth of the Sebastian river for the night. While Carlin was cooking supper, Sutton and self went on shore for a fishing. Sutton caught catfish, and having no luck, I was about to coil my line, when I felt it moving out. We had cast lines about seventy-five feet out. I let some twenty more move with the slow pull of the bite, and then I pulled myself. I found I had hooked something heavy, but could not make out what it was. It adds not a little to this long-line fishing, the anxiety to know what is on your line when it is strained like the lines to a runaway horse, and as the game comes nearer and nearer shore, our two eyes do their best service to catch a glimpse of the struggling fish. The water was rough, and I could not see my victim until just at shore up "flopped" a twenty-pound turtle! He "fought nobly," but I landed him, and got him on his back, and secure. You may reckon Capt. Carlin gave us a grand feast on turtle steak this morning. Stopping at Turkey creek for our bones, and a new supply of oranges, we made a fine run over to Rockledge for the night.

26th.—Before we laid up last night, we had some warnings of a "norther," but the wind died out, and we laid at anchor perfectly quiet until, about four o'clock this morning, we heard the roaring of the wind coming, and ere long a furious gale from the north struck us. We were exposed to the direct force of the storm, and no shelter near, so the captain threw out another anchor and "let her blow," and we rocked and rolled and pitched in the swells in a not very desirable way for any one inclined to sea sickness, but as I am not of that kind, Carlin lit up his oil stove, and by taking half a cup at a time, we took our coffee and "flap jacks" with a good relish.

28th.—The norther blew a gale for forty-eight hours, and the mercury from 53° to 60°, and detained us at Rockledge until this morning. Abating somewhat, we beat against it to Titusville, where we arrived just at dark. We have been twenty-eight days on the *Ella,* and every day a pleasant one until this three days' norther struck us. We move on to Sanford next.[19]

GROWING THE ORANGE

St. Augustine, March 14th.—From Indian river our first stop was Sanford, where the next day we took the cars of the narrow gauge railroad, running through Orange county, to "Kissimmee City," on Lake Tahopekaliga [Tohopekaliga].[20] I hope no one will hold me responsible for damage if injury result from an attempt to pronounce this name, for I did not make it. On this road we passed through the high pine lands, and found several villages in embryo. Orlando is a growing and pleasant village with a population of several hundreds. From Sanford to Orlando, and a few miles beyond, we passed in sight of fine orange groves on both sides, every mile or so. Very pretty lakes are also numerous. As we came near Kissimmee, the land became low, level pine land, unsettled, and only valued for the pine timber on it, and several gangs of hands were collecting logs to send out to the mills by rail. Nearer the "city," which consists of a dozen or so houses and cabins, the land changed to rich, low hummock [sic] land. Orange county is considered one of the best orange sections. One man, Mr. L. Stebbins, has the largest grove in the state, 160 acres, and over 9,000 trees.[21]

The crop in Orange county is this year about $100,000 worth of oranges. The desire of northern men to own orange groves was never greater than now. Thousands of trees are being set out, and thousands of dollars being invested in the work. Marvelous stories of great receipts are repeated by land agents, and visions of large incomes are pictured in the minds of investors. My own investigations satisfy me that a few succeed, where many fail, and lose their investments. I can only refer to a few facts. A gentleman from N.Y. told me he had sunk twenty thousand dollars in working up a grove of a thousand trees, and had received no income yet, while the future was uncertain. He had worked at it ten years. I know of another shrewd business man of the north, who bought a grove at San Mateo, near Palatka, twelve years ago, ran it nine years at a loss, then sold it, and wants no more such investments. Another man paid $20,000 for a very fine grove, the annual *receipts* from which are very large; but a man well posted in this business says he does not think the net profit is over two per cent on the investment.

It costs heavily to buy or make a grove, and keep it up. A gentleman told me he had fifteen acres he was putting into oranges. The land cost him four hundred and fifty dollars. He paid out the first year $800, the next $1,000, next $1,200, and thought it would take this year $1,500, and thus it goes on for five years more before any return begins, and with the return increased expenditures. This same gentleman, who expects to succeed himself, told me that three-fourths of the investments in making orange groves in Florida were failures. Think of a man who would invest in a farm, in our county, if it took ten years, and a thousand dollars a year expense and living, before it returned any crop. Of course there are many successes, and these stimulate to[o] many failures.[22] If I were sentenced to Florida for life, I would prefer these high pine lands, like the land around Orlando, for a residence. Passing down the river to Palatka, we concluded to take in the trip up the Ocklawaha, and secured state rooms on the steamer "Ockahumkee" [*Okahumpka*], fully expecting before we returned to fall in with "Humpty-dumpty," and "Hunckadory." Other writers have fully described the trip up the Ocklawaha, so I shall be brief, and only repeat that we turned and twisted up a stream just wide enough for the steamer, a hundred miles, through a cypress and palmetto swamp. Large numbers of the cypresses were from three to four feet in diameter, and straight and free from limbs for sixty to eighty feet. A dense growth of many kinds of smaller trees, shrubs, vines and weeds, lined the shores and filled in the woods. Our steamer ran directly into "Silver Springs," which cover about three acres, and is from ten to fifty feet deep, and the water as clear as that of Lake Superior. Its source cannot be nearer than the mountains of North Carolina. The bottom as we passed around it in a small boat, could be seen fifty feet down, as distinctly as if there was no water there. From Silver Springs we went by rail back to Palatka through parts of Marion, Alachua and Putnam counties, directly through the highest lands in Florida. Like Orange county, the rolling pine lands predominate, with many beautiful lakes. Here we saw a few cotton fields and many orange groves. On two fine lakes eighteen miles from Palatki [Palatka], a company from Springfield, Ohio, has located a winter resort called "Interlachen," on the plan of Petoskey with us for summer. In every part I have visited, in ten counties from Jacksonville to Jupiter, and through the interior, one answer is given to the inquiry, "If this is a good section for oranges?" "The best in the state," with plenty of proof for the assertion, in every instance. I do not wish to be understood that failure is a necessity in orange culture. A large proportion of the ventures are by northern men, who are absent ten or eleven months in the year, and leave the care of the grove to hired help, and very few northern men will live here even for an orange grove. A few days at this old city and we leave for home. Florida is full of visitors this winter; every hotel and boarding house is full.[23]

Adrian, March 23.—Messrs. Stebbins and Sutton returned from their Florida trip night before last. It would seem not to be a favorable time to go "from lands of sun to lands of snow."[24]

Adrian, May 31.—The large whale's rib and vertebra brought from Florida by Mr. F. R. Stebbins are now on exhibition at the rooms of the Scientific society.[25]

8 1884 Where Summer Lives

L. D. Watkins, of Manchester, wants me to *pilot* him to Florida this winter and I shall probably go.[1] I intend to make the grand tour of the south end of the state, and among the hundreds of "keys" on that coast, perhaps as far as Key West.[2]

Manchester, Jan. 17.—L. D. Watkins went to Adrian on Monday afternoon, where he remained one night with F. R. Stebbins, and on Tuesday the two gentlemen started for Florida where they will stay until about the 1st of April. They have chartered a yacht and intend to sail down the Indian river to Key West, and anticipate having immense sport. They will visit Jacksonville, and numerous places on the St. Johns river, St. Augustine, etc., and we learn that they have gone prepared to open one of those mysterious shell mounds. We expect to hear from them often.[3]

FROSTY WEATHER IN FLORIDA

We make the following extract from a letter sent by Mr. F. R. Stebbins to Mrs. Stebbins, in this city. The effect of the cold upon the orange crop, has been denied in some of the Chicago papers, but the statement of our intelligent and observant townsman, will settle the fact that great damage has been done, at least in the sections he has visited:

Sanford, Fla., Wednesday, Jan. 22
We arrived here an hour ago. Monday night we stayed at Jacksonville. The ice formed there an inch thick, and laid in gutters on the shady side of the street all day. The unpicked oranges in the latitude of J., and many miles farther south, were all frozen and ruined in the earlier freeze, and most of the young orange groves are either killed, or almost ruined. Up here and through this section, little or no damage was done, the freeze was so light.

We start up the river, to-morrow, for Rockledge, 135 miles to Indian river.

The weather is warm to-day, and will probably remain so the rest of the winter. The swamp maples are blossomed out here, and are as red as peona [*sic*]. They are profuse, and look very beautiful. I saw other flowers on the river side. I can hardly realize that we have not yet begun our cruise, it seems so long since we started, but it is only eight days. I have been well all the time.[4]

INTERESTING REMINISCENCE

Sanford, Fla., Jan. 23, 1884.—Eight days from Adrian to this point, two hundred miles beyond Jacksonville, up the river, and down further south, may require explanation not without interest. Forty-eight years ago, two boys played together a week in Granby, Conn. They were cousins, and while their parents were having their visit in the house, the boys were busy playing "store," with nuts and apples, in a little booth by the yard fence, or roaming the fields, and feasting on the wild grapes of a beautiful October in Connecticut. The visit ended, and these two boys parted, never to hear from each other for nearly a half century.

One settled in the south, and the other in the new west, and until this winter, we knew nothing of the existence of each other. And when we learned our locations, and that I was soon to pass through his city, he invited me to stop off on my way to Florida and pay him a visit in Macon, Ga. I gladly accepted, and met Henry L. Jewett at his elegant home, adorned most by his excellent wife, daughter, son and relatives. Mr. Jewett is the president and largely owner of one of the heaviest banks in Macon, and has been for many years a leading light in the best, and especially educational, enterprises, in his adopted city, notably as trustee and business manager of the Wesleyan college there, an institution of the Methodist church. We parted as happy boys in the years ago, careless of the coming years; we met with hairs greyed by the pares [sic] of those years, and looked into each other's faces, beholding wrinkles made by the toils and battles of life's experiences, but happy "boys" yet.

Macon is a city of about twenty thousand inhabitants, nearly one-half colored persons. Much attention is paid to educational institutes. The Wesleyan female college is a large and I think prosperous one, and is said to be the first institution in America, and probably in the world, to grant diplomas to females. The electric light has been introduced in the streets, upon nine lattice work towers, 180 feet high, costing $500 each. The cost of lighting the streets is $4,800 a year. Each tower has four lights. The works are erected by a private company. While in Macon we visited a newly discovered mica mine, about four miles out, which promises to be a very extensive and valuable mine. Gold is said to be found also, near by. Bidding adieu to our hospitable cousin, we moved on, losing connection at Jessup [Jesup], and nearly freezing over night, with two sets of the usual bed covering, at the hotel. The night of the 21st we were obliged to have a fire in our room, at Jacksonville, and ice formed an inch in thickness, and remained in the shaded gutters all day. As this was the second freeze this winter, it found little to damage; all the oranges in that latitude, with early vegetables, and all tropical foliage, having been ruined by the first freeze. In the latitude of Sanford and Orange counties, little or no damage was done. I can see that many improvements have been accomplished since last winter in the river sowns [*sic*], and to-day word comes that the railroad from Sanford to Tampa, on the gulf, is finished.

To-morrow we take steamer for Lake Poinset [Poinsett], one hundred and thirty miles further up the St. Johns river, where we take "stage" three miles across to Rockledge, on Indian river, where Tony Conover [Canova] awaits us with his sail yacht, for a six weeks' cruise. We will soon be beyond communication with the world "outside" for some time.[5]

FROM THE LAND OF FLOWERS

A Letter Written to the Novell Farmers' Club
[Lucius D. Watkins]

To write you a pleasing and entertaining letter would be a great pleasure to me, but I fear that I shall fail in both respects. Still as I promised your President to write, I will give you the narration of my journey, leaving home with the thermometer at 8°, Toledo at 6°, Cincinnati at 29°, Chattanooga at 38°, when we left the snow and most of the ice.

At Macon we stopped off three days to look over the country and make a study of the very center of the upland cotton lands. The growing of cotton as compared to our farming is for you to compute, I will give you the cotton side. Upland cotton is quoted here at about ten cents per pound. It takes three acres of an average crop to make a bale of 500 pounds. The labor cost is about one-tenth more than corn here, but they have to apply two dollars in fertilizers per acre annually. I have failed to see an acre of grass since I left Tennessee. The whole aspect is that of a worn out, run down country. Ploughing is done here with one mule and sometimes one ox to the plow. I think our manner would not improve theirs, for the land is so light and sandy and liable to leach, that surface treatment would be the most satisfactory. We visited the cotton compress of which many of you have read. I cannot describe it, but it is the most tremendous machine I have ever seen yet. The Corliss engine at the Centennial was a baby's toy beside it.

From Macon to Jesup, and from Jesup to Jacksonville is one continuous pine plain used only for lumber and the manufacture of tar, rosin and turpentine. The undergrowth is mostly saw palmetto and young negroes. They seem to fill the whole country. The common team is one mule or ox which the driver rides.

From Jacksonville we take a steamer to Lake Possette [Poinsett] 365 miles up the St. Johns river. The banks are very heavily timbered, the pines and cypress predominating, though the cabbage palm or palmettoes are very common. Above Sanford the country is a wilderness and we see more and more of the coming beauties. The whole forest is festooned with moss. The maiden cane is twined and festooned with vines in full bloom, common among which is a white convolvulus (morning glory), air plants, festooning the trees. While here a great snapping occurred; I had seen all along occasionally something drop from an overhanging branch that I could not make out, but finally by close looking I got a fair view, and behold it was a water turkey. Imagine the most impossible bird in all the range of ornithology and you are not up to his standard. He is absolutely all neck, except perhaps some small annexes, I am not sure of this, and appurtances [sic] thereunto belonging, as may be needed to nourish and support said neck, and you have a water turkey.

The river has widened to about five miles which includes the channel and level water covered lagoon. This broad space is divided by open pools the space between which is a perfect network of vines, and white and yellow lillies [sic] now in full bloom. Here we see our first alligators, and all is packed with a vast variety of water birds. These last I hope to describe in another letter. We have disembarked, gone over the land from the St. Johns to Indian river, and are now at Rockledge, a place surrounded by orange groves. We have chartered the champion yacht *Arrow*, Captain Corwa [Canova]. Our future will be of much greater interest. We are fully prepared with material for handling the largest fish, and our Winchester rifles for alligator hunting, and a little iron or harpoon for shark and saw fish.

Perhaps I had better tell you what kind of a craft the yacht *Arrow* is. She is 27 feet long, 12 feet beam, 5 tons capacity. Her main-royal boom is 32 feet long, five feet longer than her length over all. She spreads 125 yard of canvass and is the fastest yacht on the coast; we have on board the yachting club's champion and first prize flags. We have two cozy little state rooms, and plenty of room for all our stores and collections.[6]

WHERE SUMMER LIVES

Indian River, Off Merritt's Island, Jan. 28.—We left Rockledge, on Indian lagoon, this morning after breakfast, on the sloop yacht *Arrow*, Antonio Canova, master. The *Arrow* is twenty-seven feet long, and twelve feet beam with a shelter cabin four feet six inches, and seven feet six wide, with center board casing in the center, and our cots are placed each side of center board.

Our skipper is a very good-natured young man, of Italian descent, born at Augustine, and is a good sailor, who told us frankly that he had just brought to a successful issue the courtship of a Rockledge girl, and as they were Catholics, he had some anxiety lest the priest should come and go before we should get back from the Keys. As the priest makes only occasional visits to this section, and the "engaged" have to improve these visits to get married, we ran over to Merritt's Island to lay in some sweet potatoes and eggs.[7] The rest of our stores we have aboard. You hear much about the advantages of Florida in raising vegetables but we could not hear of any sweet potatoes anywhere. One storekeeper thought we could "get them in New York." We found some on Merritt's island, also a few eggs, and we are now booming along before a strong fair wind. Our boat was the winner of the prize in the last season's race, and makes good time.[8]

30th.—Monday night laid at anchor at the foot of Merritt's Island; near the large shell mound. Yesterday, called at a settler's store on the west bank of the lagoon, at Crane's creek. The owner, Mr. Hector, an Australian Englishman, showed us some carvings in stone, said to be taken from a mound near here, which was in slate stone.[9] They were sinkers and bills of ducks, and executed in the highest order of modern skill; so much so, it does not seem possible that they were executed by barbarians. He would not sell them.[10] We tied up for our 4 o'clock dinner in the east channel of the narrows. We get but two meals a day. We had some Indian river oysters fried, which were four inches long and very fat. On our way we visited our old ground, Pelican island. As in former years, the pelicans were nesting, and the young ones were in all stages of growth, and the old birds all around us in countless numbers. During the day we came to the mouth of Turkey creek, where is the last orange grove, and picked a bushel of these grand oranges, all averaging ten inches in circumference, and of most delicious sweetness and very juicy, at two cents each.

31st.—Laid at anchor last night at St. Lucie, near old Ft. Capron, a Seminole war post. This place is also called "Paynes." It consists of four or five houses, owned by the Paynes brothers, the father, who lived here many years a noted character, having died last year. These brothers keep accommodations for tourists, but their principal business is cattle raising. They have now a herd of about 500 cattle, which are scattered in the wilderness which lies back and extends to the Kissimmee river. They keep no herders, but let the herd run wild; and about the middle of February a large tract of land is fired, burning off the old wild grass which grows in the pine woods and the open plains. The new grass immediately springs up after the burning, and the poor winter starved herd gathers from all directions, and feeds upon this young grass, and by May gets in order for the Cuban market. Then the flies and mosquitoes become so ravenous, the cattle huddle together, are easily driven and penned.[11]

There are but few settlers in this section, and all are on the coast of the lagoon. Everything in foliage is green here, there having been no frost to do any damage, as far down as this point. We left Rockledge with the mercury at 75°, and it has averaged about that ever since. We drop our anchor to-night on the west side of the lagoon.

This afternoon we went over to the ocean; on the beach we found a "loggerhead" turtle. I put my rule to him, and found him to be five feet long and nearly three feet broad. He was too dead for our use.

We have made only about fifteen miles to-day, against a strong head-wind, but clear sky and beautiful air. We were much pleased to get the *Times* up to the 17th, at St. Lucie. We shall not hear from home again for weeks.

Feb. 1.—We went on shore this morning at Richards' place, while "Tony," our skipper, was getting breakfast, and young Mr. Richards showed us over the plantation. We saw here fields of pine apple plants, many of them just setting the fruit, containing in all over sixty thousand plants. On this place is probably the oldest and largest orange tree in southern Florida. It is about fifty years old, and is about fifteen inches in diameter, and bearing the very finest of fruit. Thousands of ducks and coots cover the river below here.[12]

Before entering the lower narrows, we left the *Arrow* at Gilbert's bar, an old inlet now closed by a bank of sand ten feet high and ten rods wide, and walked down the ocean beach two miles to "Peck's landing," another closed inlet, where our boat again took us aboard on Indian river. We secured a number of "sea beans," shells and sponges. We saw about half a mile from shore what seemed to be a large section of a broken up vessel afloat. We thought we could discover persons on the wreck, but there was no signal hoisted, and we must have been mistaken.

2d.—We entered the lower narrows with no fair wind and our prize yacht had to be poled along ignominiously like an old scow. Night overtook us at "Indian camp," the only dry ground in the narrows, and we tied up there last night, as the water channel runs through a mangrove swamp for miles. Some large animals prowled around nearby in the night, but did not make close acquaintance. We rounded into Jupiter river, and tied up to the lighthouse about noon, where we have to remain for favorable wind and sea; for our course southward from here is "outside," or on the ocean, for sixty or seventy miles, with occasional inlets; one at Lake Worth, one at Hillsboro one at New River, and then Biscayne bay and Cape Florida. This trip south of here is taken by very few tourists, or really by none at all, and we are aware is not without danger; but the interest it promises us is such we decide to risk the danger. The one coconut tree at Jupiter has on it over a hundred nuts.

The bluff in front of the lighthouse is completely covered with a beautiful bed of pink wild flowers, fine leaved blossoms, and nearly two inches in diameter, called "Old Maid."

Mr. Watkins caught two large crevalle, trolling, as we came in, and we have just tried to do justice to one of them for dinner.

4th.—We had hoped to go on our way immediately, but an east wind set in soon after our arrival here, and raised so much sea and surf across the bar, we could not go. Wind the same this morning, but the sky is clear, and the mercury runs from 64° to 75° through the day.

After breakfast we took the small boat, and Antonio rowed us about four miles up Lake Worth creek, which empties into the river near here. We found no game, but had a delightful ride between mangrove and "coco plum" banks, with the usual variety of palmetto groves. The coco plum is very plenty, is just ripening, is about as large as an average hickory nut, with a rather large stone for the amount of pulp, but is quite pleasant to the taste. We picked also some beautiful high stalk, wild white lilies in full blossom.

On our return we find the high surf still rolling on the bar, and we remain "prisoners of hope." If the wind holds, we shall try fishing to-morrow.

From the top of the light-house, this afternoon, we had a most complete birds-eye view of a large "sacred enclosure," and mound of the prehistoric race. The light-house is built on one side of the top of the enclosure, and we could take in the whole work at a glance. This embankment enclosure is six rods through on the base, and twenty-five feet high, and is built in the form of a horse-shoe; the open part resting on the river. In the center of the bend of the enclosure is a round mound, some sixty or more feet in diameter, and twelve or fifteen feet high, the whole bend forming a grand amphitheater, full forty rods across, where the central mound is located. I do not know if this work has ever been described in the scientific works, but if not it is well worth investigation.[13]

5th.—We had a fine catch of sea bass and crevalle, this afternoon, in surf and inlet cast-line fishing, and returned early, and I initiated Antonio into the mystery of a fish chowder, he having never seen one made. Mr. Watkins pronounced the chowder a success. We have to educate our skipper in several branches. He could not conceive, at first, how I was going to cook a pancake without dropping it into a lot of grease or butter in the pan, but admitted my cakes, which came out free from soaking butter, were the best with the butter put on when we ate them. Like a great many cooks he was horror stricken when he saw me breaking eggs into a cold-buttered fry pan to fry. "Why," exclaimed he, "you can't fry eggs that way; they must be dropped into a hot pan with hot grease in it." "My dear Tony," said I, "let me show you the difference between a well-fried egg and the usual illy-fried, leather-edged, indigestible nuisances, frizzled-up 'fried eggs.'" When my eggs came out, tender and toothsome in every part, with no leather edges, he stared at them, and only remarked, in a half-soliloquy tone, "Well, I suppose I will learn a heap about cooking when I get married." Evidently that girl at Rockledge, whom he is going to marry as soon as he returns from this trip, is running in his head more than fried eggs. Mercury 73° at 6 p.m., 80° at noon.

One boat, impatient at this delay, tried to go on to Lake Worth to-day. She succeeded in getting through the surf on the bar, but with a head wind and a three mile current against her, she could make so little headway she gave it up, and returned.

7th.—The mail goes north to-morrow, and we must close our notes. We are still held here by adverse wind, but manage to pass our time reading, fishing and strolling on the beach.

No news from the north later than the 20th of January. We are isolated from the world and all its cares, except the wind.

We had a fine catch of crevalle yesterday, trolling from our sail boat. In a short time we caught about sixty pounds of fine fish.

The mail passes here twice a week. The carrier brings it down to Jupiter with a sail boat, leaves his boat here to take on his return, and carries the mail on his back, down the ocean beach afoot, ten or twelve miles. The mail often weighs over fifty pounds.[14] The carrier is here, and I must close.[15]

WEATHER BOUND

Jupiter Inlet, Feb. 8.—We were weather bound here at the close of my former letter, yesterday, and as we are still enjoying the same delightful condition of rest, we decided to go "a shelling" on the south beach. The *Illinois,* which tried to go on the other day, and had to come back, determined to try it again, and went fast aground on the sand bar, and it took four hours to get her afloat, and she is now back inside at anchor. We had a grand shell hunt, and found many rare varieties, some of them on the beach, and we poked some of them out of recesses in the rocks, at low tide. One who has never enjoyed the picking "live shells" out of the waveworn pockets in the sea side of the old rocks, when the tide is out, has missed a rare pleasure. The beautiful pure sea air and the incoming surf near by, roaring and foaming as if angry that it cannot quite reach its domain at high tide, and engulf the invaders of its rocky playhouses, and its children, the shells, in its foam and fury. Then the collecting rare and beautiful shells adds a zest to the climbing over the rocks, even if you do sometimes slip into the little pools of water left by the tide in the "pot holes." The live shell fish we have to boil and draw the meats before we can pack away the shells. A single overlook in this process, and an undrawn shell put in your collection, will soon give you an odor quite different from that of roses.

11th.—"Thus far and no farther," is the decree of old ocean. We started on this tour with the determined will to visit Biscayne Bay and the Keys. The night we arrived at Jupiter inlet there sprung up a strong east wind, which raised the sea on the bar so that no boat could get out in the face of the wind; and for nine days we waited in vain for a change.

Yesterday the *Illinois* twice tried to make out, but both times had to give it up. We stood on the beach and looked on. She rolled and pitched in the surf, the breakers at times going over her cabin deck, and every time beating her back. She had a close cabin, so that the water did not get into her, but ran off the deck. Back she came again inside, and when we realized that our own cockpit boat would have been swamped in a minute, we read our doom, and having been waiting nine days and no signs of change, we turned our prow into Indian river, and bid adieu to visions of corals and the Keys, and decided to do the St. Lucie river, and the beaches between Jupiter and Cape Canaveral. Had Jupiter inlet been the only one to encounter on our trip to the Keys, we had not let twice nine days east wind turned us back, but when we knew we had three other inlets of the same character to encounter, and over eighty miles ocean unsheltered sailing, we saw it was of no use to attempt the risk.

After we got back through the lower narrows, we went ashore at Gilbert's bar, and walked the ocean beach north four miles up to life saving station No. 2, collecting shells, sea-beans, &c. Our bags grew heavy, and our legs weary, but it was worth all the toil. On our way, the tide being low, we waded out to a sunken old coral reef, over which the surf roars at high tide. It was the rotten massive coral which forms the known foundations of Florida. It is beautifully marked with the cell structure of the coral, but gradually disintegrating, and adding to the shore sand.

12th.—We anchored ten miles up the Lucie, last night; some one has started a pine apple field here, and has about an acre in plants. A palmetto thatched hut, and a pole bedstead covered with palmetto leaves for bedding, but deserted, is on the place. Moving on farther up the river to-day, we tied up to a high sand bank, with dry pine forest back, and about fifteen miles from the mouth of the river. This river, for eight miles up from Indian river, is about a mile wide, above, it divides into north and south branches, both running from interior swamps, twenty miles more above, and gradually growing narrower

Fig. 12. An unidentified Florida Indian mound photographed in the early twentieth century. (Florida State Archives. Used by permission.)

as we go up. My former visits have been to the south branch; this time to the north. The features of this branch are very similar to the other. Shores fringed with saw grass marsh, backed by dry pine land, with occasional palmetto groves. This saw grass is very stout in the stalk, with sharp saw-teeth edges, and from five to eight feet high. One would not find a journey through it one of pleasure. We took the small boat, and rowed up a narrow branch of the river, this forenoon, between saw grass shores and palmetto, and many other varieties of wet hammock land trees hanging over the water. The large air plants cover the trees and are starting to blossom. Many wild flowers are already in bloom. The weather for two weeks has been the most charming summer temperature. A few showers to-day. About one-fourth mile out, in the pine woods, is a mound some eighty feet broad on the base, and about twenty-five feet high, very symmetrical in shape.[16]

13th.—The depth of water in these interior fresh water streams is remarkable. Indian river does not average six feet deep. This river where we are is about one hundred feet wide, and soundings show a depth of twenty-five feet. Many of the little lily-pad side channels cannot be sounded with an oar. We had a most charming row this morning. Running in from the main stream through a bed of yellow lily pads, called "bonnets" here, we came into a dark deep stream, or lagoon, overhung with a high sand bank covered with a dense growth of saw palmetto, and young pines, fringed at the water's edge with several kinds of lilies and other water plants, some of them in blossom, dense masses of morning glories, and other climbers. On the other shore, not thirty feet across, a dense dark hammock of large old palmettoes, mangroves, oaks, water maples, all festooned with these tropical climbing plants, hanging over the water, which, near the low shore of that side was decorated with many beautiful water plants and lilies in blossom; the dark shadows of the tall hammock trees casting a deep somber shade over all, which might delight the night birds at noonday. A large tarpon, some six feet long, broke water as we came out into the main channel. We anchor to-night at life saving station No. 2. These stations are merely houses of refuge, for shipwrecked sailors.

14th.—Mr. Watkins takes the beach and walks up three miles to a crossing from the old Cuba place, while Tony and self go up with the *Arrow,* and take the trail over to meet him. We left the *Arrow* at anchor, and found the trail a fourth mile from our larger boat. We got over to the beach and met Mr. Watkins, and at the same time discovered a fear-ful looking wind and rain storm coming up from the southwest. We made the best time back the saw-palmetto roots and leaves would permit, but the storm struck us just as we reached our small boat, and we barely saved our hair by taking shelter behind a dense clump of mangroves.

The wind made such a noise in the tops of the palmetto grove near us we had to shout to be heard by each other. At a half lull of the wind, we took to the small boat, with the rain beating upon us in torrents, for we saw the *Arrow* had dragged her anchor and gone ashore.

When we reached the *Arrow,* you may reckon we were slightly moist about our clothes, but we found our boat unharmed. Her sails not being clewed up, the jibsheet had filled and taken her into a thick growth of mangrove bushes, bows on.

The storm was soon over, our boat hauled off, and we were on our way with a fair wind, our wet clothes spread in the sunshine, and we are now sailing peacefully on our way, as happy and contented as if there were no storms in this land of beautiful sunshine, evergreen shores, and balmy air.

Two ducks shot this morning, Tony has just dressed for dinner, as I sailed the boat for him. We have just secured, at the old Cuba place, the first bananas of our trip.

A most delightful sail of twenty miles, brought us to St. Lucie post-office in time for our dinner, and a most welcome lot of mail matter, and the *Times* up to February 2d.

Just before night we saw coming up the river beach three Seminole Indians, an old man, his squaw, and boy, of about fourteen. The old Indian courteously walked, while his squaw and boy rode ponies. These Indians have evidently Spanish or Cuban blood in them. The woman had on a calico dress, a long and shorter skirt over; the boy a sort of short thin cotton frock. The old man had a sort of double shirt with a kind of cape, and band sash, the dress of the males coming down to the middle of the thighs, and the legs and feet bare and symmetrical. How they manage to keep unscarred limbs, tramping through these saw palmettos and thorn vine and shrubbery, is past my comprehension. The males had colored turban head dresses; and such eyes as were in that boys head! Full, round orbs, dark as jet, but with a vacant look, sad to see. Both the boy and man had coal black hair, dressed in the most approved modern style of bangs; in fact the man rather crowded the fashions, and parted locks hung lower than his eyes. They could understand and talk a little English. These Indians live in back of St. Lucie, about twenty miles, cultivate a little land, and subsist largely by hunting. The settlers here treat them kindly on their visits.[17]

Tony is washing the breakfast dishes, from which we have just feasted on venison, and we move over to the ocean shore near Indian river inlet. Storming yesterday, but beautiful so far to-day; soft balmy air as could be desired for out-door life.[18]

BAD MAIL SERVICE

Banana Lagoon, Feb. 19.—Since leaving St. Lucie post-office, where I mailed my last letter, we have been cruising leisurely up the Indian lagoon, and entered this water at the foot of Merritt's island to-day. There is much complaint of the bad mail service in Florida, and it could hardly be worse. I received a letter from home at St. Lucie, which was fourteen days on the way, when you can travel over the same distance, by the same conveyance that carries the mail, in six or seven days. I think the Jacksonville postmaster must retain the matter for this lower country until he gets a bag full, before it is sent on. We never get over half the papers sent to any point. At Jacksonville the papers are thrown away if not called for very soon after arrival.[19]

From St. Lucie we ran over to Refuge Station No. 1, and turned from sailors to tramps on the ocean beach again. We were told there was a trail back to a landing on the lagoon, two miles north, and we took to the beach with our collecting bags, and sent Tony on with the boat to meet us at the river end of the trail. We walked over two miles, but found no trail; still on a half mile farther, and found a trail leading into a dense palmetto forest, and we decided to investigate.

Taking the trail through one of the grandest palmetto forests I ever saw, at about a half mile we came out suddenly into a clearing in the midst of the forest, with a good house as Florida houses rate, in the wilderness, a croquet ground and garden, with cabbages nearly grown, tomatoes, and other varieties of vegetables ready for the table. On entering the house, we were welcomed by an old man, and a younger one, the lady of the house, a young lady, and other younger children. A cup of warm water—cold water is not known in Florida—after our long walk in the sun, was nectar to us. The old gentleman, Mr. La Roche, was from South Carolina, with his family, and settled in this out-of-the-world place to end his days, with no neighbors, except the station keeper, for many miles; and no roads except a trail to Indian river. We were on the wrong trail, but Tony had found our steps, and followed us to La Roches. Our trail was a mile farther on, and we reached our boat after a tramp of five miles. I cannot help an unpleasant sadness coming over me, continually, as I visit these buried homes in the wilderness, and see women and children shut out entirely from society, and the common advantages of civilized life. We asked this man what he did for schooling his children. He said they had to teach them at home; for if they had schools, the children being miles away, they would not like to risk their going through the woods, for danger of wild animals. This teaching at home, of course, depends upon the education of the parents; and very many of them never very seriously wore out the seats of the school-house. Oh! children of the north, thank God every day of your lives, that your lot and life has been cast in such different circumstances from these children exiled to the depth of a Florida wilderness.[20]

On the 20th we moved up the Banana lagoon and anchored near Mrs. Hall's place. Here this lady and her daughter, from Boston, have a grove and spend their winters on it.[21] We caught here a twenty-five pound bass, and our chowder fails not.

After a long walk among the shells on the ocean, at Hogan's trail, we moved on to the vicinity of two boats at anchor, where we found Commodore Welch and lady, from Boston, and Mr. Reed, from Neponset. Both of these gentlemen I met at Jupiter last winter. They have both purchased land here for a winter resort.[22]

The firing season has commenced. Last night we had a grand illumination on Merritt's island, about four miles across the water from us, and coming down to the shore, a line of fire a half mile long was leaping, tree top high, before a strong breeze, and the dense smoke covered the southern sky, and smokers are starting in many other places.[23]

On the 21st we called on Capt. M.A.[O.] Burnham, the keeper of the Canaveral light, which is only five miles from this point. Here is the celebrated Burnham-Wilson orange grove. Capt. Burnham has kept this light-house thirty-one years. He has here a fine sugar cane field, which has grown twenty-six years without fertilizing, and has been reset only three times during that time. The land is a low, flat field, subject to overflow, and has thus been enriched in the ages past.

Outside here I caught a sea bass which weighed nineteen pounds. It "makes music" to play and take such a fish. We have a curious way to catch the mullet, which we cut up for bass bait. We take a good lantern, and row out the small boat, and the mullet jump into the boat. I know of one case, where with a strong light, a young man caught over a hundred in a short time in that way. This statement may seem a little "fishy," but it is a fact.[24]

The weather is still fine, with occasional night showers. Our daylight hours are all spent in the open air, and we sleep with shelter but plenty of air.

22.—Laid at anchor last night in the broad lagoon, a mile from either shore. The phosphorescence of the water was very remarkable. Striking the water with an oar, a bright flame of "white heat" color fire flashed as the water flew upward. Dipping a pail of water we had a display I have never before witnessed. Small illuminated spots about as large as peas were thickly scattered through the water like little globules of fire, which retained their luminous property for a long time, if we jarred the water in the least, presenting a very curious and interesting sight.[25]

A long tramp to-day over Baker's trail to the beach, where we saw the stranded whales last year, completed our tenth and last visit to the ocean beaches.

On this last beach, where we saw last year the carcasses of ten sperm whales, forty-five feet long each, the only vestige of remains were a section of vertebrae, and two of the rolling plates. We brought these away. Stopping for dinner in the mouth of the channel which connects Banana with the Indian lagoon, Watkins caught a shark and five large catfish. I hooked a six-foot shark, and had him nearly ready to shoot, when he bit off my line and escaped, but he made it lively for me while he held on. We seldom secure a shark of that size on our bass lines. Mr. Watkins soon after caught a four foot shark, and I put a ball through him. Then came a lull in the biting, but ere long one of my lines began to run out. I had about eighty feet of line out, and when I gave the jerk to hook him, I saw, or felt, that I had a big one, and he made a strong fight until I tired him out, then pulled alongside the boat, and not daring to risk lifting him in, Mr. Watkins put three balls into his head, and I lifted him in by his gills. It was a sea bass, three feet nine inches long, twenty-seven inches girth, and weighed thirty-five pounds. I would have given a round sum to have shown him in Adrian. He was a beautiful fish, a little brownish on the back, but the rest of him was like burnished silver.

23.—A fine sail to-day brought us through the "creek," out into Indian river, opposite Titusville. We ran five miles over to Titusville, and anchored for the night.

On the last ocean beach we found large patches of the "singing sand." The drawing of a stick across the sand gave out a peculiar metallic sound; and a little dragging of our boats, gave us the same music.[26]

A fine chowder of our big bass, for dinner, left us only a lot of his scales to show of him, a specimen of which I send the *Times*. I don't mean to say that we ate the whole thirty-five pounds.

24.—Twenty miles sailing, and we tied up at Rockledge, our starting place.

On the way down to Fabers, where we stopped to lay in moss with which to pack our shells and other gatherings, our boatman showed us the mettle of the *Arrow*. We run all the way on the port tack, and a strong northeast wind, with our starboard scuppers under water most of the way. We made the twelve miles in two hours.

25.—Our barrels of curiosities, picked up on the ocean beach, are packed, and we take our way to Augustine to-morrow; and thus closes our four weeks' cruise on our boat, during which time we did not sleep under any roof but that of our little shelter cabins.[27]

Adrian, March 8.—Mr. F. R. Stebbins returned from Florida last evening. He looks as hale and hearty as many a younger man, and there seems no reason to doubt that he has enjoyed his trip as much as anyone could.[28]

Manchester, March 13.—L. D. Watkins returned home from his southern trip last Friday night. He was unable to continue his cruise to Key West on account of heavy seas and ba[d] weather.[29]

9 1885 Northerners in the South

Adrian, Mich., January 5, 1885

Editor of *The Florida Star:*

It is with much interest that I greet the weekly appearance of the *Star,* and look over the local news of Indian River settlements, where a winter visit for six or seven years in succession has given me a pretty fair acquaintance with many localities and individuals. Indian River Lagoon, as I had seen it on the map during my school-boy days, always brought to my imagination a romantic charm of strange and tropical beauty, which I longed to explore, but never dreamed I should enjoy, but in 1878 a friend and myself being on our first visit to the South, in New Orleans, and having a few days to spare, this Indian River romance took possession of me, and I said: "Let us go over to Florida," and my friend said, "all right," and so we crossed the gulf, pushed up the St. Johns and inquired about Indian River. "Yes," they told us, "an old tub ran up to Salt Lake but nobody went there. Lake Monroe was the end of all desirable visit to Southern Florida. Mosquitoes, sand-flies, snakes and all the other plagues of Egypt would meet us and make life miserable." But I had started to look upon Indian River, and as Luther said about his journey to Worms, I was determined to go if all the "devils" of the vermin creation stood in our pathway. I need not tell of the charm of that trip from Sanford to Salt Lake, and across the land on that mule tramway, to Titusville, and my first look out upon your beautiful lagoon and the three weeks trip on it, as far as Jupiter, in 1879 on the *Ella,* with Captain Charles R. Carlin, filled all the old pictures of my early imagination; and similar trips in each successive winter, have left a record of pleasant memories time cannot efface.

> Those days are passed, and sleet and snow
> Are tapping on my window pane;
> But in my room, with fire aglow,
> I live those joy-days o'er again.
>
> And while I live, in sun or storm,
> In forest camp, or gay saloon;

I'll ne'er forget the days we sailed
On thy blue waves, O, fair lagoon!

And now the day is set for another visit to Indian River, and for the Keys. I had hoped to start from Titusville, but our negotiations there have failed: but we hope the first of February will see us afloat again on your beautiful river.

We have been having cold weather in December, I suppose 20° below zero cannot hardly be realized by persons who know nothing about our northern freezings. Continued for a few days, it would freeze over Indian River so that you could haul the heaviest loads across on the ice, and it would kill every tree and shrub in Florida, possibly excepting a few pines.

Times are hard in the north this winter, many persons out of employment, and with some aid to the poor, we will "worry through" and hope for livelier times in the spring.

I see my old skipper, Charles R. Carlin, with whom I have spent so many pleasant hours on his boats, during my several winters, is fitting up a fine, large boat. I had hoped to sail with him this winter, but was unable to secure a party large enough to charter so large a boat, but you can assure any of our northern tourists that they will always find Captain Carlin's skill and boat-comforts first class in every particular.

I wish to congratulate you, and the Indian River country, on the settled establishment of a paper like the *Florida Star,* and that your advertising columns show that the people there appreciate the advantages of such a paper.

A word in comparison between northern and southern Florida. At my first visit in 1878, I found that the orange lands lying between the latitude of Lake George and Jacksonville were considered very largely the most valuable, and settlers were pushed farther south, principally because of their pecuniary inability to purchase in the favored district. At that time I predicted that opinions and values would change, within twenty years. My prediction was based upon my experience of a change of climate incident to a clearing up of a new country, in Michigan, and I believed the same cause in Florida would produce the same result there as it did here. This part of Michigan was settled about fifty years ago, and I have resided here forty-seven years. Twenty years of settlement and clearing up the timber lands so changed the climate that for thirty years our springs are fully and uniformly thirty days later than before 1854. Previous to this change our winters were mild, and our peach crop almost always sure and of such abundance that thousands of bushels rotted on the ground, in our gardens. For thirty years the rule is so certain that the crop, and even the trees are so often killed by severe winter cold, in this part of the State, that the "peach belt" is pushed back to the Lake Michigan shore, and almost all of our peach orchards are destroyed and no attempts made to renew what the next winter is almost sure to kill, and we get our supply of peaches from the west shore of the State. Has not the experience of orange culture during the two previous winters in Duval, Putnam, St. Johns, Clay, and other counties given strong premonitory symptoms of a fulfillment of my prediction in 1878? From the north line of Orange county, south, is to be the great orange land, and all the world knows that although the fruit of other sections is good enough for anybody, the Indian River orange is the best in the world.

I would not have any one infer that this coming change of climate, pushing back the north line of the orange belt, as I suppose, will permanently injure the value of the lands north of that line. Our farmers here had to abandon the peach-raising; but we are still the richest part of the State, in agriculture.

The easy access of this northern section of Florida, to transportation, and the nearness to market, will give an advantage over Southern Florida in the production of many early fruits and vegetables, to which, attention will be given, and produce returns which will fully compensate for the loss of the orange.

Of course my opinions may be worthless, but I think that in less than ten years more the orange growers on Indian River will be more than ever thankful that they located in southern Florida.[1]

Titusville ought to be the great central depot for your section, but your citizens must be awake, for other points are striving for the same distinction. That tramway to Salt Lake ought to be rebuilt, and the road pushed unto the marsh, to deep water; then with the Coast Canal improvement, you have not only facilities but competition and would be masters of the situation.[2]

Adrian, Jan. 27.—Messrs. F. R. Stebbins and Peter Coller,[3] of this city, accompanied by Mr. L. D. Watkins, of Manchester, started for Florida this morning.[4]

Titusville, Feb. 5.—F. R. Stebbins, of Adrian, Mich., who has spent several winters in Florida on Indian River, arrived at this place yesterday on the steamer *Fox*. Mr. Stebbins will be accompanied by a party of three or four, consisting [of] L. D. Watkins and son,[5] and Mr. Collar [Coller]. They have engaged the sloop *Mattie* and C. R. Carlin, and expect to make quite an extensive trip down the coast.[6]

SOUTHERN FLORIDA

Titusville, Fla., Feb. 9, 1885.—We arrived at this point, where we take our sail boat for our cruise further south, on the 3d, one week from home. We laid over one day at New Orleans, for railroad connection to Jacksonville, a run of 750 miles. We went up to the exposition grounds, but did not go in, reserving our examinations there until our return. It may be fine inside, but it is a sorry looking place outside; ditches full of water, and mud covered in part by planks for landings and walks. But the street car management is very fair, and you are landed at the gate of the grounds.[7] Florida this winter is "blue" in every aspect.

The weather has been unpleasant, and large hotels so far cannot be paying expenses. I am sure from close observation and private enquiry, that there are only about half the visitors of last winter, yet I saw in a Jacksonville paper a compiled tabulated statement showing that the arrivals thus far have been nearly four thousand more than last year. This is a fair sample of the exaggerations resorted to in all things to boom Florida. A statement is going the rounds of all the papers, that a man in the orange business "picked 50,000 oranges from a grove three years old." No such grove could produce 5,000, and probably not 500. This is only another sample of efforts made to deceive and entrap strangers into investment. I saw one of the practical examples of these deceptions. I met an old gentleman on the boat who was going up to Lake Harney, where he owned an orange grove. Excited by these stories of the great fortunes in orange groves in Florida, during a visit here two years since, he bought this grove, which, at this time, stands him at a cost of a little over six thousand dollars. He is now trying, in vain, so far, to sell the grove for less than two thousand. Oranges have already met the depression many looked for. Choice Floridas, wholesale, are only $3.00 per box, and good ones for $2.50 in Boston and New York. By the single box, about the same price in Florida—one firm in Jacksonville advertises "good oranges" for $2.00. One man here shipped north four hundred boxes, and received in return only enough to pay the freight. Prices will rally a little later, but a sad gloom is over the former rosy-hued sky of orange raising.[8] The weather has been chilly here, and we had a strong white frost the morning of the 6th, but a southerly wind has now given us the old delightful temperature, and the mercury to-day stands at 75°.

Last night we had one of the grandest displays of "fireworks" I have ever seen. Our hotel is on the shore of the lagoon, which is here over three miles wide. On the other shore is a wet prairie, miles in extent, and covered with a tall, coarse grass, standing very thickly, and five or six feet high, and at this season very dry. Some hunters set the grass on fire, and soon after dark the display in a strong wind was one of rare grandeur and beauty.

Imagine, if you can, a mass, or as it appeared to us, a continuous wall of flames at right angles to our visions, over three miles long; the upper surface leaping skyward twenty or thirty feet in broad tongues of flame, with a crackling and roar which we could distinctly hear three or four miles away. I could think of no comparison but a telescopic view of the electric storms in the sun.[9]

The orange trees are budding for the blossom, and roses and many other flowers are in full bloom in the open air. We expect to get our stores aboard our yacht to-morrow, and the next morning start as free rovers for the next thirty days.[10]

SAILING SOUTH

On Board the *Orient,* February 11, '85

> Although the day be never so long,
> At last it ringeth to even song.

After a delay of seven days at Titusville, which was very tedious, our stores and cruising baggage, and ourselves, are all aboard, and with a new six-feet "stars and stripes" flying gallantly at the topmast, we move off before a fine breeze, for the south. Under our flag floats also a pennant inscribed in bold letters "Orient," the name of our yacht. The *Orient,* which is to be our home for the next thirty or more days, is a slooprigged boat, thirty-five feet long, and thirteen feet beam. Our cabin is enclosed on all sides, with companion way, side and end windows, and hatchway, ensuring plenty of ventilation. Each side of the centre-board are located our spring bottom cots, with good mattresses, sheets, pillows, and blankets. Our cabin being six feet high, fifteen feet long, and ten feet wide, affords us fine quarters, where we hope to enjoy our indoor trip, which is principally confined to our meal hours twice a day, and our rest at night; nearly all the daytime being spent in the open air on deck or on shore. Our little kitchen is forward, and supplied with a fine small cooking range, made expressly for boats. A good folding leg table is running across the cabin at the foot of the centre-board, extending into both sections of the cabin, and of ample size to accommodate our party of four, consisting of L. D. Watkins and his son, Whitney, Peter Coller, and your correspondent.

12th.—About noon to-day we ran into Turkey Creek for a supply of oranges and lemons. The lemons were very large, one of them measures lengthwise 14 inches in circumference, and 12½ inches around. Three boats are in shelter here for change of wind, while we go on, beating against a strong southeast wind. Blossoms are opening on the orange trees here. Mercury on the boat 67°; on land, 74°.

13.—We came to anchor last night in the open lagoon, in about four feet of water. About midnight a furious blow and rain storm came down upon us. No wind could move the two anchors which Capt. Carlin had cast, but such a fall of rain is seldom recorded. An open, straight-sided tin pail on the open deck, showed a fall of six inches in five hours. A few little leaks in the cabin did not materially disturb the serenity of old cruisers.

Toiling all day, beating against a head wind, we have made slow progress, and we come to anchor off "New's cut," where old Mr. New has been trying to open a new inlet to the ocean, where the crossing is not over two hundred yards. We found the old gentleman at work on his cutting in the sand. He is very sanguine of success, and expects eventually to have a ship canal from here to the gulf of Mexico; Mr. New is seventy-five years old, but looks hearty and rugged. Last night, during the high wind, we had one of the most remarkable and beautiful displays of sea phosphorescence I ever saw. The darkness was intense. The "white caps" were breaking for miles in all directions, and the crests of the waves as they broke into foam, lighted up with their phosphorescence, and it looked like thousands of small, distant, pale-flamed forest fires, rising and falling in quick succession, as wave after wave rose and broke and fell. It was a scene of weird and wonderful beauty no description can portray.

14th.—The date reminds me that it is St. Valentine's day. Many a staid matron will to-day remember how, in the old days, the girlhood days, she "wondered if she would get a valentine;" and visions of hope that she would, were with maiden coyness, connected with a rosy-cheeked boy youth, of her school playmates. And when the lace-edged message adorned with a display of every possible, and some impossible, flowers, and its wondrous verse of poetry, came, how she wondered again if *he* sent it. Oh, those old girl days! How old memories will at times, awaken at the appearance of some trifle. One day as we were sailing lazily along, I saw a little boy and girl strolling on the beach, hand in hand, swinging the[ir] clasped hands back and forth; both of them barefooted, but evidently happy and contented, and the long-ago time of my boyhood came back to me, and I was a boy again. . . .

It has been rainy and squally to-day, and we have been running under close-reefed sail, and made St. Lucie, 90 miles on our way, about 3 p.m., passing through the Indian River narrows, our centre-board grinding over a great many banks of oyster beds, which shoal the way, in these narrows.[11]

A TRAVELLER'S DIARY

We reached Jupiter on the 16th, five days coming from Titusville, 135 miles. My first fish was caught trolling as we sailed in Hope [Hobe] sound, and was an eleven pound crevalle. With the boat running six miles an hour such a fish pulls hard. When I first hooked him he perversely took it into his head to go in the opposite direction to our sailing, and for a short time I could only hold the line fast and let the fish try to stop the vessel. He soon tired of that, and by hard pulling I brought him in, my new and strong cod line holding him safely, though he made a gallant, gamy fight for his life. His meat made a fine fry, and a smaller one, caught by Mr. Watkins, made a good chowder.

Did you ever notice this curious system of lagoons all along the Atlantic coast, from New Jersey to Biscayne Bay, at the south end of Florida? A glance at a good map will show that they extend along the coast, more or less, the whole distance, and would have no doubt extended the whole line of the New England coast, had not the rocky nature of the land there changed the lagoon formations of the sandy coast of the south, into the fiords, or inland channels and bays of the northern coast. The waters of these southern lagoons are generally shallow, but having occasional inlets from the ocean, and being more or less subject to the movements caused by the action of the tides, they have channels of considerable depth. Steamers as large as our lake steamers, but flat bottomed, run at times between Savannah and Jacksonville through the lagoons or "inside route." How were these lagoons formed? Any geologist can probably tell you to the entire satisfaction of the scientific world, and he may be right; but the actual sight of the formation of small lagoons has satisfied me how they were formed.

At St. Lucie, on this lagoon, I have seen the construction of small lagoons on the flat sand shore there, every winter of my visits here. A storm will throw up a sandbar along the shore, which is left above water when the waves of the lagoon subside, two or three rods long, parallel with the shore, wider in some parts, with regular inlets admitting the water of the large lagoon into the new-formed miniature lagoon between the sand bars and the shore, the whole a perfect illustration of the lagoon system and formation. A new storm, with the wind in another direction, removes these sandbars, and destroys the little lagoons, but reforms in new bars and new lagoons, different in position and outline, but of general characteristics of the others. Now, if the storm, which here formed the first small sandbars and lagoons, had never recurred from any direction, these sandbars and lagoons would have never materially changed, but become permanent land and water.

Now you see my argument, based upon these illustrations, is that the large lagoons were formed precisely as the small ones, by the waves throwing up, in some long ago age, these sand ridges and fields which protect these lagoons from the ocean now as they have done since their first formations. The fact that the winds in some sections have drifted these shore sands, does not affect the fact that the formation of the sand barriers outside these inland waters, although they may change the features of a locality, was the work of some great tidal action, the magnitude of which has never been repeated, because a rush of waters which formed these barriers, would remove and reform them; but, save local changes in the great storms of this age, these barriers remain unchanged as they have evidently for ages, and make it evident that no such wave storm as the one which formed these barrier lands, has ever been repeated. And now comes in an interesting inquiry what caused the tidal waves of this storm? And this will explain why I introduce this subject. Have you ever read Donnelly's "Atlantis?"[12] To one who takes any interest in the questions, evidences, and theories about the prehistoric condition of the earth, the arguments and evidences brought forth in "Atlantis," in regard to the tradition of the former existence of an island continent between Europe and North America, are at least worthy of an earnest attention. Mr. Donnelly's evidences of the existence of such a continent, and its sudden subsidence in the ocean by a great disruption of the earth's crust in that locality, had almost convinced me of the truth of the tradition, and a study of these lagoons has fully converted me to the opinion that "Atlantis" existed, and when it went down, the great tidal waves that came rolling in succession upon the sandy low shores of the American coast, perhaps a hundred feet in height, formed these sand barriers, and the lagoons; and there never having been anything like it since, the barriers and lagoons have remained materially unchanged. When those great waves rolled back from the land on the coast of Maine, the waters dug out those fiords on that coast, which remain as arms of the sea; and I can see nothing unreasonable in the theory that these great tidal waves existed and were caused by the sudden subsidence of this island continent "Atlantis," as tradition has handed down to us its existence and destruction.[13]

We hear that the central government is intending to establish a life saving station at Jupiter inlet. From Jupiter south our course is "outside," on the ocean, eighty miles, to Biscayne bay, with three inlets into lagoons on the way.

Feb. 19.—This morning, with the wind northwest, Capt. Carlin decided that we could cross the bar and make for lake Worth, ten or twelve miles south. We hoisted our row boat on deck, and lashed it firmly, and with a fair, strong wind, moved out into the breakers, which were beating over the bar, the large waves eight feet high. We were nearly through, with only some grand pitching and rolling, without taking any water on board, but just as we were congratulating ourselves upon our dry passage, a huge wave uprose and broke directly upon us, covering our quarter-deck, and rolling with a broken force completely over our cabin. We were all in the open cockpit, and ducked our heads below the top of the cabin, and took the compliments of old Neptune with shouts of laughter; and let the water roll off our backs as it would off a lot of ducks. But little water got into our cabin, and we squared away for lake Worth, with a strong wind and a pretty heavy sea rolling, which by the time we turned into the lake Worth inlet was showing the "white caps" in earnest, and we came to anchor inside none too quick to suit us. We were not long in making for the beaches, and came in from our long stroll with our collection bags fairly stored with "beans" and shells.

One of the large Havana steamers has just passed, some three miles out. Mercury 70°.

Feb. 20th.—A great change has taken place at this inlet since my visit here three years ago. A sand bank many acres in extent, has been formed directly where the inlet channel was then, and the new channel is formed twenty rods below. The "norther" has settled down to a cold strong wind. I find quite a number of new settlers have located on lake Worth since my visit here. We went ashore at the places of Messrs. Dimmick [Dimick], Geer and Moore.[14] Hundreds of cocoanuts [sic] are flourishing here, some of them bearing in seven years from the seed. We laid in also a lot of bananas, at fifty cents a bunch of a hundred and fifty and over.

A stiff norther is still blowing; we must remain here until a change of wind, and we take occasion to get out our letters, as this is the last office this side Miama [Miami].[15]

NORTHERNERS IN THE SOUTH

Feb. 23.—"How can I sing the Lord's song in a strange land?" asked the old Hebrew, and how can I write pleasant things about Florida without pleasant weather? There is no use denying the fact that the weather thus far in this state this winter has been generally a succession of cold, rainy northers, and the really pleasant days, for Florida, very few. As I write we are at anchor inside the Lake Worth inlet, wind bound, and the rain falling, as it has been all night; but our cabin is dry, and our cakes and coffee and ham and sweet potatoes, and good appetites, fail not; and most of us take it as it comes, and make the best of it; but I have seen more unpleasant weather in three weeks here this winter than in seven former winters here all together.[16]

But with all this, the winter here has not brought as cold weather as was recorded last winter. At Lake Worth there is seldom even a light frost, on the east side of the lake. We find here pine apples half grown, cabbages nine inches in diameter, tomatoes full grown; but the tomatoes are picked green, for the northern market. We get an introduction to several kinds of insects here, but owing to the cool winter, the mosquitoes and sand flies have annoyed us but a little. We have spread our nettings but two or three times. A gentle centipede, however, gave Capt. Carlin a lively time to capture him, on the cabin floor, just now. It came on board with our fire wood, and was only two inches long. They seldom disturb anyone, if let alone.

"The best laid plans of mice and men oft gang aglee." Our new boat, prepared expressly to take us to Key West, came to grief an hour ago. We have again given up Key West, and shall start north as soon as the wind comes right, and Capt. Carlin succeeds in repairing his boat. Key West isn't much of a place, anyway. Nothing there but a lot of cigar makers, and sponge fishers— and then, the sea fans are horrid smelling things. We don't want them, now; and those sponges and corals, we intended to collect, are useless things. Who cares for them? But why this? This morning the wind and sea were all right for us to go on, and we took an early start, with bright sunshine, and high hopes of a grand run on the ocean as far at least as New River inlet. But as we were passing through the channel into the ocean, with a furious tide running out, all at once a thumping and grating told us the boat had struck a "snag," and the water began to pour through the cabin floor. We immediately ran the *Orient* into shore, and it took three of us to bail water so as to keep her from sinking. We succeeded, however, and with the help of a boat's crew near by, on shore, towed our boat along the shore to our starting point, and putting timbers under her, pulled her on to them, and proceeded to examine the damage. On ripping up the cabin floor, where the water appeared, we found the ribs sprung from their fastenings to the base frame of the centreboard, and forced upward, and the hull planking with them, opening a seam through which the water came through so lively that from the time she struck until we had her on the skids in shallow shore water, it made so many of us work pretty lively to keep the water down. We had our stores and baggage all secure in dry places, and did not let the water rise to do any damage. As soon as the tide is low, we expect to repair the leak, so that we can sail again; but the vision of the Keys and their treasures has again vanished, as it did last year, from another cause. We do not believe now there are any Keys except on the map.

Feb. 24.—Last night the north wind whirled suddenly into the east, and has been blowing a gale all night. Watkins and Coller were up at daylight, and have gone over to the ocean beach to see what the waves may have thrown up. About two o'clock this morning Capt. Carlin and his mate, Harris, it being high tide, floated the *Orient* from the skids into deeper water, where she lies, and is as tight seamed from the repairs, as ever; but we dare not risk her "outside," only to get back to Jupiter, when the wind and waves are all right. The other party anchored near us, includes three ladies. They have a tent ashore. This party have been waiting to go to Jupiter, and two days since started to run up there with an east wind, but when about half way, all hands being sea sick, they turned back to the old anchorage here. It was very fortunate for us they did, for we needed the help of all the men to aid us to save our boat from filling before we could get her into shoal shore water. In the shoal water here are hundreds of those large thick star fish, some of them twelve inches across, but we have no way to cure them, and have to leave them. Some fine specimens of the long and short-spined anemones we have secured. Our mate caught a curious fish, if it was a fish, here. It was about three feet long, three inches in diameter, and mottled all over like these southern rattlesnakes. It is called the "mory" [*sic*]. Mercury to-day, 77°.

Feb. 25.—This morning the wind was still heavy, and the sea rough. One boat manned by three colored men went outside, but she will have a rough, wet time. We saw one wave break all over her, and at times she "stood on end." We shall exercise a little more "discretion." About 9 o'clock the wind came from the southeast, and the waves running down somewhat, we worked the boat down to the inlet, and one of the sailors from the other boat here, at the tiller "helping." He put us directly on to the same snag that stove us the other day; but luckily the keel struck it, and we warped the boat safely off and started no leak. We think you will not catch us again in Lake Worth inlet.

We came to anchor after our clearance from the snag, to wait for the right state of the tide, and Mr. Coller has taken to the beach to walk ten miles to Jupiter. He does not think much of ocean sailing. We were much gratified to find the last mishap had not started anew the old leak, and about noon we up sail and moved out through the crooked channel and breakers, into the high but regular swells of the ocean. We had a delightful sail through the grand ocean swells, with a fair wind and sunshine, and a temperature of 80°. We passed a large whale and two large loggerhead turtles, on our way, and in less than two hours we crossed the bar into Jupiter river; and if anybody is longing for Florida inlets, we know of two or three, and will give anyone needing them a good quit claim to their valuable cussedness, we have no further use for them. I caught a crevalle, trolling with a rag on my hook, as we came into Jupiter, and Mr. Coller arriving soon after us, we celebrated our escape from the snags of Lake Worth, and our safe incoming again into Indian river, over a capital chowder.

Feb. 27.—We passed the Jupiter narrows yesterday, and laid at anchor opposite the mouth of St. Lucie river last night. We have had two old-fashioned Florida days, and went to sleep last night with the mercury at 80°. Before daylight we pulled our blankets over us; and this morning, with another "norther" on us, and the mercury at 64°, we are wondering if you are not all freezing to death at home. We have not heard a single word of what is going on away from the immediate vicinity of our boat, in any part of the world, since February 8, but we expect to get mail from Lucie P.O., twenty-five miles from here. A large steamer, loaded with sugar, went on shore near here a few weeks since, and her wood-work is strewn along the ocean shore for miles, for she soon went in pieces. Even with so much chilly weather, we find the beautiful Hybiscus [*sic*] and many other flowers, wild and cultivated, in blossom as usual.

Feb. 28.—We came to anchor near St. Lucie post office last night, and went ashore for our mail. We found news as late as the 13th of February, and of your great storm, and we are beating against the norther to day. Fair weather, but the mercury only 59° this morning and 74° at noon. I have just weighed one of our sweet potatoes, and found it three pounds. It grew at Lake Worth. We paid $1.30 a bushel for them, and they are of very fine quality. I find some improvements in settlements here. Below St. Lucie, pineapples, tomatoes, coconuts and bananas are the leading enterprises.

March 2.—We have been having two days perfect weather, but this morning another cold norther sends the mercury down to 54°. Are you never going to break up your winter in the north and stop sending down here these miserable "northers?" I finish my letter on board the *Orient,* fifteen miles below Titusville, beating against a strong head wind and wave, but we expect to arrive to-night, and bid Indian river good-bye, and move on to New Orleans and the exposition.

We have been twenty days on our boat. If my letters have failed to interest some, this winter, I regret that the failure to reach the keys, has deprived them of descriptions which the new field would have furnished. If they have pleased some of your readers, I am content.[17]

Titusville, March 5.—Mr. Stebbins, and party, returned on Monday afternoon from their trip down the coast having gone as far as Lake Worth. They expected to have made a longer trip but their boat having encountered a snag near Lake Worth Inlet, they preferred to return to continuing their trip down the coast. They started for their homes yesterday.[18]

10 1886 Florida's Freeze Up

Adrian, Feb. 3.—F. R. Stebbins, Dr. J. S. Johnson, W. K. Choate, of this city, and N. M. Sutton, of Tecumseh, started for Florida yesterday.[1] They go by way of New Orleans direct to Jacksonville, from which point their routes of travel will be determined by circumstances.[2]

Adrian, Feb. 8.—A card from F. R. Stebbins and his party for Florida, dated Cairo, Ill. February 3, states that they have been held there thirty hours by the snow storm.[3]

IN THE SUNNY SOUTH

Banana Lagoon, February 16.—It was a cold day when we left Adrian; colder at night when we claimed our berths on the Pullman sleeper in Chicago; and still colder when we ran into the depot at Cairo, with the ten inches of snow on the level in southern Illinois, being piled up in huge winrows [*sic*] along the tracks, with the usual alacrity of a gang of colored shovelers, all of whom had shawls tied over their heads and ears, and large wraps of rags tied and wound around their otherwise considerably conspicuous feet, to save their comely persons from freezing.

We hailed the arrival at Cairo with delight, and we were at least equally rejoiced when we left it, for we laid there in perfect quiet thirty hours. South of us, for sixty miles, down into Tennessee, the road was blockaded with over twenty inches of snow on the level, and the trains abandoned. After this long delay, with four engines on our train, we pushed through the blockade with only our sleeper off the track, on slow motion; changing to another, we in due time found ourselves beyond the snow, and safely landed in New Orleans.

A two days' tarry in that city convinced us that the exposition this winter is a complete and emphatic failure, both in exhibit and attendance. In comparison with last winter, one there

> Feels like one who treads alone
> Some banquet hall deserted.

I think more than half the area of space is vacant, on the lower floors. The galleries, full last year, are entirely deserted. All the best exhibits are gone—the fine Mexican saracenic, or Moorish building, which cost fifty thousand dollars, empty and closed—all the Mexican goods gone—the walls of the art building half bare—the best pictures having been all removed—nothing in the furniture and carriage department. The horticultural building contains nothing but a few cactus plants, dead banana stalks, and withered tropical plants, all killed by the "great freeze," and everything around the grounds is looking like the ruins of some badly dilapidated gentility.

The visitors are very few, and the scattered male and female attendants of a few show cases, and state exhibits, inside, in their enforced imprisonment, scarcely look up as you approach them, or if they do notice a visitor, it is with a half vacant, uninterested stare, as if in wonder what the stranger is there for. At quite a number of the exhibits there is no one in attendance—they are simply left to run themselves.[4]

The seven hundred and thirty miles from N.O. to Jacksonville, we passed with only one detention, of ten hours, beyond Tallahassee, by a double freight train wreck.

Everywhere the great disaster of the freeze is apparent in Florida. The great fire in Chicago was no worse for that city, than this freeze for Florida. All the millions of unpicked oranges, except a few groves in lower Florida that you can count on the fingers of one hand, are entirely lost, or rendered nearly worthless, and over three fourths of the groves north of Indian river are very badly damaged in the trees.[5]

We are now quietly tied up at Burnham's wharf, five miles from Canaveral light house, awaiting the abatement of a "norther" now raging. The oranges in the two groves here are unhurt, and the lemon trees still green, and the golden fruit uninjured, while nearly all the lemon trees through other parts of the state are killed. All the pine apples, even here, are killed for one season. All the many tropical fruit trees and shrubs, are killed everywhere north of St. Lucie, sixty miles south of here. Many a poor fellow who has been some years hard at work and just beheld in his oranges his money to clear him from debt, has met ruin in this freeze. We inaugurated the fishing season this morning, with a twenty-five pound sea bass, on my hook, and soon after, a fifteen pounder by Mr. Choate.

February 18.—Yesterday, the norther still blowing, kept us tied up at Burnham's wharf, and the weather being pleasant on shore, we planned an excursion to the light house. Chartering Burnham's one mule and two wheeled cart, with one seat and two chairs, we four took our seats and moved out into the great plain of scrub oak and saw palmetto over a good sand trail for the five miles ride to Canaveral. Sutton drove the mule, and we all fell in love with that dun mule, for a more faithful mule never throve on the coarse fare of his daily food. We were told it would take an hour and a half to reach the light house, and we might have used that mule for a timepiece; for taking a steady walk all the way, both going and returning, that mule brought us through in just that time to a minute. We are all ready to affirm that Burnham's dun mule, for a five-mile trip, is old reliability itself.

How well do I remember the "Cape Canaveral" of our school boy days' lesson in geography, and how little did any of us dream we should ever walk on its wide sand beach, and with what delight did we now stroll along this beach, collecting shells and starfish. In many places the upper part of the beach was covered with clusters of fine star fishes. We brought away all we could carry, but we left thousands more on the sand.

Canaveral light house is over one hundred and fifty feet high, and thirty feet diameter at the base, built of boiler iron, filled heavily with brick work on the inside. But this noble structure is doomed to go into the sea, unless the government takes prompt measures against the encroachment of the waves. The light house is now only about twenty rods from the tide water, and the land is being rapidly eaten up by the waves, they having at times this season been advanced over fifty feet in one month.[6]

We found at the keeper's house a lady and her daughter from Iowa. They gave each of us a fine rose from the garden as we mounted into our mule cart, and in the exact time that mule landed us at our boat on the lagoon, all well pleased with our visit to Canaveral.

This morning Mr. Sutton pulled in a 15 pound bass, making, thus far, 55 pounds of meat in three fishes. This is the seventh day of our cruise, and we are now moving south with a fair breeze and a beautiful summer air, and we are all writing up our notes to get letters in the mail at the Georgiana postoffice for home, and we go on for a hundred miles further south.

Choate says he hasn't time to write; he is busy fishing; but he tells of a good joke played on him by a barber in New Orleans. Just before we left the sleeper there he gave his neck a thorough washing and a clean collar, but wishing his hair cut, after our arrival, he stepped into the parlor of a first class tonsorial and neck-cleaning artist. After cutting the hair the barber said: "You came off the cars, I reckon. Your neck needs washing badly." "Guess not," says Choate: "washed it well before I left the sleeper." The barber gave a towel a wipe across Choate's neck, and holding it in sight, it was black with coal dust! The barber had "a splendid preparation which would soon remove it," and, of course, friend Choate could not be easy with a neck that developed good signs of a coal mine! and he said "clean her up!" After a vigorous application of the "remover," the neck was pronounced "clean." After the usual dust broom operation Choate called for his bill, and it was eighty-five cents! fifty of it for washing his neck, brushed over with a prepared coal dust towel, as Choate discovered by seeing a row of them, just as he left, ready for use on northern visitors "just off the cars!"

Our party this year consists of N. M. Sutton, of Tecumseh, Dr. J. S. Johnson, W. K. Choate, and F. R. Stebbins, of Adrian. Our boat is named the *Lillian,* Capt. Dick Rhodes, and is twenty-eight feet long, and eleven feet beam, and draws eighteen inches water. Our little cabin is eleven feet long and nine feet wide, all open aft, and we have free air all the time, night and day.[7]

FLORIDA'S FREEZE UP

Jupiter, February 27.—After closing my last letter, at Burnham's, near Canaveral, we started south along the east side of Merritt's Island, and went on shore at a trail which leads over to Georgiana P.O., on Indian river side. The government having neglected to put up a street corner receiving box, we were obliged to go over the trail, three-quarters of a mile, to post our letters, and we had to wade a long ways in the shoal water in our rubber boots to reach the trail. These little varieties of life, which we might at home think great inconveniences, are all taken, as a matter of course, and are turned to real enjoyments. We sailed on to St. Lucie, where we found papers from the *Times* up to February 11. Our friend Choate went ashore for some eggs in one of the channels near Indian river inlet, just at sunset, one night, and before he got back to the boat he received his first lesson in the peculiar amusements of "sand flies," which abound near the ocean inlets. When he returns he will relate his experience with the little festive insect, in much more graphic and emphatic style than I can write it. We found one hundred and eighty thousand pineapple plants at "Eden" below St. Lucie, sixteen miles, not killed, but the leaves partly frosted and withered. The few coconut trees at Eden were scorched, but not killed. At Jupiter and Lake Worth only the strictly tropical plants were seriously injured. One of the remarkable effects of this winter's freeze here, is the destruction of fishes, of all sizes, in the lagoon and river waters. All along the shores of the lagoons the dead fish strew the beach in such quantities as to foul the whole atmosphere, in their decay. Occasionally, a very large fish, the jew fish, was killed. But what is the most strange, when we consider that these waters were only chilled, we found in passing through the lower narrows the carcasses of three manatees, or sea cows, dead on shore; killed by a simple chilling of the water. One of them was over ten feet long. By careful estimate we make out over fifteen hundred tons of fish must have perished.[8] Another surprise meets us at this point. Jupiter inlet is closed—where we last year sailed out into the ocean surf, there is now a wide sand beach of acres in extent.

The U.S. government has just completed a new life saving station, a mile below this place, but has not yet furnished the apparatus. We caught some half-dozen crevalle, surf fishing to-day; they were from five to eight pounds weight. We have had only one light shower of rain for the seventeen days thus far on our boat.

28th.—The weather has been very comfortable, ranging from 65° to 75°; to-day the mercury stands at 86 at noon, but a strong breeze makes it very delightful weather. The charm of the wilderness we found in Southern Florida in our first trips here a few years ago, is gradually passing away. Settlers are now found where then we found wild turkeys and alligators plenty, but now getting scarce.

March 1st.—We rested yesterday, taking occasion to thoroughly air our mattresses and blankets and sheets on deck. To-day we have had another grand ocean surf fishing; after catching eight or ten large crevalle, ranging from five to eight pounds each, a shark took one of the hooks, and he made a rare fight before we succeeded in landing him. He was five feet four inches long. Inside the bar we catch pampano [sic], sheepshead, grey snappers, and some other kinds. Another "norther" last night, and to-day, and we wait for a change of wind before we can get through the narrows, going north. Four large steamships passed yesterday, about two miles out, just this side the "Gulf stream."

2d.—Not much success in our surf fishing to-day. I had on my "string" only a six-pound crevalle, and a shark only two inches short of four feet. But I had a fine play with the shark on my hundred feet long strong line, and I landed him without rising from my comfortable seat on the sand bank, for I was just then too tired to lower my dignity by rising to receive a shark of that size. Sutton soon after hooked one large enough to bring a Tecumseh man to his perpendicular in a hurry, and there was some lively antics on Sutton's part, until his line parted. Dr. Johnson caught a fine crevalle, and Mr. Choate a ten-pound crevalle. All this under a blue sky, and a ocean breeze just cool enough to be exhilarating, gives us a daily pastime of much enjoyment. An old Lake Michigan fisherman has just drawn a small gill net across a little bay near by, and brought out a lot of fifty or more of crevalle, pampano [sic], grey snapper, sailor's choice, mullet, &c.

3d.—Our mild norther still continues, but the weather is beautiful and the air superb. This morning we drew the net again, and caught about forty fishes, estimated at about three hundred pounds weight. All except a few of the choicest we returned to the sea.

4th.—We left Jupiter this morning, after breakfast, and now we are moving slowly along through the beautiful, but to boatmen vexatious Jupiter narrows. Doc. Johnson has just heated up the oven, and is boiling a fine sea trout, and I have mixed up a shortcake, which we would not be afraid to set before any cook in the world, when it is baked; and with these and good coffee all will be well relished by hungry, roving, aquatic tourists. Sutton and Choate are helping Dick navigate the boat, and they are all busy in poling and sailing, as the wind may be. At times our boom rakes along the green mangroves, showering on our deck many of the waxen leaves and broken twigs, which line both sides of the narrow channel. We have had a very pleasant five days' pastime at Jupiter bar, dealing with the sharks, and the half-dozen kinds of large and fine eating fish.

5th.—Laid at anchor off Eden last night, where we filled up our list of stores—Irish potatoes at twenty shillings a bushels [*sic*]—and set sail after breakfast with less regret than did our ancestors the older Eden, with our mainsail under one reef, but soon lay to and put in another reef. With a heavy west wind rolling the white caps upon our deck in fine style, we are now tearing along, anxious to reach St. Lucie P.O., only ten miles distant, where news from home awaits us. All of us seem to enjoy the boisterous sail but Mr. Choate. He "don't care a darn if there is a ton of mail for us." He thinks it can wait while we run into the shelter of the high palmetto hammock on the west shore. But the rest of us want our mail, and the spray still foams and flies astern from our bows, and Choate gracefully bows to his fate. The air is soft and pleasant, even with the high wind, with the mercury at 75°.

6th.—St. Lucie P.O. came in view just as another norther struck us last night, and we had to beat against it three miles. We soon came to anchor, and went ashore for our mail, and were glad to find accumulated during our eleven days' absence quite an amount of letters and papers, having heard nothing from the outside world since the middle of February. A dozen numbers of the *Times,* up to February 20, were received as rare treasures, and letters from home, like precious jewels. To-day the norther still howls, and we rock finely in shoal water, while we read up our mail matter; mercury 70°.

8th.—A five miles tramp through a hammock trail, and on the ocean beach, prepared us to relish well a fine oyster stew, Dick had ready for us on our return. The oysters here are very fine, and in many places we can pick them up with our hands, from the row boat. It was amusing to see Dr. Johnson, at the hotel, take out his pocket rule, and measure one in his stew, it was three inches long. We found on the beach here a bale of cotton, and a nine foot shark; we did not bag them, but were content with a peck each of fine shells.

The skeletons of dead fish line the shores. The question which for years vexed the learned men, as to what at various times has caused the death of thousands of fishes in the Gulf, in times past, is settled by this last killing. But another arises, why is it that a simple chilling of the water, a few degrees, can cause the deaths of fishes large and small, and the huge manatee of a thousand pounds weight, and many of the fishes the same kind that live through and thrive in the ten times colder waters of the north? Many of them actually migrating from these warm waters, in the spring and summer, to the waters of the New England coast, which are at all times many degrees colder than these waters can ever become, in the coldest weather ever known here.

10th.—A fine run, yesterday, off forty miles, in a westerly wind, brought us to anchor near Eau Gallie, for the night, well out from shore. This morning, just as our breakfast dishes were put away, a furious norther came down upon us, and made things lively for a time. Fearing our anchor would not hold in our position, exposed to the full force of the highest waves, we determined to run in shore with the jibsail. We had a lively time for a few minutes while raising anchor, and when we rounded to into the trough of the sea, and we could hardly tell if our boat was on her beam's end or her fore and aft ends. Most of us took the antics kindly, but one of our party is not a sailor, and his hastily selected positions [sic] on the cockpit floor, in not a particularly grace-ful position, and holding on to the mess chest for dear life, with a very com-mendable energy, brought forth some very unpolite remarks.

He very earnestly replied, "Oh, you fellows may laugh as much as you please; but I am not *prepared* to go up just yet;" and the mess chest was not released until we got the boat on her course. One of the fellows was so thoughtless as to "improve the occasion" as the wind howled and the water broke over the cabin, to exhort the member in distress to be "prepared to go up" next time before a "norther" struck his boat. But no harm was done, and our Adrian friend took our chaffing in good part, and will, with a little more experience on this lagoon, make a "brave sailor boy" to beat all of us. To tell the truth in this affair, I could see that our skipper was alarmed for his boat. The rest of us didn't know enough to be frightened.

12th.—After rolling at anchor in the storm all night of the 10th, our anchor dragging several rods, we went ashore, the squall having abated, but the

norther raged with white caps all day, and some of our party showed un-
feigned delight at the stepping on white sand in safety, and walking up three
miles to a boarding house at Melbourne, where at 4 o'clock this morning, the
wind changing, we routed them from their beds, and took them on board
again, and we are sailing finely along now, hoping to finish our voyage to-day
at Titusville.

18th.—Starting with a fine wine [*sic*] to-day, the wind gradually increased, and
we ran fifty miles before the wind, a part of the way at ten miles an hour, and
bid adieu to our boat home of thirty days at Titusville, before dark, and soon
had our sea shells and blankets safely stowed in our rooms at the hotel, well
pleased with our trip. We had no rain during the month to call for an um-
brella, and the temperature, most of the time, just cool enough to be pleasant.
We did not have occasion to put up our fly and mosquito nettings during the
trip, a thing never recorded before. We start for Augustine to-day, and hope
to be home by April lst.[9]

THE SUNNY SOUTH

We are permitted to make a few extracts from letters that Mr. N. M. Sutton
has recently written home from Florida, and which we think will be interesting to our readers.

Titusville, March 12, 1886.—When I wrote the enclosed I expected to be here
as soon as the mail boat, but we were struck by a Norther and detained near
St. Lucie two days, and then we got a nice wind that sent us up forty miles,
and during the night a Norther struck us and it was a regular tearer; so we
laid there two days. The first night the boat jumped and pitched about lively
and the Adrian man that Mr. Stebbins will speak about in his letter, was badly
frightened. We had about 100 feet of cable out, and she drew the anchor
100 yards that night. The wind quieted down last night and we went aboard.
This morning at two o'clock I awoke and found the wind was in the south. I
called the captain, and we got up, set sail, and went up about three miles and
got two of our party that thought they would rather take it on foot and stay
last night on land. The captain went ashore and woke them up, got them
aboard and started, but by that time a calm struck us. We did not know but
we must get another Norther; so we floated and got our breakfast, the last
meal we took on our little boat. About nine o'clock a brisk wind sprung up
from the south that sent us right along, and we sailed up fifty miles in seven
hours. The waves rolled high and we had full sail on, and one hour we ran ten

miles; so we arrived here at 4 o'clock, and just had time to wash and change our clothes before supper. We conclude we had a good time and feel it has done us good. We will take the noon train to-morrow for Sandford [*sic*], and steamer from there to Jacksonville, arriving in Jacksonville Sunday morning in time for a train for Augustine.

St. Augustine, March 17, 1886.—We arrived here first day morning at about eight o'clock for breakfast. Came to our old boarding place, though a new landlord. Found things about the same in the house though they are not as much crowded as they were three years ago. Get our board for eight dollars per week. I have a room all to myself, but not as large as we had. I have a good bed and that is the main thing. The weather is very unpleasant, as it has rained every day since we have been here, though some days it rained but very little. It rained yesterday afternoon and nearly all last night. It has rained but very little to-day, though dark and cloudy, and wind north. I never saw the streets as muddy as they are now; but it is just sand and water, not like the Ridgeway mud. I saw a lady picking her way along to-day and her husband told her to come along as she would not drown. They must have had a heavy freeze here, as the date palms, that have looked so nice in former years, seem to be entirely killed; also the sage [*sic*] palms. They are digging up many orange trees that are entirely killed, some of them sprouting out a little like our peach trees do sometimes after a hard winter. The peach trees are in full bloom and the fig trees are just leafing out. They say they do not get many peaches, as they blast or something. The mercury here is between 60° and 70° most of the time. I see by the weather reports that it is not very cold North. I saw the account of the M. & O. smash-up in a Chicago paper. We also read of the sinking of the *Oregon*. I hope the weather will not be bad for wheat. I see by the papers that it is winter-killed some in Virginia. They have one very large hotel this winter, the San Marco, and are building a much larger one to be ready for next winter, to cost two million.[10] They are making many improvements on the strength of northern visitors. We expect to remain here until Monday at least, and then work our way towards New Orleans.

Hope the rainy weather will let up and give us some sunshine. It is nearly six o'clock standard time, and dark and cloudy. It is dull times for the owners of sail and row boats, as people do not wish to sail [in] such weather.[11]

Adrian, April 9.—When Messrs. Stebbins, Sutton and Johnson were at St. Augustine, Fla., they had their photographs taken, in good positions, at the picturesque old Spanish gateway. Then they bought the negative, and brought it home with them, and Mr. Stebbins is having some copies struck off for distribution among his friends. The *Times* is pleased to acknowledge the receipt of a copy.[12]

Tecumseh, April 15.—Mr. N. M. Sutton brought home with him from Florida a rare curiosity in the shape of a nautilus shell which he picked up on the sea shore. The shell is perfect, very delicately formed, and in every way a beautiful specimen, and Mr. Sutton considers himself very fortunate in finding it.[13]

11   1888 Roving on Indian River

CORRESPONDENCE

Adrian, Mich., Jan. 1, '88

Editor of *The Florida Star:*

Three years ago, in a letter to the *Star,* I made this prediction, "In less than ten years the orange growers on Indian River will be more than ever thankful that they located in *Southern* Florida," and I based that prediction upon a conviction that the same cause, *viz.:* the clearing up the country in the destruction of the forest growth, which changed the temperature of Michigan winters, thirty years ago, from a record hardly ever below zero, to an almost regular record since, to twenty or more below, would in Florida destroy *all reliability* as an orange growing country, [in] that part of the State north of Orange county; and even *all* sections north of Indian River, would be somewhat uncertain ground for *maturing* the orange crop. Have the experiences of your orange growers in the State for three years past confirmed my prediction, or not?

Do not the orange growers of Middle Florida know that since the freezes of three and four years ago, and to a still greater extent since the "great freeze" two years since, thousands of immature oranges have been picked and rushed into northern markets, to save them from a probable frosting or possible freezing?

Of course this may be, and probably is, wisdom on the part of Central Florida growers; but where this must be done to be certain of saving something out of the new crop, it does not leave a very enthusiastic estimate of such a section for orange raising.

The effect of this flood of unripe oranges upon the northern markets has been to almost destroy the former great reputation of "Florida oranges," and to degrade them to a level with the ordinary cheap imported article.

We have had genuine Florida oranges in our market for a month, most of them the color of a lemon, and but little sweeter, or with a dawning russet hue, and also sour.

When I taste of one, and think of a *mature* Indian River, I declare that we would not in Florida insult the reptile by offering the like to an alligator.

I trust no orange raiser on Indian River will be induced to a too early picking of his fruit. Fully ripe, and properly sold, every box of Indian River oranges will net the grower five dollars a box, or more.

Is not Southern Florida the only place east of California, to which we can look with any *certainty* of supply, for sweet and luscious oranges? If these suggestions have weight, ought not every available foot of orange land be occupied at once in your part of the State? The North wants such oranges as your latitude alone can raise, and is willing to pay for them; while we desire to be relieved from the flood of immature and sour fruit Central Florida is pouring in upon us, at any price.

I see by the *Star,* Titusville has been improving very much during the two years since my last visit. Titusville has been my headquarters every winter but two for ten years past, and I feel no little interest in her welfare; and while her citizens are alive to all other good influences, I trust they will not overlook the great benefit and influence of your paper. No one thing gives a town so much aid as a well-conducted newspaper, and I see by your advertising columns some of your citizens are aware of it.

I hope to see you early in February—if I escape the dangers of "Middle Florida," where I wish there might never be another frost.[1]

Adrian, Jan. 31.—Mr. Fred Bury left this morning for Kerr City, Fla.[2] He will visit there a week and then join a party composed of F. R. Stebbins, A. Worden and D. Metcalf, which leaves here, we believe, next week.[3]

Adrian, Feb. 4.—Yesterday while Mr. A. Worden sat in Treat's drug store, he was attacked by a fainting spell, and but for the timely assistance of those present might have received severe burns from the stove, which he fell towards. He has been so attacked several times before, but the cause of the attacks is not known. He will shortly start for Florida, and hopes to regain health by the trip.[4]

Adrian, Feb. 6.—A Florida party composed of Mr. and Mrs. David Metcalf, F. R. Stebbins, Daniel Edgar and wife, Mrs. Dr. Baker and A. Worden started for the land of oranges this morning via the Lake Shore.[5]

Titusville, Feb. 16.—Messrs. Stebbins, Worden and Metcalf, prominent business men of Adrian, Mich., arrived here last Friday to spend several weeks on Indian River. Mr. Stebbins has spent many winter seasons on Indian River as well as in other parts of the State, this being his favorite retreat. The party started down the river Monday with Capt. L. M. Gardner, and expect to be gone about 30 days.[6]

ROVING ON INDIAN RIVER

Off Merritt's Island, Feb. 13.—As I shook hands with my old friend and neighbor, Alanson Worden, on my return from the east last fall, he inquired, "Do you think any about Florida now?" and I said, "I think of Florida all the time." He replied, "I will go with you there this winter, if nothing happens."

For years I had been looking for the time to come when he would join me in my Florida boat life of a free rover on Indian river, and I rejoiced that the time had come; for Alanson and myself had been companions in many pleasant travels and fishing trips, from lake Superior, and Grand Lake, to the cod banks of Maine, the tidal wonders of the bay of Fundy, and the curious waters of the St. John's river, in New Brunswick, which runs down stream half the time, and up stream the other half, on account of the twenty-five feet tide at its mouth, and I know how well he would enjoy a trip to my old hunting, fishing and sailing grounds on the lagoons and tropical wild woods, and orange groves, in southern Florida. And here we are; in forty-eight hours from the bitter cold of the north, to the land where flowers are blooming in the open air, and we start forth on a month or more excursion on land and water, where no house roof will cover, or house walls enclose us during the whole time.

In many winters past I have tried to picture to the readers of the *Times* the great enjoyment of this roving life under the summer skies and semi-tropical air, over the ocean beaches, and beautiful lagoons of southern Florida, in February and March, and once more I propose to record whatever of good or evil may befall us on a trip like this.

Our party this year is made up of A. Worden, David Metcalf, Fred Bury, and F. R. Stebbins. Our route was by Cincinnati, Chattanooga, and Atlanta, to Jacksonville. At Chattanooga we remained some four hours, and looked over the city made prosperous by Yankee enterprise, and the fostering care of the protective tariff in the iron and steel industry. Making enquiry of an intelligent colored man as to points of interest, he called our attention to a collection of war curiosities, in the shape of sections of trees in which cannon balls and shells were firmly imbedded; and he at once volunteered to, and did, attend us a half hour, to show us various localities of interest.

At Jacksonville we visited the "Subtropical exposition," where there was a show of fruits and other productions.[7] At Titusville we engaged our boat, the *Mary J. Lewis,* Capt. Leonard M. Gardner, for short called "Len." Leaving our "best clothes" and our trunks at the "Grand View" hotel, our valises, bags, bedding, guns, and stores were soon safely stowed away aboard the *Mary,* and away we went before a fine breeze. Some fifteen miles below we ran over to the shore of Merritt's island, and came to anchor for an early supper and the night's rest.

Our yacht is twenty-six feet long, and thirteen feet beam, with a comfortable close or open cabin, as we choose to adjust it, and two wide double cots, with mattresses, sheets, blankets and pillows.

Our fine boatman's yacht stove, soon cooked our supper, and when the dominoes ceased, we turned in, well pleased with our start for the first day.

February 14.—This morning, before the sluggards were out of their sheets, the two "boys" of our party, Mr. Worden and Fred Bury, took their guns and the small boat and "went" for the ducks. Mr. Bury secured a fine shot from the shore, and when the hunters returned for breakfast, they brought in six ducks from that one shot. Fred also shot a fine blue heron, which he is just now skinning for preservation of the skin.

After breakfast, and the fixing up of our cots, we up sail, and in the beautiful sunshine and fine air, with the mercury at sixty-five, we bear away south. About noon we went ashore at "Cocoa," and walked down a wide, well beaten pathway, through a beautiful palmetto grove, flanked by fine cottages and orange groves, a mile or more to Rockledge, where there are two good hotels, and many guests, procuring there a bag of the superb Indian river oranges. Mr. Worden says this walk afforded compensation, alone, for a visit to Florida. A fine sail of twelve miles brought us to the foot of Merritt's island, and we rounded to in the mouth of Banana lagoon, and abreast of the great shell mound.

While "Len" has been making a duck pot-pie, and myself a corn-cake for supper, Metcalf, Worden, and Bury have been ashore to examine the mound, and get some wild oranges.

February 15.—After a quiet night's rest, with no mosquitoes, and a good breakfast, our party took a trail over to the ocean, a mile or more distant. The trail ran through a wide spread savanna of "saw palmetto," beautiful for prospect, but decidedly objectionable for a pleasant stroll, where it has overgrown the narrow trail; though a fine friend to the clothing merchant.

A mile out and in on the trail, and a mile each way on the beach, with the grand breakers roaring in our ears, and the pure cool sea air gave us complete and satisfactory exercise for the day. Very fine wild oranges grow here, and Mr. Worden and Fred Bury have secured a liberal supply for "orangeade," which is as good as lemonade. A man from Ann Arbor, Mr. Moscley, has a cabin near the mound, and has cleared up a large garden-spot where he has his tomatoes, cabbages, &c, well started. He lives alone.

Mercury, to-day, highest 78°.

February 16th.—Another night's rest in our "little beds," and we are ready to move on up Banana lagoon, and cake and coffee dispatched, by 9 o'clock we are under sail, with a favorable wind, and a slight fall of rain. We did not anticipate a settled storm, and we bore away for Dr. Wetfeld's [Wittfeld] place, some twelve miles up the coast of the Merritt's island shore of the lagoon. The wind increased, a heavy rain set in, and some eight miles out we came to anchor, in a rough sea, but fearing a wild night, we ran over to the shelter of the east shore, where we found complete security from a wild east storm, and had a quiet boat. The aroma of coffee, and ham, and baked sweet potatoes, soon made us forget the wild wind and waves of the storm, and we sleep as sweetly to-night as if in our own beds at home.

February 17.—The mercury this morning stood at 70°. Metcalf and Bury went after ducks, while Worden and myself stayed on board, to help "Len" get the breakfast. Mr. Metcalf shot a fine specimen of the large bittern, and the first thing the hunters inquired for on their return was about breakfast, and the quantity. Worden was anxious about the same thing, while I was mixing the corn cake. Well we expect good appetites here, but Alanson was well pleased to find the corn cake was of ample size.

A six miles' sail, and we anchored in shallow water, at Dr. Wetfield's [Wittfeld] place.

I had in former times visited the doctor's plantation many times, and was greeted by him as an old acquaintance, and shown the great improvements since my last visit. All sorts of garden vegetables, pine apples, and oranges, are in fine condition. Our next run was across the lagoon, four miles, to a short trail over to the ocean, where a two mile stroll, collecting shells, made us ready again for cakes and coffee.

I find through this region great improvement within two years. The great freeze two winters ago, which gave a sad check to the enthusiasm of central Florida, gave southern Florida an emphatic "boom" on account of its climatic advantage.

February 18.—After dark, with a locker door across the top of the centre-board frame, for a table, we often concentrate our skill upon the highly intellectual game of "dominoes." We had "set" our fish lines before dark for over night, and while Worden was about to exclaim "ten for me!" with the usual exultant tone of success, the skipper put his head through the hatchway and announced "a fish on somebody's line."

Dominoes were at once abandoned, and all of us rushed on deck to look to our lines. It was Worden's game, but "only a shark!" Not a very large one, but a shark, sure, and added variety to our experience. I find our skipper is one of the Gardner brothers to whom Cloudman sold the *Outing* for his passage to Rockledge.

The weather to-day seems to be settled into our old-fashioned beautiful Florida weather, with mercury at 70°.

February 19.—A quiet night at East Melbourne, and a clear morning, with a soft wind directly from the warm waters of the Gulf stream, a stroll on the shore, under the grand palmettoes, and along a fine display of the moon flower, which grows wild here, we accept as a glad harbinger of a day of rest.

Running over to the west shore of Indian river, we tie up for the day at Melbourne, and attend church. We are now forty miles south of Titusville, one week on our cruise, and thus far had four beautiful days. There are three small steamboats laid up here, over Sunday, a good-sized hotel on shore, and a dozen houses, and a large wharf, where two years ago there were only two small buildings.

We have heard nothing from the outside world for a week.[8]

BALMY OCEAN BREEZES

On Board the *Mary J. Lewis,* Feb. 21.—This morning we started early from our anchorage under shelter of a point on the east side of the lagoon, where we rested cozy and secure from a strong southeast gale. The gale over, a charming soft air from the ocean cheers us as we sail over to Turkey creek for a fresh supply of water. A beautiful old orange grove here, in charge of Mr. Minor, of Tecumseh [Michigan], gives from 250,000 to 350,000 oranges yearly.[9] There are 1,800 trees, and fifteen tons of commercial fertilizer, at $27 a ton, are used each year. We are only forty-four miles from Titusville, and a week out, but we have sailed three times that distance, including our trip up the Banana lagoon.

By the time our breakfast was over the heavy wind set in again, and compelled us to remain in this shelter. Our boat safely moored, we took the row boat and went up the creek a couple of miles. We found two or three settlers, Georgians, were "commencing life" on a fine elevated pine ridge. Tomatoes were a foot high, and bid fair for a good crop. The settler we visited with was a young man with a comfortable home, very pleasantly situated on a fine elevation, but all alone. As we bade him good-bye, I advised him to get him a wife at once, and break the solitude of the situation.

February 22.—The sweet perfume of the orange blossoms greeted us this morning from the land, as we made an early start, to take advantage of a light, fair wind, anxious to reach St. Lucie to get our first mail from home since our start over two weeks ago.

We passed the mouth of Sebastian river, about noon, and tied up at a

Fig. 13. Frank M. Chapman photographed at Pelican Island by his bride, Fannie Embury Chapman, on their 1898 honeymoon trip to Indian River. Frank Chapman was instrumental in Theodore Roosevelt's establishing the island as the nation's first federal wildlife refuge. (*St. Nicholas,* September 1899)

"store," on a shell palmetto hammock, where there was a young Englishman and his family. The wife said they were here four years, and their young children and their parents had never been sick. We met here, on a cruise like our own, a party of ladies and gentlemen from Illinois. We anchor to-night in shoal water near Pelican Island.[10] There are plenty of pelicans and men of war hawks, but no nesting now—and after our capital chowder from a crevalle, caught by Mr. Metcalf, we seek again repose.

February 23.—The mercury, last evening, stood at 74°, and the mosquitoes put in their bills lively, but we put up our large, roomy nettings, opened all the cabin windows and doors, and with only sheets the first half of the night, and thin blankets the other half, we had peaceful sleep, the music of the insects outside making only pleasant harmony. Blessed be the mosquitoes—outside the nettings. Now we blow the horn for Worden and Bury, who, with the small boat, went early to the shore agunning. The hunters returned with a very fine specimen of the grey pelican, shot on the wing, with a rifle, by

Mr. Worden, measuring 6 feet 10 inches from tip to tip of wings, and four feet six inches from end of bill to end of tail. We eat breakfast "in our shirt-sleeves," with doors, windows and hatchways all open, with a soft air breeze and glorious sunshine. After breakfast we took an east channel through the islands of the narrows, landing at a rude log wharf where we found another of these Florida hermits, a "Dr. Sill," a roamer of the world over, now settled here all alone in a rude palmetto thatched log cabin, ten feet square, in a small clearing, in the midst of a dense palmetto forest. The inside of his cabin was enough to give a civilized person the horrors. A rude side bunk to sleep in, a rusty cook stove, rude board table, a few shelves on the logs, filled with bottles, cans, etc., all the inside smoke-colored and dirty. It made me feel sad to think it was the domicile of a human being.[11] From this we took a broad trail over to the ocean, three-quarters of a mile, filling our bags with a few shells, and a large number of those large and small sea beans. At this point a large freight steamer, the *Panama,* went aground last October. After throwing over most of her cargo she got off. Some of the cargo was saved by the underwriters, but the settlers from all this section took good care to get "their share."

After one visit to the ocean we moved out into the west channel, through a beautiful and changing panorama of islands and headlands, all the shores lined with a wall or bank of the dark green glossy foliage of the mangrove, backed by the dense palmetto forest. We cast anchor to-night in shelter of one of the mangrove islands, in a stretch of water a mile or more across, and with a view of quiet tropical scenery unsurpassed. Fred has skinned the pelican, but does not fancy the job. Mercury this morning, 72°.

February 24.—The mercury this morning at 8 a.m., 76°. A strong wind en-abled us to reach St. Lucie post office this afternoon, with but one mishap. The wind was very puffy, and Len lost his head for an instant, when a puff heeled over our craft so that the water astonished Mr. Worden, by pouring through the little cabin window at his back, as he and Metcalf sat on their couch. Most of the two buckets of water that came inside went on to and deluged our little cook stove, but we heard some grumbling from our friends about "wet sheets" and blankets, when they turned in at night. We found plenty of mail, papers and letters from home, at Lucie. We were pleased to hear from home, but deeply saddened to hear of the death of my brother's wife, at Lansing. No truer-hearted, nobler lived woman ever walked the earth.

February 25.—Rain this morning, but Len has been netting mullets for bait, and enforced by a fine oyster stew, we moved over to Indian river inlet, across the lagoon, and cast our lines for the fishes. We had to wait an hour for the tide to run in, when a seven-foot shark took Metcalf's hook. Metcalf was on shore, and Len took the line. The shark made him a lively time for ten minutes. The line catching around Len's foot, he went sprawling on the deck, but soon recovered and held on, though the shark finally bit off the braided wire, and carried off the hook.

February 26.—Laid at anchor last night, inside the bar of the inlet. This morning brought a settled rain, and we remain at our anchorage, read up our papers, and watch the flight of the pelicans and other large birds.

February 27.—Before leaving the vicinity of the inlet, Mr. Metcalf caught a fine sergeant fish, which weighed twelve pounds. It was a beautiful fish, covered with scales, which glistened like burnished silver on the back; and it had a black stripe about a fourth of an inch wide running the whole length on its side. He furnished us meat for a fine fry, and a pot of chowder.

We lost several hooks and parts of lines, in the channel near the inlet, by the sharks, which afforded some lively work in the operation. We suspect there is cold weather in the north, for our mercury stood only 62° this morning; but the rain of yesterday gave way to a clear sky and welcome sunshine to day. We are now some eighty miles from Titusville, and move on with a fair wind.[12]

Adrian, March 2.—The Adrian contingent wintering in Florida, is having a good time. It comprises F. R. Stebbins, A. Worden, David Metcalf and Fred Bury. Of course, Mr. Stebbins is the General commanding. They are enjoying summer weather with plenty of hunting, fishing and fruit gathering. Gardens are in their prime, vegetables plenty, strawberries in the market and oranges ripe. They are spending considerable time on a vessel, cruising around, and Mr. Worden had the exciting experience of catching a shark on a hook baited for other fish. The entire party seems to be improving in health and renewing their energies.[13]

FISHING AND FEASTING

The experiences of our townsmen on the waters of the St. John's river, have been read with general interest. The distressing news received Friday, that one of the party had been suddenly taken away, while they were en-route home, gives a saddening interest to the accompanying letter:

On Board the *Mary J. Lewis,* Off Eden, Feb. 27.—I mailed my last letter at St. Lucie, after leaving the inlet, and a strong north wind bore us away from old "Fort Pierce," where we laid in a new invoice of sweet potatoes, and various other supplies. We inquired for eggs, and the man at the "store" had but two. We found, however, in a back room, where we were hunting for a box, a real hen's nest, which had three eggs in it, and we secured two more and sailed away proudly with four eggs!

Away we went, ten miles before the wind, with our peak lowered, to a trail to the ocean; we had to land on a beach where the waves were beating heavily. But we were bound to take in the ocean beach at that place. Only two at a time ventured in the small boat, the skipper keeping the bow of the boat to the wind and waves, and landing us stern on, we jumping as soon as the boat touched the shore. A long stroll on a fine shell beach, and we went back to our yacht a little wet from the heavy sea for a small boat, but a four mile run gave us a perfectly quiet berth behind a point for supper and sleep.

February 28th.—The mercury this morning was fifty-four, with the norther still blowing, but with a clear sky and pure air. Len gave us a grand breakfast, this morning, and our keen appetites did ample justice to the freshly dug sweet potatoes, ham, corn cake, griddle cakes with Florida syrup, and good coffee. Our skipper makes our cakes and coffee, under early instructions, as good as we could ourselves.

A fine run of five miles before the wind, and we turned into shelter at the "Old Cuba" place, now occupied by "Old Joe," a Portuguese, who showed us through his "plantation." He has growing cabbages, onions, potatoes, squashes, bananas, limes, citrons, coconuts, and several other fruits.[14] Near by Joe's land, our boatman has a place, where we went and took a trail over to the ocean beach, and walked down it three miles to the house of refuge.

If any one thinks a three miles' tramp hunting for specimens along an almost continuous winrow [sic] of shells thrown up by the storms and tides, is not a tiresome job, let him come and try it. Len sailed the Mary down to the station, and met us on our arrival.

Just as we sat down to supper, the somewhat notorious yacht Outing came to anchor near us, but sailed before we arose from our "mahogany," for our little tables are actually mahogany.

February 29th.—We laid quietly tied up to the little landing plank walk wharf on the lagoon bay at the station, while over the ridge, on which the station is built, and twelve rods away, old ocean was "loudly roaring," as the heavy surf beat against a coquina limestone ledge of rocks. The cold norther "blew out" last night, and instead we have this morning an east wind and mercury 70°, and we move over to the mouth of the St. Lucie river, three miles opposite. A fifteen miles' sail up this fresh water stream, takes one into the wilderness. The north branch runs through a dense growth of deep green foliage, of the mangrove, palmetto, rubber tree, maple, oak, etc., coming down to the water's edge, with huge ferns, six feet long, the bayonet-pointed, radiating leaves of the saw palmetto, all adorned with vines and air plants. Some of the plants are covered with their yucca-shaped form, and the red-spiked blossoms give a fine contrast to the universal green. After terribly frightening a huge alligator in the lily pods [sic] but getting no shot at him, we returned. We anchor to-night in the middle of the river, which is here for miles uniformly about a hundred feet wide, and twenty-five or thirty feet deep. The tall pines on one side, the palmettos and mangroves and live oaks and other tropical plants on the other side, all reflected in the mirror surface of the river, form a twilight scene of rare beauty, at our anchorage.

March 1.—Early this morning Worden and Len went with the row boat for bass, or alligator, or anything that might turn up. They brought us no alligator, but a seven-pounder black bass, and two or three smaller ones. Breakfast a little late, but the fish excellent. We beat about eight miles, and to the main river, where we found a manitee [sic] net stretched across our course, but a vigorous blowing of our horn brought out in a row boat four men from a schooner that laid off shore around a point.

We managed to get over the net, and anchored. Taking our row boat, we went over to the schooner, where the men in charge had a captured manitee [sic] in the water alongside, securely held with a rope tied above the large round flat tail. This manitee [sic], or "sea cow," is getting very rare, and there are very few localities in the world where they are known. This one was nine feet long, and would weigh probably a little less than a thousand pounds. It was a rare sight to see a large manitee [sic], as it is almost impossible to keep them alive in captivity.[15]

[Boating] down five miles opposite a solitary cabin, we anchor near the shore for the night. On shore we found the settler, a Floridian. He had a half acre in pine apples, which were coming on finely, the young fruit being some three inches long, and a beautiful pink red. This man lived here with his wife, and no near neighbors, and no roads but the river.

March 2.—Our little "range" does wonders for our ravenous appetites, and is worthy of notice. It is only twenty inches long, and twelve inches deep. The oven is ten inches by nine, and seven in clear, with grate. On top two "griddle holes." This morning Len gave us ham, potatoes, hominy, corn cakes, griddle cakes, warmed-over chowder and coffee. Our housewives would think they could not cook thirty days for five persons with only such a stove as this, but we do it nicely, and all our food comes to our little tables hot.

A few miles run after breakfast, and we tied up at the wharf of the Bessie brothers, from Oberlin, Ohio, where we refilled our water cask. The mother

Fig. 14. A St. Lucie River manatee in its drained Central Park tank in 1873.
(*St. Nicholas*, February 1874)

of these young men is spending the winter with her sons.[16] While here we saw an Indian on the river in a large dugout. We called him in and purchased a fine ham of venison for seventy five cents. He was a fine muscular fellow, and his entirely nude legs showed well the muscular development of a Seminole.[17] Mr. Bessie gave me the rib of a large manitee [*sic*].

We rest to-night on the east shore of the lagoon, ten rods from the ocean, and our venison well satisfies our appetites. In the center of the little bay here is an island three or four rods across, covered with saw grass and a beautiful cluster of mangroves. It is called Ballast island. Some seventy years ago there was a fine inlet from the ocean here, and a vessel in ballast was driven over the bar in a storm. She could only get out by throwing over all her stone ballast, which in time gathered the sand and formed this gem island.

March 3.—With our haunch of venison hanging to our shroud—what is left of it after two meals—we moved on for the Jupiter narrows. Delightful weather—mercury ranging from 70° to 75°—with a head wind, or a dead calm, through the narrows. Len had to resort to the pole, for four miles, to the "Indian camp ground," half-way through, where we tied up to the bank for the night, but an alligator in the woods near by persuaded us to move on a mile further, not a very ferocious 'gator, but strong enough to move us. A grand venison "pot pie," or stew, for supper, closed a delightful day. I shall have to confess what many a cook has done before, that the dumplings were a failure; unless we look upon them as an effort to manufacture grape shot, which they resembled in shape and texture. In that missile of war line they were a great success; and so we "fired them" down the center board casing, and enjoyed the capital stew, all the same.

5.—Another delightful morning finds us in Hope [Hobe] sound, four miles from Jupiter inlet. As we laid at anchor last evening, Len, who is a fine singer, went ashore to visit a new settler, and we heard a fine concert over the water from the cabin on shore of good old Methodist hymns and tunes. We arrived at Jupiter inlet before noon.

The mercury on shore stands at 85°. I find some change here. My old captain, Mr. Carlin, has built a good house of entertainment.[18] I also had the pleasure of meeting Com. Welch and wife, of Boston, who have cruised these waters many years. We found mail here from home, and the *Times* up to February 21st, containing our last news from the north. We expect to stay here a day or two, and then move on to Lake Worth.

March 6.—Since yesterday, we have been anchored against a great low sand bar, in a fine cove near the inlet. This morning, after breakfast, on invitation from Superintendent Carlin, of the U.S. life saving station here, we all went to the station and witnessed the weekly drill of the men with the life boat—Capt. Carlin, with a long oar, guided the boat through the breakers, while six sturdy men pulled the oars. The surf is not very high but yet enough to make the thirty-feet boat take some fine leaps skyward as she mounted the waves.

The government has established a signal station here, giving telegraph communication with the rest of the world, while only ten years ago, at my first visit, there was no post office within forty-five miles. The station is in charge of Henry Pennywill and T. J. O'Brien.[19] We found on our arrival here that Jupiter and Lake Worth inlets were so uncertain, and the numerous and widespread bars and shoals inside were so certain, that we could not with safety go outside to Lake Worth, so we concluded to start on our home trip.

Mr. Metcalf decided here to take the little steamer to Titusville, and the rest of us remain to finish our trip on our boat.

March 8.—This morning we started with light baffling winds, homeward bound. We expect to be a week in reaching the end of our cruise. Anchored last night in the north end of Hobe sound, near the narrows, and this morning a strong "norther" is blowing, and we cannot get into or through the narrows, until a change. Meanwhile the cakes and coffee fail not, and we are "happy still." As we sit at our breakfast table this morning, we look out of our wide cabin doors upon a group of twenty or more palmettoes, a fourth of a mile away, which with the low mangrove bushes below, the clean body of the palms and the round, close of the tops, at different elevations, standing in full relief against the sky, form a beautiful picture of tropical charm worthy the pencil of Bierstadt.[20]

Although two reliable guns have left us with Mr. Metcalf, we are yet prepared to appreciate the advice contained in an article from M. Quad, sent us in a newspaper, *marked,* by one of our wives, under head of "Advice to boy Terrors." The "advice" marked for our notice says, "You must have an outfit Don't be stingy in buying yours. It will be all the better if you have a Spencer carbine, and a double barrel shot gun, to go with your Winchester, and don't scrimp on Bowie knives. You should take at least two hundred pounds of ammunition. I should scalp every Indian I shot. It not only looks more business-like to do it, but that's what you got your Bowie knives for." Now, when we consider that our party brought three shot guns, and three Winchesters; and two pistols; one knife, with a twelve-inch, and another an eight inch blade, and lot of powder and shot, our wives may rest assured we are well "outfitted." We haven't seen but one Indian, and we preferred his venison to his scalp; but the buzzards have suffered extremely; and we have ammunition left.[21]

We are a little modest on the "Indian" question; for when we look in a glass we realize our danger of being captured by the government for Indians on the warpath, and sent to a "reservation." Our color, from thirty days exposure to sun and wind, is certainly against us. But we expect to fade out by the time we reach home, so as to be safe.

March 9.—A fierce norther blew all day yesterday, so we rested at anchor in a good shelter and went again to the ocean. The wind this morning is changed a little, and we move off for the narrows. Seven hours going ten miles through the narrows, we cannot claim as very fast sailing; but Len made it, most of the way, with a pole, with either a bad wind or no wind; but we come to anchor to night at our old anchorage near Ballast island.

March 10.—After breakfast this morning, Fred Bury and I took to the ocean beach, and "combed" it two and a half miles up to the house of refuge. A strong easterly wind had raised a heavy sea, and a grand surf broke and roared for our delight, as we strolled along the beach, bagging sea beans, shells, etc.

Leaving the station with our water cash [cask] refilled from the rain water cistern, we bore away before a fair strong wind, for St. Lucie postoffice, where we arrived at 2 p.m., and after receiving our mail ran over near Indian River inlet, and anchored for supper and the night, in a bay almost completely sheltered from the wind by islands on every side.

It must be written that the fishing this winter, in comparison with other years, has been a failure. We caught very few on our down trip, and at Jupiter, where formerly we caught them to a surfeit, we could scarcely get a bite. The old fishing places are all changed, and sand bars and new channels formed. Large quantities have been caught by the commercial fishermen in seines, and they may have frightened the schools away.[22]

As we approach the end of the cruise, our garments show signs of wear and tear. One pair of pants is nearly out at the knee; two other pairs show too many "bay windows" to be available for short skirt coats. One "fellow" called for some patching material, some days since, and the only available material being a piece of red and white checked table cloth, when in his shirt sleeves, he has the appearance of having been sitting on a bed of Florida flowers of bright and varied hues, and some of them had "stuck." We bring fine sharp sand aboard the boat with our shells and our boots, and one cannot sit without more or less of it gets in its work of destruction on our clothes.[23]

DEATH OF A. WORDEN

Adrian, March 19.—We received to-day a letter of Mr. F. R. Stebbins, postmarked at Melbourne, Fla., the concluding portion of which we copy as follows:

Melbourne, March 15.—Alas, for human hopes and enjoyments! Mr. Worden's death has cast a crushing shadow of sorrow over all our trip. He was taken on the 10th with a slow approaching paralysis, which attacked the brain, and finally rendered him insensible. We made all haste to this place, the nearest to medical advice, and a good hotel. All the care that could be taken anywhere was given him, but he remained insensible until 3 p.m. to-day, when he went to sleep as easy as the sleep of a child. He suffered no pain during his sickness, had good medical advice and nursing, but of no avail.

My own heart is deep in sorrow for his loss, and the anguish the news must have given Mrs. Worden.

Fred Bury has acted like a noble young man, working over Mr. Worden day and night, with myself and nurse.

Dear, kind neighbor, farewell.

F. R. Stebbins

Melbourne is in Brevard county, Fla., and is in the south part of the state. But a letter written on Thursday last reached here to-day, and it seems safe to expect the remains to-morrow.[24]

Adrian, March 23.—Last Friday morning a telegram from Florida, announced the death of Alanson Worden, at Melbourne, in that state, from paralysis. Mr. Worden was one of Adrian's pioneer residents and oldest business men, having been in active business here continuously for a great many years, and only last summer retired from the field where he had been so long a successful and prosperous merchant. Close attention to business together with his advanced years, had impaired his strength, and a few months since in company with Mr. Stebbins, David Metcalf and Fred Bury, he went to Florida where he has thoroughly enjoyed himself, and the news of his sudden death came like a thunderbolt from a clear sky. The remains reached this city Tuesday.[25]

Adrian, March 23.—The funeral of the late Alanson Worden, was under the auspices of the masonic fraternity, of which he was an old and respected member. Adrian lodge has adopted appropriate resolutions of respect.[26]

Adrian, March 28.—Mr. and Mrs. David Metcalf and Mrs. V. A. Baker returned from their Florida trip last evening.[27]

Epilogue

Francis R. Stebbins's shock and grief at the passing of his good friend and neighbor Alanson Worden were profound. After escorting the body home, Stebbins assisted Worden's widow in settling his friend's estate.[1] Performing this role under such circumstances would have seemed slight penance for luring his friend away from family and home to die in a faraway place. Stebbins's deep remorse for his part in Worden's death was surely intense. His own dread of expiring alone in a strange land, often expressed in his Florida papers, must have compounded his feelings. This fear and its realization may well have terminated Stebbins's winter cruises on Indian River.

Stebbins never returned to Florida following the ill-fated 1888 expedition. He had no more to say to the public about Indian River. No further travel articles of any sort from his pen were published in the *Adrian Daily Times and Expositor*. Without a stated reason for discontinuing his customary excursions, Stebbins's latter-day reader is left with two likely explanations: a deterrent in Florida and restraint at home.

Certainly a situation arose in Florida following Stebbins's return that severely depressed general tourist travel to all parts of the state the next season. In the warm summer months of 1888, yellow fever, an irregular and dreaded affliction in port cities, especially Southern ports, moved rapidly north out of south Florida. It had entered Florida the previous year from Key West and reached Tampa by the fall, where it subsided during the cooler months. It was on the march again when temperatures rose in the spring of 1888. By the end of the summer, even inland towns such as Gainesville were in its grip. All the eastern Florida resort towns came under its pall. Despite its efforts to avoid the coming plague, Jacksonville, the state's economic capital and premier tourist destination, knew it had not escaped when the first cases appeared there in early August. The disease spread rapidly among the city's population, and it became clear that the yellow fever outbreak of 1888 would be a disaster to health and prosperity. As the disease progressed and quarantines were inaugurated in more and more towns and cities, commerce ceased, and supplying not only Jacksonville but the rest of the peninsula with necessities became difficult. Jacksonville's city government ran through its resources and was forced to issue a national appeal for assistance.[2]

If the epidemic alone were not sufficiently devastating, Florida's woes became front-page news around the country. The major northeastern newspapers followed the story throughout the disease's course, relaying statistics on how many people were infected and daily death counts along with accounts of hardships in the cities and outlying quarantine camps. Principal regional newspapers followed the northeastern papers' lead and gave the Florida news the same prominent coverage. The *Detroit Free Press,* then as now the leading Michigan journal, reported the unfolding events each day, as did the *Adrian Daily Times and Expositor.* During the height of the epidemic in September and October, it treated the dispatches as a continuing story, placed first on the front page but later relegated to the back pages. The editor picked lurid titles for the updates. Readers were confronted with headlines such as: "Florida Depopulated," "Death's Harvest," "Yellow Jack's Victims," and "The Fearful Fever."[3] When signs the epidemic was finally abating in Jacksonville emerged the end of September, they were duly welcomed, but the numerous setbacks and outbreaks elsewhere in the South were all recorded. The first of November, election coverage dislodged the yellow fever story from the headlines, but the paper's last word on the subject, "The Yellow Fever: It Still Has Its Grip on Florida Towns," hardly encouraged prospective travelers.[4]

Such detailed coverage signified the importance Florida and its gateway city had achieved. Had thousands of Northern and midwestern tourists not already experienced the sunshine state's gentle winter climate and thousands more read about it and wished to go there in coming winters, Florida's misfortune would not have been so glaringly spotlighted. But by 1888, Florida was the nation's winter resort. Those wishing to elude the cold season's miseries in the far South scanned the reports intently, wondering if they should hazard the 1888–89 Florida season. Despite newspaper proclamations late in the fall that yellow fever was over in Jacksonville and the rest of the state, the majority of potential tourists decided not to take the risk. Months of sensational coverage effectively checked the usual torrent of travel. Although Indian River was relatively unaffected by the disease or its complications, the Titusville editor felt obliged in mid-November to publicly reassure hesitant seasonal residents that it was safe to return. But he added, "Titusville still maintains a strict quarantine, and as the cool weather is fast approaching, we hope to be free from any more 'scares' this winter." Two weeks later he jubilantly announced that frost had formed as far south as Melbourne and that it was now safe to travel anywhere in the state. Nevertheless the season was largely a failure. Looking back on it, one traveler recalled that very few Northerners had ventured south and hotels and passenger trains did little business. He noted, "There was one compensation, the trains ran promptly on time, and there was plenty of room."[5]

Stebbins's medical condition also prevented him from traveling. His general health had deteriorated despite his precautions. Repeatedly he had cited improving his health as the main motive for his winter vacations. Everyone in Lenawee County who read his Indian River articles knew this, and it cost him the 1883 mayoral race. The Democratic *Weekly Press*'s editor used this common knowledge to successfully label Stebbins an invalid, whose therapeutic junkets would permit him only to serve part-time.[6] By the 1888 excursion, he showed definite signs of diminishing strength. He did not participate in strenuous diversions, such as hunting or mound digging, and frequently remained aboard the rented yacht while the others left for side trips. When he returned home in the spring of 1888, he was sixty-nine years old, an age then considered elderly. At that time, Stebbins himself had nearly five more years to live.

The first news of Florida's yellow fever epidemic came just a few months after Stebbins's return with his friend's body. Surely it must have alarmed his family, who might have feared he would attempt yet another Florida cruise. Perhaps they were not certain the circumstances of Worden's death had entirely quashed his Florida yen. If his wife and adult children were now determined to keep their aging loved one home and safe, word of so great a calamity befalling much of the region he must traverse to reach his destination would furnish them a compelling argument against more winters on Indian River. Concern for his safety after the 1886 trip's dangerous boating incident may have caused him to cancel his 1887 trip. If this was the case, they could use this dread disease even more effectively than they had the earlier misadventure, for they well knew his phobia about a solitary death in a distant place. They would have been convincing, under the circumstances, even if Stebbins wanted to continue his Indian River cruises.

And he may have, at least until 1890. He had not entirely lost his urge to travel. Indeed, during the winter of 1889 when he usually would have departed for Indian River, he appears to have grown restless. Stebbins and his family reached a compromise of sorts. Instead of traveling to Florida, he would tour Washington, D.C. in the company of N. M. Sutton and Tom Applegate and his wife. This was his last sight of the South. It is significant that his escorts were the man who most frequently joined him on Indian River and the man who solicited his Indian River travelogues. Catering further to his wanderlust, his family indulged him in summer trips to Boston to visit his daughter and to Vermont to see the old Stebbins home, accompanied only by his wife and his oldest son Frank.[7]

After his last Florida trip, little was said of Stebbins's activities in the *Adrian Daily Times and Expositor,* indicating that if he attended social events and professional society meetings he no longer took a leading role in them. His son Fred's letters to his Lansing cousin suggest Stebbins was also largely retired from his business after 1888. He had placed his three adult sons in charge of the store during his Florida junkets. By 1888 they handled all the day-to-day affairs, although they publicly attributed business changes and store improvements to their father. As long as F. R. Stebbins could, he summered at his north Michigan cottage at Grand Lake in Presque Isle County, but after 1888 he seems to have escaped the city heat at area resorts. In 1890 he built another cottage closer to home at Sand Lake, Lenawee County.[8]

The fall of 1890, Stebbins and his family mourned the loss of his youngest daughter, Lilla Louise Stebbins Pierce, who died at her home in Hingham, Massachusetts. Stebbins and his wife had regularly visited her during summers, and she returned to Adrian for extended visits with her parents as well. In late spring of 1882, the Pierces made the long journey from Boston to Adrian for Lilla to give birth to her first child under her parents' roof. The next summer Lilla's mother and half-sister traveled east to be with her at her second child's birth. The young mother's sudden demise stunned her family. Two months later her brother Fred wrote his cousin about his father saying he was "glad he has built [the Sand Lake cottage] for it furnishes him something to think of in this time of our great bereavement." Almost two years after his daughter's death, Francis Ranna Stebbins himself died peacefully at home on September 29, 1892. He had been declining through the summer from what his doctor diagnosed as heart disease. Like his friend Alanson Worden before him, Stebbins startled his friends and family by suddenly collapsing in the midst of a conversation the previous May. Stebbins was almost seventy-four. Nehemiah M. Sutton, his former Indian River companion, served as an honorary pallbearer at his funeral.[9]

When Stebbins's estate was settled, the fifth item listed in his will was his private museum, made up of a great many articles collected during his leisurely winter visits to Indian River. It was valued in his estate inventory at seventy-five dollars, just twenty-five dollars less than the Grand Lake cottage, lot, and furnishings. Stebbins left the collection to his three sons "to be equally divided between them as they shall agree."[10] Fred B. and Edwin J., his two youngest sons, shared their father's enthusiasm for collecting and natural history.[11] Thus F. R. Stebbins confidently bequeathed his sons his personal trove of natural curiosities and antiquities, knowing they would treasure its contents as well as their association with him. To him it surely represented, especially after the spring of 1888, a tangible link with a place as dear as a friend. Though in the end it revealed to him its perils, Indian River was his earthly paradise.

Notes

PROLOGUE

1. Stebbins, "An Interesting Letter."

2. Ibid.

3. For details of Stebbins's journalism career, see F. R. Stebbins, "The Pioneers"; C. Stebbins, "Sketch of My Life," Stebbins Family Papers, Michigan State University Archives and Historical Collections, East Lansing, 58, 63; Geddes, "Memoir of Francis R. Stebbins," 214–15; "Stebbins, Francis Ranna," 66; and Bonner, *Memoirs of Lenawee County, Michigan,* 1:551–53, 556. Stebbins penned his first travelogue in 1867 on a combination business and vacation trip to the Northeast. He sent others home while on similar later junkets. F.R.S., "At Sea."

4. *Florida Star* (hereafter *FLAS*), 14 May 1885, 1.

5. The life of Francis R. Stebbins (October 26, 1818–September 29, 1892) is well documented. "Stebbins, Francis Ranna," 66–67; Whitney and Bonner, *History and Biographical Record of Lenawee County, Michigan,* 1:493–94; "Francis R. Stebbins, Memorial Paper"; Geddes, "Memoir of Francis R. Stebbins," 214–17; Knapp and Bonner, *Illustrated History and Biographical Record of Lenawee County, Mich.,* 225–27; "Francois Rene Stebbins (Francis R. Stebbins)," 1:542–47; and Bonner, *Memoirs of Lenawee County, Michigan,* 1:554–55. His older brother Cortland B. Stebbins provided important insights into F. R. Stebbins's early life in his unpublished "Sketch of My Life." The various contemporary Adrian newspapers, particularly the *Adrian Daily Times and Expositor,* are the best sources for Stebbins's life after the Civil War.

6. Federal population census figures show that by 1860 Lenawee County's population was stabilized at 38,112 and by 1870 it was stagnating. Its citizens numbered 45,595 in 1870; 48,343 in 1880; and 48,448 in 1890. U.S. Department of the Interior, Census Office, *Ninth Census, 1870,* 58; U.S. Department of the Interior, Census Office, *Eleventh Census, 1890,* 1:24; DeNovo, *The Gilded Age and After,* 97–98; McKelvey, *The Urbanization of America,* 61–63.

7. *Tecumseh Herald,* 19 April 1883, 5.

8. Atherton, *Main Street on the Middle Border,* 8–17; Stonehouse, "The Michigan Excursion for the Founding of Riverside, California," 197.

9. Perejda, "Sources and Dispersal of Michigan's Population," 365. The 1870 federal census found 4,857 native-born Michiganders residing in Kansas, Dakota, and Texas but only 35 in Florida. There were 17,669 in Kansas, Dakota, and Texas, and 215 in Florida in 1880. The 1890 census shows 21,775 Michiganders in Kansas, North

Dakota, South Dakota, and Texas, and 802 in Florida. U.S. Department of the Interior, Census Office, *Ninth Census, 1870*, 378–79; U.S. Department of the Interior, Census Office, *Tenth Census, 1880*, 466; and U.S. Department of the Interior, Census Office, *Eleventh Census, 1890*, 3:16.

10. "Wintering in Florida"; H., "In the Florida Pines"; Mrs. H., "The Prairies of Florida"; Mrs. A. H., "The Sunny South"; and Mrs. A. H., "The Captive Redskins."

11. Adams, "The Land of the Sky"; Adams, "Educating the Negro"; Adams, "A Delayed Letter."

12. Crow, "Florida University (1883)"; Proctor, "The University of Florida," 193–220; Proctor, "The Early Years of the Florida Experiment Station," 213–14.

13. For another account of guided excursions for potential settlers, see Stonehouse, "The Michigan Excursion for the Founding of Riverside, California," 193–209.

14. "Facts from Florida."

15. Stebbins, "The Pioneers," 1.

16. Stebbins, "Roving on Indian River."

CHAPTER 1

1. Stebbins, "Indian River Longings."

CHAPTER 2

1. Frank W. Clay was a successful banker, self-made businessman, and local politician. Strangely enough, he was running on the Democratic ticket for city treasurer when he left for the South with Stebbins, a Republican Party stalwart. Stebbins's lengthy detour and slow progress home ensured that the candidate would have no time to campaign, and both reached home after the April 1 election. Despite being regarded as invincible, Clay came in third in a field of three. "Frank W. Clay"; *Adrian Daily Times and Expositor* (hereafter *ADT&E*), 1 April 1878, 1; "The Shake Up!"

2. *ADT&E*, 1 March 1878, 1.

3. This statement is not entirely correct. Both Spain and the United States required American citizens entering the Spanish colony of Cuba to carry passports. These were issued in Washington, D.C., and visaed by Spanish authorities at the port of departure. When Stebbins wished to visit Cuba, Spain had just ended a ten-year conflict with Cuban insurgents on her terms. From 1867 she exerted her authority through restrictive policies governing the island's trade with the mother country and others, particularly the United States. Spain seemed in no hurry to lift these encumbrances; the requirement of a Spanish visa on foreign passports lasted well into the next decade. In 1885 railroad magnate Henry B. Plant, who had recently completed a railroad and steamship route to Cuba and saw his investment threatened by this regulation, petitioned the State Department to persuade Spain to lift its visa requirement on travelers to Cuba. H. B. Plant to Mr. Bayard, April 30, 1885, *Papers Relating to the Foreign Relations of the United States* (Washington, DC: GPO, 1886), 711–12, and T. F. Bayard to Mr. Foster, May 6, 1885, *Papers Relating to the Foreign Relations of the United*

States (Washington: DC: GPO, 1886), 711. See Perez, *Cuba and the United States,* 49–54, for a summary of Spain's handling of Cuba from 1867 to 1878.

4. Stebbins, "Way Down South," *ADT&E,* 11 March 1878, 1.

5. Stebbins, "Notes on the Gulf."

6. For more about Cedar Key during the Civil War and the movements and motives of Union sympathizers and disenchanted Confederates, see Fishburne, *The Cedar Keys in the 19th Century,* 65–77, and Shofner, *Nor Is It Over Yet,* 1–3.

7. Such structures were common along the Florida Gulf coast. Designed for fish processing, the buildings were called ranches locally. An ornithologist described one south of Gasparilla Pass where he stopped to clean his specimens. Scott, "The Present Condition of Some of the Bird Rookeries of the Gulf Coast of Florida," 273.

8. Stebbins, "Way Down South: Cedar Key and Jacksonville."

9. Colorful Hubbard L. Hart turned Palatka into a major tourist stop on the Florida grand tour through a program of relentless self-promotion in the North and Midwest. The former New Englander opened his showcase orange grove opposite the river from town to tourists and regaled them with his portrayal of a Southern aristocrat. Thanks to his specially designed Hart Line of steamers, tourists could extend their St. Johns River cruise with a side trip up the twisting Ocklawaha River. Cabell and Hanna, *The St. Johns,* 250–53.

10. Such acts were the norm. Male tourists expected to amuse themselves firing from steamboat decks at wildlife along the riverbanks. A correspondent stated, "Every man and boy feels called upon to do some 'sporting' in Florida, and all are armed with as varied a lot of guns as would adorn an arsenal." He further noted, "[I]t amuses all but the timid people, and is a custom of very great value to the Union Metallic Cartridge Company." L.W.L., "Florida Sketches—Yachting Down South," 83.

11. Green turtles yielded two nineteenth-century delicacies, turtle soup and turtle steaks. The turtles were common on Indian River, the principal supplier. So profitable was the business that the first commercial fisheries on the lagoon divided their efforts between turtles and fish. The ones Stebbins saw were on their way to Jacksonville agents, who shipped them north and paid their captors after deducting commission and transportation expenses. Federal fishing monitors reported Indian River turtlers realized about 11 cents per pound and that the average size was 50 to 60 pounds in 1879. The largest ones caught reached 200 pounds. Earll, "Eastern Florida and Its Fisheries," 527; True, "The Green Turtles," 150–51.

12. Harvard professor Jeffries Wyman published several widely read papers on his excavations and analysis of the St. Johns River mounds. His pioneering work caught the public imagination by offering some insight into the mysterious prehistoric structures glimpsed along the shore from steamer decks. Stebbins, an antiquities collector and amateur excavator, surely thought of Wyman on first seeing these mounds. Wyman, "Fresh-Water Shell Mounds of the St. John's River, Florida," 4–87.

13. Stebbins, "Boating in Florida," *ADT&E,* 27 March 1878, 1.

14. These cages had been entertaining visitors for decades. Ralph Waldo Emerson saw the devices and related much the same tale about them in 1827 as Stebbins did in 1878. However, a contemporary Florida author, Abbie M. Brooks (Silvia Sunshine),

offered another interpretation. Elderly St. Augustine informants told her Minorcan settlers moving into the city found the cages holding the remains of pirates executed by the English when they governed St. Augustine. After the British left in 1785, the cages and their contents were buried outside the city gates. Workmen rediscovered them early in the nineteenth century, and the cages were displayed to tourists as examples of Spanish cruelty. Gilman and Ferguson, *The Journals and Miscellaneous Notebooks of Ralph Waldo Emerson,* 3:116; Griffin, *Ralph Waldo Emerson in St. Augustine,* 7–8; and Silvia Sunshine, *Petals Plucked from Sunny Climes,* 188–92.

15. In 1874 the U.S. government sent a number of captured Cheyennes, Comanches, Kiowas, Arapahos, and Caddoes to Fort Marion (Castillo de San Marcos). In May 1878 they were released. The adults were shipped to Fort Sill, Oklahoma, but the children were sent to the Hampton Normal Institute in Virginia to be educated. Stebbins narrowly saw them before their departure. While held in St. Augustine, the Indians became a tourist attraction. Silvia Sunshine, *Petals Plucked from Sunny Climes,* 192–97; Lanier, *Florida,* 51–54.

16. A few years later John Simons, a Georgia commission merchant, discussed Northern sweet potato preferences and the problems of marketing Southern varieties in the North and Midwest. He remorsefully observed: "Our Georgia yam, while it is the sweetest and best potato I know of, will not ship well or sell well. What they want is the Jersey potato, something like our Spanish potato. It is white, mealy and dry, resembling the Irish potato in these points. . . . This potato is what we need" ("What Sweet Potatoes to Grow for Northern Markets").

17. Stebbins, "From Far Florida," *ADT&E,* 1 April 1878, 2.

18. Stebbins, "From Florida Home."

19. *ADT&E,* 4 April 1878, 1.

CHAPTER 3

1. *ADT&E,* 18 December 1878, 1.

2. Nehemiah M. Sutton, an avid sportsman and eleven years Stebbins's junior, enjoyed the 1879 trip so much he accompanied him in 1880, 1883, and 1886. Sutton was a prosperous Tecumseh farmer, hardware merchant, opera house owner, and family friend. He visited Florida on other occasions as well. His son-in-law J. B. Swan owned property at Kerr City near Sanford, and the Sutton family shared winter vacations there with the Swans. "Nehemiah M. Sutton"; "Loveliest Village of the Plain"; Waldron, *One Hundred Years a Country Town,* 99, 132; *Tecumseh News,* 4 June 1885, 1; and Hause, "The Land of Flowers."

3. "Tecumseh Topics."

4. Herman F. Eberts and Chester R. Hulett kept their excursion agency offices at 1 Walker Block in Detroit. They escorted three different groups to Florida in 1879 and again in 1880, taking one a month in January, February, and March. Their clients also received reduced rates for meals, berths, hotels, and side trips to popular watering spots beyond Jacksonville. *Michigan State Gazetteer and Business Directory 1879,* 378;

"Florida," *ADT&E,* 29 January 1879, 1; *ADT&E,* 4 March 1879, 1; *ADT&E,* 8 January 1880, 3; and *ADT&E,* 23 February 1880, 3.

5. *ADT&E,* 16 January 1879, 1.

6. *ADT&E,* 20 January 1879, 1.

7. An eyewitness, camping on the Sebastian River, described his experience of this earthquake: "I heard a peculiar rumbling and roaring sound proceeding from the eastward . . . but as it rapidly came nearer it became louder, and the ground began to tremble and roll. . . . The heavy rumbling seemed to pass right under me with an oscillating and wary motion, and disappeared in a westerly direction." He also reported, "At Cape Canaveral light-house it threw oil out of the lamp onto the reflectors, and it shook the solid brick tower of Jupiter light from base to dome, while the keepers of both lights made the best time on record for a hundred feet downward" (Henshall, "A Winter in East Florida: Fourth Paper").

8. *ADT&E,* 21 January 1879, 1.

9. "A Southern Memory."

10. *ADT&E,* 27 January 1879, 1.

11. *ADT&E,* 30 January 1879, 1.

12. Stebbins, "Way Down South: At Savannah and the Journey Thither."

13. Stebbins, "From Florida," *ADT&E,* 7 February 1879, 1.

14. *ADT&E,* 8 February 1879, 1.

15. A contemporary writer summed up the matter: "The alligator, bear in mind, has no friends. People seem to take supreme delight in worrying him by all manner of expedients . . . he is timid and harmless, except when his life is imperilled. . . . [And] the fact that the hunting of them is by no means a perilous amusement, so-journers here are generally quick to accept of any opportunity that may present itself for experiencing the sensation of an alligator hunt" (P.H.A., "Alligator Shooting in Florida").

16. Since the colonial period, Northerners commonly compared themselves favorably to Southerners in terms of energy and ambition. Still, the charge that Southerners lacked drive rankled, and Southern newspaper editors repeatedly and hotly denied it. Jacksonville resident Dr. Charles J. Kenworthy, a specialist in Florida's climate, offered reassurance to prospective Northern emigrants by remarking: "[T]he emigrant will not become indolent unless he is constitutionally lazy. . . . In our many wanderings in the Southern States we have met with numerous Northern people who, after years of residence in the South were as active, industrious and enterprising as before they left a more inhospitable climate" (Al Fresco, "Southwest Florida—No. 4"; and Woodward, "The Southern Ethic in a Puritan World," 333).

17. Stebbins, "Wintering in Florida."

18. Captain Charles R. Carlin knew the Indian River from Titusville to Jupiter Inlet thoroughly. A former officer in the British navy, he served from 1872 to 1876 as assistant lightkeeper at the Jupiter Lighthouse and worked for the U.S. Geological Survey from 1876 to 1886. He was active in local efforts to improve area transportation facilities. Just before he took the Jupiter Lighthouse position, Carlin married Mary

More Joyner. Thereafter, he augmented his income by boat building for permanent and seasonal residents and gained a national reputation among sportsmen wintering in Florida as a premier pilot and game guide. White, *History of the Carlin House;* and the following in *FLAS:* 13 October 1880, 1; 26 January 1881, 4; 23 February 1881, 4; 25 May 1881, 4; 5 April 1882, 3; 14 June 1882, 4; 12 July 1882, 4; 20 September 1882, 4; 7 December 1882, 3, 5; 7 June 1883, 8; 13 December 1883, 8; 20 December 1883, 8; 31 January 1884, 1; 2 April 1885, 4; and 9 July 1885, 4.

19. Francis Le Baron, who conducted a field survey of ancient earthworks in east Florida for Harvard's Peabody Museum of Archaeology and Ethnology, considered this mound manmade: "South of Titusville, 12.3 miles by the new Titusville and City Point road, as I located it, is a large sand mound in the hummock [*sic*] now belonging to Charles R. Carlin, but formerly to Albert Faber. It is on the west side of the river, about 500 feet from the bank, in T. 23 S., R. 35 E. It is about 25 feet high" ("Prehistoric Remains in Florida," 783).

20. George M. Barbour, accompanying Seth French, the State Commissioner of Immigration, on an official tour of south Florida, called on Mr. Spratt within days of Stebbins's 1880 visit. He recorded his observations in his popular guide to the state. Barbour, *Florida for Tourists, Invalids, and Settlers,* 38–39.

21. Florida's birdlife was decimated in the nineteenth century. Amateur and professional naturalists, recreational and market hunters, and ordinary shooters seeking targets went to Florida expressly to shoot large numbers of birds. The majority were large water birds, such as egrets and herons, and small birds with brightly colored feathers. Some went into scientific or private collections, but others became parlor ornaments in tourists' homes. The principal trade, however, was not in bird skins but in plumes and feathers, which were in great demand by the millinery industry. In the last three decades of the nineteenth century, fashionable women wore hats adorned with feathers or plumes, wings, or entire stuffed bodies of small birds. The style persisted into the early twentieth century despite the best efforts of the Audubon Society and conservationists of all stamps. State laws regulating the business came late and were not enforced until the twentieth century. For more on the subject, see Doughty, *Feather Fashions and Bird Preservation,* 10–12, 81; and R. Williams, "History of Bird Protection in Florida," 54–58.

22. This mound's conspicuous size and location made it well-known to Indian River residents and visitors. Le Baron personally investigated it and described its condition in some detail. He noted that the Coast Survey had used it for a triangulation station. Le Baron, "Prehistoric Remains in Florida," 783–84.

23. Sea beans were fabricated into fashionable Florida mementoes and widely sold in Jacksonville and St. Augustine souvenir shops. Damon Greenleaf, proprietor of the well-known Jacksonville establishments Greenleaf's Museum of Florida Curiosities and Greenleaf's Jewelry Store, listed them first among his stock in a full-page advertisement. Greenleaf claimed he had, "[c]onstantly on hand, the largest stock in the State of Sea Beans, mounted in every style." Rambler, *Guide to Florida,* 169.

24. The ruins of Fort Capron intrigued other visitors to Indian River. Both James A. Henshall and Dr. Herman Herold left descriptions of the fort's condition.

Henshall, "A Winter in East Florida: Sixth Paper," 763; and Herold, "Log Book," 26–27.

25. Stebbins, "Indian River, Florida."

26. Enough of Fort Pierce's ruins survived to attract sightseers. For accounts of the place from nearly the same time as Stebbins's stop, see Henshall, "A Winter in East Florida: Seventh Paper," 783; and Friar Tuck, "A Winter's Cruise in Eastern and Southern Florida."

27. Large steamboats frequently were subjected to worse conditions than they were intended to handle. It was not unusual for river steamboats to make long coastal runs. For instance in 1888, the large St. Johns River steamer the *Chattahoochee* was leased by the Jacksonville, Tampa and Key West Railroad for a floating hotel and shipped to Jupiter. Its pilot took five days to maneuver the large craft through the inlet and up to the wharf. Avast, "Jupiter."

28. In Florida, recreational fishermen tended to become "fish hogs" in the presence of an apparently endless supply and no game laws and limits. They took all the fish they could. Most brought their catch back to their hotel kitchen or gave it to nearby residents. Frequently, the hotels could not use all their guests caught nor was there anyone living in the vicinity to whom they could give the fish. Even with no takers, fishermen felt few qualms about wasting their entire catch. Al Fresco, "Florida Again"; J. W., "The Homosassa River"; and J. W., "Notes from Florida."

29. Stebbins, "On Indian River," *ADT&E,* 14 March 1879, 1.

30. F. R. Stebbins was more observant than the average traveler. Only Dr. Herman Herold, a physician from Newark, New Jersey, who dogged Stebbins's trail down Indian River in 1884, said anything about Jupiter Inlet's extensive prehistoric middens and earthworks. He also photographed one of the shell mounds in the vicinity of the lighthouse. Residents knew about the Indian constructions area, but so familiar were they that locals seldom alluded to them. However, in the early 1880s, several settlers informed Francis Le Baron of their existence when they learned he was conducting an archaeological survey of the region. Herold, "Log Book," 34; and Le Baron, "Prehistoric Remains in Florida," 784.

31. This site, perhaps occupied as early as 1000 BC, suffered as the area was settled, and the walls and the sand mound no longer exist. They were leveled before the turn of the century like many area mounds. Some were removed to clear the way for the railroad. Others were mined for their shells, which were carted off as paving material. Over the years, construction on the military installation built around the lighthouse effectively destroyed and scattered whatever antiquities were left. Furthermore, persistent stories of pirate treasure prompted unauthorized excavation on the site. On one occasion, Department of the Interior officials surprised a group of servicemen digging at the lighthouse base with a road grader. In 1973 the Jupiter Inlet Light House was placed on the National Register of Historic Places. Thomas and Weed, "Jupiter Midden #2"; Hoffman and Hughes, "Cultural Resource Assessment"; DuBois, "Jupiter Inlet," 21; DuBois, "Jupiter Lighthouse," 11–12; and Winsberg, *Florida's History through Its Places,* 91.

32. Stebbins, "At Jupiter Inlet."

33. Le Baron visited the site but said, "I stopped at Fort Capron, opposite Indian River outlet. Here I found a large deposit of oyster-shells resembling a kjökkenmödding, but saw no mound" ("Prehistoric Remains in Florida," 786).

34. Stebbins learned that men retrieving bulky containers from the beach were wreckers, not moonshiners. Area pioneers relied on windfalls in the form of cargo washed ashore from storm-wrecked ships. Strong storms brought residents out to the beach to see what useful items may have been carried to land. Alcoholic beverages of all types were prized finds. In the fall of 1886, settlers from Indian River to Biscayne Bay discovered the beach covered with wine casks of varying sizes. There were one-hundred-gallon casks of Spanish claret, fifteen-gallon kegs of Malaga, and fifteen-gallon kegs of a wine labeled "Double Superior." Within a week all the casks had disappeared. Many were buried in the upper beach to preserve the contents for future use. Pierce, *Pioneer Life in Southeast Florida*, 202–03.

35. Five years before, Amos J. Cummings wrote about turtling methods in east Florida. Residents captured the animals by spreading nets across the coastal salt lagoons in early spring. The turtlers kept their catch alive while awaiting shipment in prepared enclosures Cummings thought resembled "pig pens at anchor." Called crawls, they "are distinguishing features of the salt water rivers. Cypress stakes are driven into the sand and water some rods from the shore in the form of a square. The water is from two to three feet in depth, and flows through the intervals between the stakes. . . . The word 'crawl' is probably a corruption of the Spanish *correl*. The natives persist in pronouncing and spelling it c-r-a-w-l" (Ziska, "The Home of the Turtles").

36. Cincinnati area doctor James Henshall met Peter Wright during his Indian River trip the same winter. He remarked, "Three miles below [Elbow Creek] is Crane Creek, where reside . . . several negro families, among whom is Peter Wright, who is known to a few Northern tourists as a good boatman and a sharp trader." Peter Wright was also remembered as a mail carrier. He purchased considerable acreage and cultivated oranges and tobacco as cash crops. Peter Wright may have been related to R. U. Wright, captain and co-owner of a small steamboat, the *Ibis*. Another traveler referred to Capt. R. U. Wright as "a very intelligent and industrious colored man of Titusville . . . who has carried the mails on this river the past eight years, as well as many pleasure parties." Both Peter and Richard Wright were among the earliest settlers of Melbourne. Henshall, "A Winter in East Florida: Fourth Paper"; Sherman, "Observations of a Massachusetts Yankee on Indian River"; Kjerulff, *Tales of Old Brevard*, 20, 28, 30, 38, 46, 104; and Shofner, *History of Brevard County*, 1:90, 134.

37. Stebbins's last guess was as probable as his first ones. During the Seminole Wars, settlers frequently evacuated their homes on notice or rumor of Indian attack. In 1849 M. O. Burnham's family with others of the Armed Occupation Colony abandoned their claims near Fort Pierce so abruptly when learning of an impending raid that "they left without their hats, and during the next four days which it took them to reach St. Augustine, having light head winds, all suffered much from the hot August sun which scalded their heads, and from scarcity of food and water." The start of the Civil War also panicked some settlers, especially those who did not support the Confederacy; many moved north to avoid the conflict. Some returned afterward but

not always to the same homestead. In their absence, William and Peter Wittfeld's property was seized, and they were obliged to petition the government for new claims. Ransom, *A Memoir of Captain Mills Olcott Burnham,* 14–15, 30; Lockwood, *Florida's Historic Indian River County,* 3.

38. The fifteen-acre grove, usually referred to as simply Burnham's grove, was a popular tourist destination. M. O. Burnham was an Indian River celebrity, known nationally as one of the oldest settlers, the keeper of the Cape Canaveral Lighthouse since 1853, and the co-owner of the second most famous Indian River orange grove. His grove had been made with budstock from the most famous grove, Dummitt grove, and other sources grafted onto an existing wild sour orange grove. It was noted for its sweet, thin-skinned fruit and its location, which protected the trees from most freezes. Burnham, who retained his position at the lighthouse until his death in 1886, resided there with his family. His son-in-law and partner, Henry Wilson, lived at the grove four and a half miles to the west on the shore of Banana River. Ransom, *A Memoir of Captain Mills Olcott Burnham,* 19–22, 30.

39. Stebbins, "Boating in Florida: Oranges, Lemons, Potatoes, Etc."

40. Fort Matanzas did indeed have a history. Invading parties frequently approached St. Augustine through its "back door," the Matanzas Inlet. Spanish governor Manuel de Montiano had the fort constructed between 1740 and 1742 to block any future invaders from that direction. Abbie M. Brooks, who visited the site around the time Stebbins did, was better informed about its past than he. She recorded its appearance and story in her guidebook. Waterbury, "The Castillo Years, 1668–1763," 74–80; and Silvia Sunshine, *Petals Plucked from Sunny Climes,* 237–38.

41. Stebbins, "Facts from Florida."

42. *ADT&E,* 27 March 1879, 1.

43. *ADT&E,* 28 March 1879, 1.

CHAPTER 4

1. *ADT&E,* 3 February 1880, 3.

2. *Tecumseh Herald,* 5 February 1880, 5.

3. *ADT&E,* 19 February 1880, 3.

4. Stebbins, "Way Down South: The Snowy South."

5. Amos J. Cummings visited Douglas Dummitt and his orange grove, the oldest and most famous on Indian River, in the spring of 1873. He devoted most of the ensuing article to anecdotes illustrating Dummitt's quirky personality. The journalist declared: "He cares but little for money and is contented so long as he makes a living. If anybody wants his oranges they must go to his grove and buy them on the trees. The Captain never looks for purchasers. The purchasers must look for the Captain" (Ziska, "Florida's Orange Groves"). Information about Douglas Dummitt and his grove can be found in Hanna and Hanna, *Florida's Golden Sands,* 236–42.

6. Stebbins, "Our Florida Letter," *ADT&E,* 24 February 1880, 2.

7. Planting citrus trees among palmettos was not as unusual as Stebbins thought. A writer commented on the practice: "[I]t has been ascertained around Daytona and

elsewhere, that the orange tree has a thriftier growth in a palmetto hammock that has been but slightly thinned out. It always grows better when near by, *not exactly at the roots* of a cabbage palm" ("Rockledge, the Beautiful, the Palmetto Grove Town").

8. Five years after Stebbins's visit to his homestead, H. S. Williams was elected to the state senate. During the intervening time, he had continued his experimentation with various fruit crops and turned his property into a show place. By 1886, Williams's orange grove was dignified with the name "Lawn Dale." "Rockledge, the Beautiful, the Palmetto Grove Town"; and "Indian River, as Seen by an Editor."

9. Amos J. Cummings chronicled Dr. William Wittfeld's pioneering trials and tribulations for the readers of the New York *Sun.* Ziska, "The Farming in Florida." See also Shofner, *History of Brevard County,* 1:84, 142, 172, 180.

10. Amos J. Cummings, a prominent New York newspaper editor and reporter, described the mound in 1873. Wittfeld honored him with an artifact from his mound for being the first journalist to visit the region. It was "a kind of dark flint, beautifully polished, and as true as if it had been turned by the most accurate machinery." Wittfeld thought it was a plumb. Ziska, "Florida's Indian Mounds."

11. In 1874 Frederick Ober visited the homestead of a single settler at the south end of Merritt Island. Possibly Ober's "Crusoe of the river" was Stebbins's Mr. Haddock. Ober commended the settler's industry but found his "shanty" picturesque. He attempted to photograph it with the absent owner's goats in the foreground: "I hardly counted 'two' before a huge goat, with wide spread horns, spied my camera and started on a tour of inspection. If he had started leisurely I shouldn't have cared, but he came in a hurry, as though he saw something in my direction he desired, and so I concluded to postpone the taking of that picture, shouldered my camera and traveled among the cacti in a way that brought tears to my eyes and tears to the eyes of my friends on the fence" (Fred Beverly, "Our Okeechobee Expedition").

12. Stebbins, "Our Florida Letter: Scenes and Incidents."

13. A cottage industry was founded on a craft utilizing sea bass scales, and area women earned needed income from sales to Jacksonville and St. Augustine souvenir houses. An observer remarked: "The scales are very large and strong, and are made into beautiful imitations of flowers and grasses in a very ingenious manner by the ladies in this vicinity. It is necessary to scale the fish with a hatchet" (Al. I. Gator, "Florida"; and Merchandise List).

14. Stebbins and Sutton's behavior impressed another Northern traveler, Milton E. Card, who reached Jupiter slightly before "the two elderly gentlemen from Michigan," then sixty-one and fifty, respectively. Card described their sport for his own readers' amusement: "They were fish maniacs. As soon as the first gleam of day was suspected of illuminating the east, they could be seen dimly through the doubtful light, casting their lines and pulling in fish, only to let them lie on the sand, food for the hundreds of buzzards constantly hovering about. They seemed to enjoy themselves hugely, and the buzzards were apparently in the same state of mind" (Friar Tuck, "A Winter's Cruise in Eastern and Southern Florida").

15. Stebbins, "On Indian River: Sailing on Summer Seas."

16. M. E. Spencer, the assistant lighthouse keeper, augmented his income by

photographing the local scenery and tourists stopping at the lighthouse. By 1883 he advertised stereoscopic views and prints of "Tropical Florida" for sale through the mail. Spencer and James A. Armour, the lighthouse keeper, were partners in the business from at least 1877, but Armour dropped out in 1883. According to his advertisement in March 1885, Spencer had relocated his business to Lake Worth. *FLAS,* 1 November 1883, 8, and 12 March 1885, 4; DuBois, "Jupiter Lighthouse," 10–11; and Rinhart and Rinhart, *Victorian Florida,* 8–9, 212.

17. The year before James Henshall also called on "Old Cuba," at the time the only settler between Fort Pierce and Jupiter Inlet. The "little, dried-up old fellow about five feet high" told Henshall he was a Cuban refugee and had fought against Spain. During the insurrection, he had earned the name of "sand-fly." Milton E. Card heard much the same story from him but discounted it saying, "His cigars were good, his fruit excellent, but his stories were frightful specimens of embroidery." Henshall, "A Winter in East Florida: Seventh Paper," 783; Friar Tuck, "A Winter's Cruise in Eastern and Southern Florida."

18. The two Michiganders were relatively moderate in their alligator hunting. As the 1880s progressed, professional hunters joined recreational alligator shooters. Harvesting alligator skins became highly profitable, and market hunters sought their prey in every corner of Florida. Due to the combined efforts of tourists, residents, and professional hunters, Florida's alligator population was so reduced by the end of the nineteenth century that many assumed the animal was close to extermination. "The Alligator Satchel"; "'Gators' Getting Scarce."

19. Annie and Benjamin Hogg were respected local entrepreneurs. In early 1880, Milton E. Card described their Fort Pierce store: "The store at Fort Pierce, is simply a palmetto thatch, fifteen feet square, the main and only room serving as store and sleeping apartment, and in it may be found the usual assortment, hog and hominy, green coffee, flour, matches and baking powder being the standards. The place is in reality the trading post for the Kissimmee Indians" (Friar Tuck, "A Winter's Cruise in Eastern and Southern Florida").

Another caller related Annie Hogg's salesmanship: "[A] short run was made down to St. Lucie or Hogg's store where a sharp, canny Scotch woman, Mrs. Hogg—by the way her daughter insists the name is spelled Hoag—took us all in one after another, in various little bargains for articles wanted and relieved the party of considerable silver as skillfully as if we were only a squad of Seminoles. . . . The latter do much trading here and furnish many articles of Indian work which some bought to take home as presents" ("Cruise of the May"; for more, see A. Williams, *A Brief History of Saint Lucie County,* 10–12, and Shofner, *History of Brevard County,* 1:91–92, 146).

20. Stebbins, "On Indian River: More Fishing and Boating."

21. The facility the two visited was the Gilbert's Bar House of Refuge or House of Refuge Number 2, and its keeper was then Ezra Stoner. It and four others made up the United States Life-Saving Service's installations in District Seven (Florida's Atlantic coast). The service's function was to rescue crew and passengers and protect any saved cargo from vessels wrecked along the coast. Houses of Refuge operated more passively than life-saving or lifeboat stations, the other types of installations the Ser-

vice operated. Their staff patrolled the beach during storms and provided havens for those who managed to reach shore on their own. They did not attempt rescues from ships.

Gilbert's Bar House of Refuge, one of the first five built in 1876, was second from the north and situated at the Saint Lucie Rocks on the north side of the St. Lucie Inlet. Ezra Stoner, a local resident and a single man, became its second keeper in 1879 but resigned May 26, 1880. However, he continued his duties until his replacement took the reins on July 7, 1880. Stoner gave an absence of activity as his reason for resigning. It was not unusual for years to pass between wrecks, nor was Stoner's short stint as keeper unusual. Most keepers and their families found the solitude at the Houses of Refuge oppressive. Likewise, many who resided at the Houses of Refuge contracted health problems of one kind or another, in some instances fatal. Thurlow, "Lonely Vigils"; Hutchinson and Paige, *History of Martin County,* 55–57; and Lamb, "The American Life-Saving Service."

22. This was the Bethel Creek House of Refuge or House of Refuge Number 1, northernmost of the original five life-saving facilities on Florida's Atlantic coast. It was located eleven miles north of the Indian River Inlet. James A. Henshall provided a description of the interior layout of these structures. Henshall, "A Winter in East Florida: Ninth Paper," 823; Thurlow, "Lonely Vigils," 154.

23. "Lord Sykes" was probably the fifth baronet of Sledmere, Sir Tatton Sykes (13 March 1826–4 May 1913). The world-traveling Yorkshireman was thirty-one in 1857, the date the Burnham-Wilson families associated with his visit to Merritt Island. He made a profound impression, for they recalled not only the exact date but seem to have related his story to all travelers. Amos J. Cummings heard the tale in 1873, and it passed down through the family to Robert Ransom, who recounted the baronet's hunting excesses on the island. Ziska, "Florida's Indian Mounds"; Ransom, *A Memoir of Captain Mills Olcott Burnham,* 22–23; and "Sir Mark Sykes," 134–35.

24. Stebbins, "Down in Florida."

25. The pelicans and their rookery fascinated Northern tourists, particularly those interested in ornithology. Another of Stebbins's traveling companions described how he found the birds in 1885: "These young were truly loathsome in their appearance, as awkward as squabs hissing and tumbling about on the rude platforms of sticks and weeds, and surrounded with dung and fishes in various stages of decomposition, from which a fearful stench arose. Most of the adults were rather shy but those having young perched upon the dead mangrove stubs and allowed us to approach, at times, to within thirty feet or even less" (Watkins, "A Disastrous Season on Pelican Island," 149).

26. Four years later, church services in Titusville were still irregular, and ministers continued to find gathering their congregation difficult. One parson illuminated the situation when he placed a notice imploring his Titusville flock to be punctual in the local newspaper. It was important because he had "to walk two miles in midday, and return to preach at LaGrange in the afternoon" (Duncan, "Church Notice for Titusville").

27. [N. M. Sutton], "Letter from Florida."

28. *ADT&E,* 5 April 1880, 5.

29. *Tecumseh Herald,* 8 April 1880, 5.

30. *Tecumseh Herald,* 15 April 1880, 5.

CHAPTER 5

1. *ADT&E,* 8 January 1881, 3.

2. Alfred H. Wood was a clothing merchant of long standing. One of Adrian's pioneer businessmen, he also held various public offices. Wood had been Senator Jerome Chaffee's brother-in-law, and the two men remained close after the death of Chaffee's wife. The senator was a frequent guest at Wood's home. "Alfred H. Wood"; "Hon. Jerome B. Chaffee," 1:122.

3. Senator Jerome B. Chaffee of Denver was a quite different sort from the others in the party. Like many in Stebbins's and Wood's circle, he had immigrated to Michigan in his youth, but unlike them, he was unable to find his niche in Adrian business. He moved west in 1857 and his luck improved. He reached Colorado in 1860 with funds from land speculating in Kansas and banking in Missouri. Chaffee made his fortune in silver mining, founded the First National Bank of Denver in 1865, and entered politics as a Republican. After serving in the legislature, he was elected a delegate from the Territory of Colorado to Congress and saw his bill to admit Colorado as a state passed in early 1875. Chaffee was elected U.S. senator for the 45th Congress from 1877 to 1879 but retired from office-seeking at the end of his term. To cap his career, his only surviving child, Fannie Josephine Chaffee, married Ulysses Simpson Grant, the second son of President Ulysses S. Grant, in the fall of 1880. "Chaffee, Jerome Bunty," *Biographical Directory;* "Hon. Jerome B. Chaffee," 1:120–23; "Chaffee, Jerome Bunty," *American Legislative Leaders;* and Kane, *Facts about the Presidents,* 122.

4. Frank W. Chaffee settled in Carthage, Missouri, where he went into business as a hardware merchant. "Sad Death of Miss Anna Chaffee."

5. *ADT&E,* 10 January 1881, 3.

6. Ibid.

7. *ADT&E,* 24 January 1881, 3.

8. Porpoise held no special status in the nineteenth century. Like other marine mammals, their sole value derived from their economic uses. Frederick W. True, of the United States Commission of Fish and Fisheries, even advocated porpoise as a dietary article but recommended only the young ones for human consumption. His idea seems not to have been adopted. Commercial fishermen sold few for food in the nineteenth century. They took the majority for their skins, which were turned into leather, or for their oil. Regardless, porpoises remained a slight percentage of the total commercial catch. True, "Porpoise Steak"; Stevenson, "Utilization of the Skins of Aquatic Animals," 339; and Smith, "Notes on Biscayne Bay," 172.

9. Stebbins, "Seeing Florida."

10. *FLAS,* 2 February 1881, 4.

11. Henry T. Titus, for many years the proprietor of the only hotel on north In-

dian River, was a controversial character and not entirely beloved by his neighbors. He had a reputation for tailoring his tall tales to fit his audience; therefore, he spoke of Fremont for the Chaffees and of Houghton for the Michiganders. Ironically, there was a Titus who left an account of meeting Houghton in Michigan, but the event occurred two years before Houghton's drowning. Hanna and Hanna, *Florida's Golden Sands,* 71–185; Clark, *Into the Old Northwest,* 79–80.

12. Jeffries Wyman first examined the conspicuous shell bluff overlooking Lake Monroe in 1860. "Old Enterprise," as he named it, then rose in tiers well over fifteen feet above the water and was extensive enough to support a hotel and several other structures. Le Baron resurveyed the site on 15 August 1877 and found that roughly half the shell bluff had been mined for fertilizer. Wyman, "Fresh-Water Shell Mounds of the St. John's River, Florida," 19; and Le Baron, "Prehistoric Remains in Florida," 775.

13. Perhaps Senator Jerome Chaffee's presence prompted the residents' unusual coolness toward the tourist party. A staunch Republican, he continued serving his party after leaving office in 1879. Though the ex-senator took up traveling, he apparently combined political chores with recreation and made several appearances in Florida to bolster state Republicans. In the spring of 1880, Chaffee worked to build support in Florida for President Grant's third term. Ultimately all such efforts failed, and James A. Garfield was nominated and then won the election. The Tallahassee press noted Chaffee's return to the state the next January but divulged no information about his activities or movements. The Democratic Titusville *Florida Star* ignored the senator's arrival on Indian River. His name was omitted from the list of new hotel guests, though his brother's appeared on it. Stebbins only discussed the group's recreational activities, although he did alter his usual itinerary to spend his entire 1881 winter vacation near Merritt Island, which possessed a Republican enclave. Williamson, *Florida Politics in the Gilded Age,* 56–57; *Weekly Floridian,* 18 January 1881, 4; "Arrivals at the Titus House."

14. Stebbins probably did not know Ralph Waldo Emerson himself had wintered in Florida January through March 1827. Emerson, suffering from a lung ailment, left New England in the fall of 1826 to restore his health in a warm climate. He spent his convalescence in St. Augustine touring the antiquities, observing local society, visiting the beach, and keeping a journal. St. Augustine then was nearly as remote as was Indian River five decades later. Emerson commented that local officials called the place Botany Bay. His initial reaction to the local culture antedates Stebbins's sentiments regarding native Floridians:

And here the dark Minorcan sad & separate
Wrapt in his cloak strolls with unsocial eye
All day basks idle in the sun then seeks his food
By night upon the waters stilly plying
His hook & line in all the moonlit bays.

Gilman and Ferguson, *Journals and Miscellaneous Notebooks of Ralph Waldo Emerson,* 3:151; Griffin, *Ralph Waldo Emerson in St. Augustine,* 1–21.

15. Stebbins, "On the Bounding Billows."

16. *ADT&E,* 8 February 1881, 2.

17. So popular did such exotic adornments become among Northern tourists that an Adrian jeweler advertised the arrival of "Alligator Teeth Jewelry, fresh from Florida" and ready for sale in his Michigan establishment for the summer seasons of 1884 and 1885. *ADT&E,* 9 June 1884, 3, and 18 May 1885, 3.

18. Two years previously, an enterprising resident of Pinellas, Florida, queried the *Forest and Stream* about the market for sea beans in New York City. Likely, he was discouraged to read the response: "Florida 'sea beans' polished and set in a score of different ways are sold in the booths on New York streets. They are beautiful, common, cheap, and have lost their novelty" ("Answers to Correspondents").

19. Ex-senator and banker Jerome B. Chaffee probably showed Stebbins the letter. At the time, Florida governor William D. Bloxham was negotiating a deal with Hamilton Disston to sell the Philadelphia industrialist millions of acres of the public domain for one million dollars. These monies were needed urgently to repay the state's chief creditor, Francis Vose, a major prewar investor in Florida railroad construction. Vose was on the verge of recalling his loan, a move that would bankrupt the state. Disston was keen to drain and improve the Everglades but did not possess the full million himself. In late 1880 and early 1881 he was soliciting investors, particularly among an inner circle of well-heeled Republican Party leaders. Chaffee, who sometimes managed party finances, was almost certainly approached. The state accepted Disston's offer of a million dollars for four million acres of swamp and overflow land in south Florida in May 1881. For a more complete account of the Disston Purchase and its impact, see Williamson, *Florida Politics in the Gilded Age,* 72–78; Tebeau, *A History of Florida,* 278–82; and "Disston's Million Dollar I.O.U.," 14–16.

20. Six years before, the situation looked bleak to one visitor, who thought, "[E]re long the cliffs will bear quack medicine names, and the old walls will fall before want of taste, and give way to *pine fences* as *has* the old and mysterious 'Treasury wall' at St. Augustine. (A disgraceful fact)." However, by the time Stebbins noticed this state of affairs, the problem was already clear to St. Augustine's residents, who were awakening to the value of the city's ancient architecture. In 1879 the editor of the *St. Augustine Press* noted, "People do not come here to see feeble and ugly imitations of New York and Boston dwellings" and urged that any modern structures should blend in stylistically with existing Spanish buildings. He argued: "The folks of St. Augustine should regard the removal of a Coquina wall, to be nothing less than sacrilege, and the older and quainter their buildings, the more carefully should they prop and preserve them. As regards the exterior of their dwellings, they should regard all innovations as deadly sins, and revel in the grotesque—so will they fill their hotels and their pockets" ("Preserve the Ancient"; L.W.L., "Yachting in Florida").

21. Stebbins, "From Florida: Sea Beans and an Epitaph."

22. *ADT&E,* 26 February 1881, 3.

23. *ADT&E,* 29 March 1881, 3.

24. *ADT&E,* 18 April 1881, 3.

25. *Weekly Press,* 20 May 1881, 5.

26. *ADT&E,* 21 May 1881, 3.

27. *ADT&E,* 30 May 1883, 3.

CHAPTER 6

1. *ADT&E,* 13 January 1882, 3.

2. *FLAS,* 25 January 1882, 3.

3. *FLAS,* 1 February 1882, 3.

4. Charles W. Gunn was, at age twenty-four, a junior member of his father's Gunn Hardware Company in Grand Rapids, Michigan. His father, William S. Gunn, had been a hardware merchant and manufacturer of tin and sheet iron since 1849. Unfortunately, Charles Gunn suffered from consumption (tuberculosis) and routinely left Michigan for warmer areas during the winter. He used these interludes from business to pursue his interest in ornithology. An avid amateur naturalist, Gunn had helped found the Kent Scientific Institute in Grand Rapids and was a regular contributor to ornithological periodicals. In 1880 he and his brother William A. mounted a collecting expedition to Indian River that Gunn described in some detail for *Ornithologist and Oologist.* Baxter, *History of Grand Rapids, Michigan,* 447–48; Gunn, "A Collector in Florida"; "Death of Mr. Charles W. Gunn"; "Wm. S. Gunn Dies Abroad"; *Grand Rapids Daily Eagle,* 19 February 1880, 1, 24 February 1880, 1, 20 April 1880, 4, 24 April 1880, 4; and G., "Chas. W. Gunn." Grand Rapids coverage of Gunn's 1882 trip to Indian River with F. R. Stebbins may be found in the *Grand Rapids Daily Eagle,* 31 January 1882, 4, and 8 April 1882, 4; and the *Daily Morning Democrat,* 31 January 1882, 3, 5 February 1882, 3, 21 February 1882, 3, and 9 April 1882, 3.

5. Amos J. Cummings visited DeSoto Grove while James Paterson was in residence. He described its appearance and the lawyer's gracious lifestyle in 1873. Commenting on his location, Cummings noted: "He is literally out of the world, being over twenty miles from a post office, forty miles from a doctor, and fifty miles from a church. There is no public road within twenty miles of his place, and his only way of travel is in cat-rigged sail boats" (Ziska, "Florida's Orange Groves").

6. Captain William H. Reed purchased property on the east side of the Banana River and wintered there regularly in the 1880s. Area residents accepted him as a permanent settler. By 1886 the editor of the local paper referred to him as "Bill" and duly reported his seasonal comings and goings. In 1889 a river traveler recalled passing his "handsome home . . . on the shore of the mainland . . . on a shell mound, surrounded by palmetto trees, with a large orange grove in the rear." *FLAS,* 15 November 1883, 8, and 3 November 1886, 3; Coon, *Log of the Cruise of 1889 D.T.S.C.,* 27.

7. J. H. Hogan had been married to Louise Shaffler, another Banana River resident, nearly two months when Stebbins beheld his improved homestead. The wedding was held aboard Hogan's schooner *Elf.* Four years later Hogan was listed as one of ten residents in the hamlet of Canaveral. By then, he had cleared five acres on which he had begun an orange grove. *FLAS,* 11 January 1882, 3; *The South Publishing Company's Florida State Gazetteer and Business Directory,* 1:98.

8. Stebbins would not have been impressed by F. C. Allen's holding; he did not

begin construction on a proper house until the fall of 1883. According to the *Florida Star*, Allen was selling ready-made and custom-made tinware and repaired damaged pieces at his home by November. Later, he enlarged his house and took in travelers. By 1886, he renamed the house the Georgiana Hotel and turned its operation over to his wife. Allen was then serving as postmaster of Georgiana (population 65). Allen rounded out his work schedule by cultivating truck and tropical fruit. *FLAS*, 27 September 1883, 8, 8 November 1883, 8, 6 August 1885, 1, 23 September 1885, 1; *South Publishing Company's Florida State Gazetteer and Business Directory*, 1:171.

9. Dr. William Wittfeld told a visiting journalist in 1888 that he was "a botanist and entomologist by profession." After settling in the wilds of east Florida, he continued his botanical studies by experimenting with a wide range of tropical plants. Dr. Wittfeld also participated in the larger scientific world. Naturalists connected with the Smithsonian Institution regularly used his boarding house on Merritt Island as a base for area study and collecting. He himself also contributed a variety of carefully preserved and packed specimens of reptiles, fishes, insects, mammals, and shells to the National Museum, an arm of the Smithsonian Institution. Sojourner, "Down the Indian River"; Smithsonian Institution, *Annual Report for 1881*, "Appendix C.— List of Contributors to the Museum in 1881," 158; Smithsonian Institution, *Annual Report for 1882*, "Report of the Secretary," 18; and Smithsonian Institution, *Annual Report for 1883*, "Report on the National Museum," 359.

10. Stebbins, "On Summer Seas."

11. The same winter James Henshall, who was on the first leg of a coastal cruise around the southern tip of the peninsula, also stopped at A. W. Estes's home and found him "laid up with the rheumatism." A "noted hunter," Estes had captured and transported two live manatees to the 1876 Centennial Exposition in Philadelphia. To his misfortune, they perished in a blaze after the first day on exhibition. Henshall, "Around the Coast of Florida"; "Indian River."

12. The Coast and Geodetic Survey was a familiar presence along Florida's Atlantic coast in the late nineteenth century. The survey obtained detailed and accurate knowledge of coastal topography and made and published geodetic and hydrographic charts of the coast and rivers to the end of navigation. Over time, the agency acquired other duties such as determining heights and geographic positions for control points for surveys and carrying out research in terrestrial magnetism, tides, currents, and gravity. Coastal development relied on accurate information, as did recreational yachtsmen. Weber, *The Coast and Geodetic Survey*, 1, 9; Manning, *U.S. Coast Survey vs. Naval Hydrographic Office*, 3–4, 13.

13. Two years later the *Steadfast*, which Charles W. Pierce described as "simply a large flatboat or scow with a cabin built on deck," was "moored close to the shell mound near Jupiter Inlet and [was] being used as a hotel with Ellsworth A. Hotchkiss as proprietor." Pierce, *Pioneer Life in Southeast Florida*, 209, 239; *FLAS*, 18 December 1884, 1.

14. Stebbins, "From Far Florida: Wintering on the Indian Lagoon."

15. Stebbins, "Among the Mangroves."

16. Charles Moore, the second pioneer known to have settled on Lake Worth,

sailed north from Miami and took possession of his homestead in November 1872. Curiously, this was the former property of the original settler, O. A. Lang, a German horticulturalist who had arrived on Indian River in 1860. Lang moved his family further south to Lake Worth, the most remote place he knew, to avoid conscription in the Confederate Army. He and his family returned to Indian River and abandoned their Lake Worth refuge when news of the war's end reached them. Ober, *The Knockabout Club in the Everglades,* 100–101; Corse, *Florida,* 230. Other details of Charles Moore's life can be found in Pierce, *Pioneer Life in Southeast Florida,* 49–50, 55, 61, 65, 111, 208, 224.

17. Stebbins stayed with Hannibal D. and Margretta M. Pierce, who left Chicago in 1871 immediately following the great fire. They first settled at Ankona Heights on Indian River, were burned out, took a position at the Jupiter Lighthouse, and migrated to Lake Worth the fall of 1873. They were the parents of Charles W. and Lillie E. Pierce and, at the time of Stebbins's visit, were living at their second home on Hypoluxo Island. Charles W. Pierce, who later wrote about his early life on Lake Worth, was nearly eighteen at the time of Stebbins's visit and was frequently away from home hunting or working for others. The two seem not to have met. Pierce, *Pioneer Life in Southeast Florida,* 20–22, 42–50.

18. Abbie M. Brooks published her impressions of Key West's inhabitants and how they managed wrecking just two years before Stebbins expressed curiosity about them. Silvia Sunshine, *Petals Plucked from Sunny Climes,* 318–19.

19. Captain Elisha Newton Dimick and his family were major figures in Charles W. Pierce's memoirs. The spring of 1876, Dimick scouted Lake Worth and after locating a suitable spot, returned to Michigan for his family. That fall he brought his parents, his married sister and her husband, and his brother along with his wife and three children back to homestead together. Discovering he could earn a larger and more reliable income from winter tourists, Dimick gave up farming for hotel keeping in 1880. This gave him leisure and means to travel during the slack season, which for Florida was the summer. Curiously, he turned up in Lenawee County in 1893, where he spent the summer with a Morenci friend, W. H. Follett. Later area historians credited Dimick with founding Palm Beach. Pierce, *Pioneer Life in Southeast Florida,* 73, 79, 107–08, 116–17, 129–30, 208–09, 226–27, 249; *ADT&E,* 15 September 1893, 4; Corse, *Florida,* 230.

20. Stebbins, "March in Florida."

21. Samuel C. Clarke also decried journalists manipulating the truth concerning their firsthand experiences in Florida. He referred to a piece in the *Atlantic* magazine: "[A] party of contributors are supposed to be boating in Florida, but their talk, as at home, is of novels, poetry, taste, and the musical glasses, with an alligator and a 'blue bittern' thrown in to give a local color. All evidently evolved from the inner consciousness of the writer, sitting within sight of the gilded dome which dominates the modern Athens" (S.C.C., "Canine Madness").

22. Three years later Stebbins had another adventure with one of the pelicans of Pelican Island. This experience was reported by another of his traveling companions, the then twelve-year-old L. Whitney Watkins: "As we left the island we noticed a fine

specimen of this species floating listlessly upon the water apparently sick, though still sitting erect. We approached easily capturing it, and found that it had captured . . . a salt-water cat-fish. . . . The fish, probably accidently in struggling, had thrust its so-called horns . . . through the skin on both sides of the pouch and there the poor bird was with the obnoxious fish permanently lodged in its throat. With some difficulty he was removed, but I fear the bird would not recover" (Watkins, "A Disastrous Season on Pelican Island," 149).

23. Stebbins echoed a current opinion about the affair that condemned it as another example of corrupt government during Reconstruction. One of its harshest critics called the attempt to found Florida's agricultural college at Eau Gallie "that bold, shameful swindle perpetrated by some shameless Solons at Tallahassee." When the scheme failed, the land reverted to its previous owner and the college site's principal proponent, former lieutenant governor William H. Gleason, in 1884. He subsequently renovated the college building for residential use. Over time, the structure was modified and used for different purposes. The college building burned in 1906, but one wall survived for several years afterward. S., "Bits of Florida Experience"; *Forest and Stream* (hereafter *F&S*), 9 October 1884, 1, 6 November 1884, 1, 7 October 1885, 1, 18 December 1884, 1, 10 March 1886, 3, and 9 July 1888, 1; Kjerulff, *Tales of Old Brevard*, 32–33. For more about William Gleason and the Florida agricultural college at Eau Gallie, see Cash, "The Lower East Coast," 60–62; Hanna and Hanna, *Florida's Golden Sands*, 164–65.

24. Stebbins, "Farewell to Jupiter."

25. *ADT&E*, 21 March 1882, 3. There was no mention of this near catastrophic event in the *Florida Star*. Why editor E. B. Wager omitted reporting it is unclear. Perhaps Wager felt reporting the event would discourage potential immigrants or investors by revealing Titusville to be in a high-risk area. Or perhaps he did not deem it as dangerous as Stebbins did.

26. *ADT&E*, 24 March 1882, 3.

CHAPTER 7

1. *Manchester Enterprise*, 18 January 1883, 3.

2. *Manchester Enterprise*, 1 February 1883, 3.

3. *FLAS*, 1 February 1883, 8.

4. *ADT&E*, 7 February 1883, 3.

5. Ten years earlier, Amos J. Cummings provided a detailed description of the famous landmark. Not a great deal more is known specifically about Turtle Mound now, for the site has not yet been scientifically excavated. Other notable mounds in its vicinity are better known. Based on evidence from them, archaeologists assume the construction of Turtle Mound began about 800 AD and its occupants finally abandoned it around 1400 AD. Turtle Mound was placed on the National Register of Historic Places in 1970, and in 1971 was thirty-five feet tall at its highest point. Ziska, "Florida's Indian Mounds"; Fryman, "Turtle Mound, 8VO109"; Winsberg, *Florida's History through Its Places*, 128.

6. New Smyrna's eighteenth-century beginning was a favorite topic with the writers who produced popular Florida literature. They realized the tale's appeal to Northern tourists. Its past was deemed nearly as romantic as St. Augustine's with which it merged. Sidney Lanier, who authored one such mass-oriented guide to Florida, twice outlined the tale of Turnbull's New Smyrna colony, saying substantially the same thing in both places. Lanier, *Florida*, 64, 194. For a modern treatment, see Griffin, *Mullet on the Beach*.

7. The editor of the *Florida Star* wrote up the fertilizer side of the business twice, first in late 1882 soon after opening and later in the following July when it had been in operation several months. He knew area truck farmers and grove owners would be keenly interested in a local source of fertilizer. New Smyrna already possessed a shark oil concern in early 1882, and perhaps this had joined the fertilizer company later in the year. Though the local press paid no heed to the shark oil operation, it was featured, complete with graphic illustrations of capturing the sharks, in a New York City newspaper. "The Halifax Fish and Fertilizing Co."; "Manufacturers of Fish Fertilizer"; "The Shark Fisheries at New Smyrna, Florida."

8. The flamboyant lifestyle of the duke and duchess did not commend them to their neighbors. Uncomplimentary stories about them circulated among the Indian River residents during their two-year tenure in Dummitt Grove. However, another Michigan tourist who traveled with them from Enterprise to Indian River "found the duke and dutchess [*sic*] kind, social people, and shall never regret having met them." B.P.S., "Another Letter from Florida." For further information, see Hanna and Hanna, *Florida's Golden Sands*, 239–42, 405–06; "The Dummitt Grove"; "The Duchess del Castilluccia Sues a Roslyn Yacht Builder for Damages."

9. Indian River residents turned abundantly available conch shells into noisemakers. They converted the shells into horns by cutting off their tip ends, and the sound these unusual instruments produced was "loud and clear." They replaced bells as farmstead signals, and boatmen on the rivers routinely blew conch horns to communicate with those on shore. Pilots of trading boats alerted their customers of their impending arrival in this way. In 1891 C. Vickerstaff Hine witnessed Titusville businessmen pursuing game after work and using conch shell horns for hunting horns. Hine, *On the Indian River*, 68–69; Williams, *A Brief History of Saint Lucie County*, 17.

10. Stebbins, "Notes from Florida."

11. *ADT&E*, 3 March 1883, 3.

12. The editor of the *Florida Star* reported: "We learn that 16 very large whales drifted ashore on the sea beach near Cape Canaveral recently, between the old *Ladona* wreck and the bight of the Cape. They are said by some to be the sperm whale. Some of them measured 15 paces in length" (8 February 1883, 8).

13. The whale vertebrae and teeth Stebbins so laboriously collected went into his private museum, but two teeth and nine hogsheads and one box of bones from the same group of whales were shipped to the National Museum, under the management of the Smithsonian Institution, by M. O. Burnham, keeper of the Cape Canaveral Lighthouse. Smithsonian Institution, *Annual Report for 1883*, "Report on the National Museum," 327.

14. Thomas New, a former Methodist minister, left Detroit for Indian River in 1881. Among his other activities, Reverend New also ran the New Haven post office out of his store. If he had not relinquished the position to Sylvanus Kitching in late 1884, a community might have grown around New Haven instead of Sebastian "situated nearly a mile below the old office." New had already sold his store's merchandise to August Parks the previous fall and planned "to devote the remainder of his days to agricultural pursuits and assist in developing the resources of the neighborhood." The last aim was a reference to New's single-handed attempt to cut an inlet to the ocean opposite his property. Thomas New died "at quite an advanced age" in the fall of 1885. *FLAS*, 11 September 1884, 1, 4 December 1884, 1, and 14 October 1885, 4. See also Lockwood, *Florida's Historic Indian River County*, 8, 44; and "Thomas New."

15. Nehemiah M. Sutton was following the fad of capturing Florida scenery on film, but he was better trained than most. In his twenties he had studied photography in Detroit and seems to have worked at the trade there for five years before returning to farming. His "little camera" was a newly developed portable type suitable for outdoor work. Sutton may have been imitating professional "artists," who produced photographs of Florida subjects for commercial use. It is unlikely he took his photographs for the purpose of selling them. Unfortunately, they do not survive. "Nehemiah M. Sutton," 478.

16. Stebbins, "Life on the Lagoons."

17. The lighthouse keepers certainly rejoiced when the federal government finally took action on a longstanding need frequently expressed. For years three families shared the one residence provided. The addition of a new kitchen to the one house in 1875 had not really addressed the problem. The government was still resisting expansion in 1879, excusing itself on the grounds of the lighthouse's isolation and poor access. Finally in 1883, it relented and substantially updated its Jupiter facility with the new two-story house and renovations to the original domicile and the lighthouse itself. DuBois, "Jupiter Lighthouse," 11.

18. The White brothers were Nathaniel P. White, a former mayor of Port Huron, Michigan, and James H. White, who had just finished his second term as a state representative. James was an active Republican and a successful businessman with interests in farming, insurance, banking, and real estate. The White party was enjoying a foray into the wilds from its winter base at N. P. White's property in Palatka, Florida, when Stebbins recognized them. James H. White sent his hometown paper a pedestrian tourist letter in which he recounted the group's experience of Indian River and made no mention of Stebbins. J. H. White, "Florida"; Howard, "To Florida"; "James H. White"; *Michigan State Gazetteer and Business Directory 1883*, 1267.

19. Stebbins, "Surf and Sea."

20. Kissimmee City was the capital of Hamilton Disston's south Florida empire and the destination of Northern visitors, who, like Stebbins, wished to view his drainage work and possibly purchase real estate in the vicinity. On the scene, a Jacksonville reporter observed: "South Florida despite the rapid approach of warm weather is swarming with land hunters, and Kissimmee has her share of them. Hardly a day passes but real estate changes hands most of it passing into the hands of strangers who

are seeking homes and places for new business enterprises. The two saw mills to this place are unable to supply the demand for lumber, one of them being about a month behind its orders" (M., "From Kissimmee City").

21. Lucius Stebbins, who had made his money as a subscription book publisher in Hartford, Connecticut, created his showplace orange grove on undeveloped pine land and "kept the grove like a garden." Stebbins's four-year-old 160-acre grove was the largest in the vicinity. He and F. R. Stebbins may have been distantly related. O'Neal, *Memoirs of a Pioneer,* 212–14; Gore, *From Florida Sand to "The City Beautiful,"* 229–30; and E.W.H., "Orange County Enterprise."

22. Adrianites and other Lenawee County residents were as susceptible to orange fever as the rest of the country. Even as Stebbins wrote his sobering assessment of Florida's fledgling citrus industry, one B.C. Adams was purchasing 410 acres with some bearing orange trees in Florida. He proudly informed the *Adrian Daily Times and Expositor* that he intended to plant a forty-acre grove on his partially improved property. That fall William Stones examined the citrus groves around Sanford and exhibited the fervor Stebbins wanted to contain: "The orange business here is sure to be a big thing. We are here in the midst of a solid block of 100 acres of orange trees, many bearing now, and all will be in a few years, and so it is all over the country. Oranges are all the talk. I cannot begin to grasp what it will mean to harvest and ship the orange crop in a few years" (Stones, "From Florida"; *ADT&E,* 2 June 1883, 3).

23. Stebbins, "Growing the Orange."

24. *ADT&E,* 23 March 1883, 3.

25. *ADT&E,* 31 May 1883, 3.

CHAPTER 8

1. Lucius D. Watkins was an affluent banker and farmer residing in Jackson County just a few miles from Manchester, Michigan. A member of numerous local and state organizations, he belonged to two groups that counted F. R. Stebbins a participant: the Grand Lake Fishing and Sporting Club and the Michigan Pioneer and Historical Society. Watkins qualified for the latter by virtue of arriving in the state in 1834. The men found they shared an enthusiasm for natural history. Watkins enjoyed botany, geology, zoology, and archaeology, all subjects that intrigued Stebbins. In the 1890s, he published several articles in the *Michigan Pioneer and Historical Collections* reflecting these interests. *History of Jackson County, Michigan,* 1006; *History of Washtenaw County, Michigan,* 1:1318, 1321–22; Waldron, *One Hundred Years a Country Town,* 33; *Manchester Enterprise,* 17 January 1884, 3; *Michigan Pioneer and Historical Collections* 3 (1881): 7–8; 7 (1884): ix; 5 (1886): 5, 90; 11 (1887): 12; and 17 (1890): 1.

2. F. R. Stebbins letter (probably to his brother Cortland B. Stebbins in Lansing, Michigan), Cortland B. Stebbins Collection, Clarke Historical Library, Central Michigan University, Mt. Pleasant.

3. *Manchester Enterprise,* 17 January 1884, 3.

4. Stebbins, "Frosty Weather in Florida."

5. Stebbins, "Interesting Reminiscence."

6. L.D.W., "From the Land of Flowers."

7. The party returned to Rockledge in time for the wedding. The *Florida Star* reported: "We learn that Tony Canova, of Rockledge, was married a few days ago to Miss Gingras, of that place. The STAR extends to them its congratulations" (6 March 1884, 8).

8. Antonio Canova's *Arrow* won the first class race at the annual Fourth of July Yacht Race in 1883. A younger contemporary of Canova, Charles W. Pierce, recalled in his memoirs that for a while the *Arrow* routinely beat all sailboats on the river and was ultimately banned from the races. *FLAS*, 5 July 1883, 1; Pierce, *Pioneer Life in Southeast Florida*, 201.

9. A visiting journalist described C. J. Hector's property at the end of 1885. Besides running a store and serving as postmaster, Hector had planted a substantial portion of his land to pineapples and a lesser amount to oranges and other tropical fruits. "Melbourne and Vicinity."

10. There were a number of possible sources for these antiquities. Le Baron found that "[t]here are somewhat indistinct remains at the mouth of Crane Creek, at Melbourne, on the north side, on the land of Thomas Fish, deceased, and on the south side on land of Peter Wright. On the opposite side of the river in Sec. 6, T. 28 S., R. 37 E, is an Indian mound" ("Prehistoric Remains in Florida," 784).

11. Judge James Paine and his sons Tom L. and James Jr. were known nationally as the hotel keepers at the staging point for explorers of the Everglades and Lake Okeechobee. They operated the southernmost hotel on the east coast through the 1870s and into the 1880s. Amos J. Cummings stopped at the Paines' at least twice, in 1873 and on his own venture into the Everglades in 1874. He related his impression of the Judge and discussed the family's cattle business. Ziska, "The Farming in Florida"; Ziska, "Adventures in Florida." For more on contemporary cattle management, see Otto, "Open-Range Cattle Herding in Southern Florida," 322.

12. Other travelers left descriptions of Thomas E. Richards's home and tropical fruit plantation at Eden. Among them were Dr. Herman Herold, who took several photographs and stereoviews while there, and two newspaper correspondents. Herold, "Log Book," 31, 44–45; "Indian River"; Irishman, "A Trip to Indian River."

13. Stebbins would have been distressed at the site's fate. This and other related ancient earthworks were well-known in the nineteenth century. Francis Le Baron first reported their presence in 1884, but, unfortunately, the information he passed along was secondhand and sketchy. He stated, "Opposite Jupiter Inlet on the west bank at Stone's Point are several large oyster-shell heaps, as I am informed by numerous observers, one of which is said to be *very* large." In 1891 Cyrus Thomas included Le Baron's remarks without additional commentary in his *Catalogue of Prehistoric Works East of the Rocky Mountains*. Finally in 1896, Clarence B. Moore, the first and apparently last archaeologist to personally investigate the site, reached the area. For whatever reason, the meticulous excavator did not publish his findings. Subsequently, the site fell victim to extensive earthmoving projects on the lighthouse premises, and the walls and mound Stebbins could see so clearly from the lighthouse balcony were destroyed without being investigated scientifically. Le Baron, "Prehistoric Remains in

Florida," 784; Thomas, *Catalogue of Prehistoric Works East of the Rocky Mountains,* 31; DuBois, "Jupiter Inlet," 21.

14. This was the beginning of the "barefoot route" and its barefoot mailman, who later became a romantic figure in local history. In 1884 the mail was carried only to Lake Worth overland, but the next year, the route was extended from Palm Beach to Miami. The carrier followed the ocean beach in the absence of roads. He chose to walk barefoot along the water's edge where the sand was firmest, for by doing so, he could cover the greatest distance in the shortest time. He kept boats on site for crossing inlets and slept in the Houses of Refuge. Herold, "Log Book," 33; Pierce, *Pioneer Life in Southeast Florida,* 194–95.

15. Stebbins, "Where Summer Lives."

16. This could possibly be the mound Le Baron identified as Mt. Pisgah, which he located three miles from the mouth of the St. Lucie River on the north bank of a large bay. He visited it in 1880 and said of it: "[It is an] immense mound called Mt. Pisgah, truly gigantic, and of the same character as Mount Elithabeth [*sic*] [large, high, and symmetrical mound of black earth and shells, which would probably be classed as a kjökkenmödding]. Near its base is the remains of the abode of some of the pirates that are known to have infested this locality in the early days of the present century. I saw no other mounds on the whole trip" ("Prehistoric Remains in Florida," 786).

17. Naturalist and explorer of Lake Okeechobee Frederick Ober described in detail the dress of Seminoles he visited in south Florida in the early 1870s. Ober, "Ten Days with the Seminoles," 143. Twelve years later his account was reprinted. Ober, *The Knockabout Club in the Everglades,* 107–08.

18. Stebbins, "Weather Bound."

19. Mail service between Jacksonville and the hinterland as well as between other Florida towns was often erratic and undependable in the 1880s. Protests abounded in local newspapers. In 1882, editor C. E. Dyke noted, "Complaints of irregularities of mails come from all sections of the State. There is evidently a screw (or several of them) loose somewhere." *Weekly Floridian,* 21 February 1882, 4.

20. Stebbins would have been astounded to hear of the "twelfth night party" at the "splendid home of Col. A. P. Cleveland on Merritt's Island" two years previous at which "Rockledge and City Point sent out their beaux and belles, and the brave and fair of the river were present. Miss Julia LaRoche was the fortunate recipient of the 'golden apple.' . . . The delightful hours of the evening sped rapidly to the sound of music and laughter" (*FLAS,* 18 January 1882, 3).

The LaRoches were not as isolated as Stebbins believed. A number of the family had immigrated to Indian River and made homes at various locations. Stebbins had stumbled onto the homestead of the patriarch, James J. LaRoche, on John's Island opposite present-day Vero Beach. The senior LaRoche had brought his adult children, John R., Benjamin, Daniel, Frank, R. J., and Julia, to Florida with him around 1880. *FLAS,* 15 January 1885, 4, 23 April 1885, 1, 23 September 1885, 1, 10 February 1886, 3, 3 November 1886, 2, and 24 March 1887, 2; "Beautiful Merritt's Isle"; Lockwood, *Florida's Historic Indian River County,* 31.

21. Mrs. J. C. Hall's eight-acre grove often appeared on lists of noteworthy citrus plantations on north Banana River. She advertised both fruit and nursery stock from her grove for sale in the fall of 1884. *FLAS,* 6 November 1884, 4; *South Publishing Company's Florida State Gazetteer and Business Directory,* 1:98.

22. Stebbins repeatedly encountered the Welches and William H. Reed. Concerning Commodore and Mrs. C. A. Welch's real estate transaction, the *Florida Star* noted: "Commodore Welch, we learn, has recently purchased a place on Banana river, just south of N. N. Penny; we suppose he will make quite extensive improvements thereon" (17 January 1884, 8, and 25 December 1884, 4).

23. Although some fires were caused by lightning strikes, many were intentionally started, keeping alive an Indian practice. Firing the woods to clear out underbrush was done annually in the winter or early spring. A similar scene was described in 1886 by another Michigan tourist: "New Year's night was spent at Titusville on Indian river, and will never be forgotten. The air was balmy as in summertime. Across the broad bosom of the river the canebrake on Merritt's island was a sea of fire and the lurid flames swept up against the sky lighting up the whole surrounding country" (Smith, "Editorial Ramblings in the South"). For a discussion of the role of naturally started forest fires in the area's ecology, see Abrahamson and Hartnett, "Pine Flatwoods and Dry Prairies," 129–33.

24. An east Florida resident corroborated Stebbins's fish story: "A torchlight is hung over the bow of the boat, one man in the stern to pole the boat, another stands in the centre of the boat, spear in hand, to capture the fish that are attracted to the light. In this way they capture half a bushel in a little while, of a variety, but rarely think it worth while to count or weigh them" (Hawks, *The East Coast of Florida,* 127–28).

25. A few years earlier Abbie M. Brooks observed this phenomenon on the Gulf of Mexico south of Tampa in water sixty fathoms deep. She too witnessed the bucket experiment. The source of bioluminescence, the current term, was discovered long before Stebbins or Brooks wrote about it. In 1868 British author George Henry Lewes summarized current information on the subject for an American scientific journal. He attributed the marine luminescence to "Noctilucae . . . little crystal balls of about the size of a pin's head" and noted that the light is "intimately connected with the contraction, spontaneous or provoked, of their substance." Modern scientists basically agree with their predecessors about the cause of marine phosphorescence. Silvia Sunshine, *Petals Plucked from Sunny Climes,* 313–14; Lewes, "The Phosphorescence of the Sea," 316; Harvey, *Living Light,* 7; Hastings, "Bioluminescence in Bacteria and Dinoflagellates," 379.

26. A number of scientists focused their attention on the phenomenon of "sonorous sand" around this time. They observed that sand from discrete spots would emit a distinctive sound when caused to slide. Both physicists and geologists were at a loss for a satisfactory explanation. Professor H. C. Bolton of Trinity College, Hartford, Connecticut, decided to solve the puzzle and requested assistance from the Smithsonian Institution in obtaining samples. Thanks to the Smithsonian's letter-writing campaign to such places as the Sandwich Islands, the Oregon coast, and Germany,

Bolton was able to report that he had amassed sufficient samples to begin his study in 1884. Smithsonian Institution, *Annual Report for 1884,* "Report of the Secretary."

27. Stebbins, "Our Florida Letter: Bad Mail Service."

28. *ADT&E,* 8 March 1884, 3.

29. *Manchester Enterprise,* 13 March 1884, 3.

CHAPTER 9

1. Stebbins's prediction was fulfilled a year later when the second great freeze of the century struck Florida. The first occurred in 1835. During the three days of 10, 11, and 12 January 1886, temperatures dropped and remained below freezing. The bitter cold was accentuated by a strong northwest wind throughout the three days. In most sections of the state, the orange crop was ruined and citrus trees sustained significant injury. Indian River escaped the worst of the freeze and land values rose there along with demand for a frost-proof location. However, northern Florida retained its reputation as a citrus region for another nine years before the more destructive freezes of 1895 ended commercial production there. Thereafter the citrus belt shifted southward. Harcourt, *Florida Fruits and How to Raise Them,* 294–98; Lewis, "Agricultural Evolution on Secondary Frontiers," 222–23.

2. Stebbins, "An Interesting Letter from One of Our Michigan Subscribers."

3. Peter Coller owned a large plum and apple orchard near Adrian. A member of the Michigan State Horticultural Society, he was an enthusiastic booster and opened his operation to visitors during local society meetings. Coller may have known F. R. Stebbins through the society to which both belonged in 1885. Though Stebbins left the organization after 1886, the other member of the party, L. D. Watkins, was a life member and possibly recruited Coller for the trip. At the 1885 spring meeting of the Lenawee County Horticultural Society held after the travelers returned to Michigan, Watkins "asked Mr. Coller how pears grew in Florida. He said he saw some beautiful pear trees there on that white sand." This was the only recorded Florida evaluation by the one professional horticulturalist who accompanied Stebbins to Indian River. "Adrian Fruit-Growers"; *Fifteenth Annual Report,* 383–88, 484, 489; *Sixteenth Annual Report,* 557; *Eleventh Annual Report,* 371; "Lenawee County Horticulturalists."

4. *ADT&E,* 27 January 1885, 3.

5. Lucius Whitney Watkins, L. D. Watkins's twelve-year-old son, shared his father's interest in natural history and later in life specialized in ornithology. While a student at Michigan Agricultural College, he helped Professor Albert J. Cook compile his guide to Michigan birds and later aided Walter B. Barrows with a similar work. In the mid-1890s, Watkins published four articles based on his field observation of birds. He was a charter member of the Michigan Academy of Science and joined the Michigan Ornithological Club and the Michigan Chapter of the Audubon Society. Years after his trip with Stebbins to Indian River, Watkins read an article on the Florida brown pelican that awakened memories of his own experiences in east Florida and inspired him to record them. He took several government positions related to natural resources and agriculture and then entered state politics in 1909. L. W. Watkins

gained fame as the gubernatorial candidate for the Progressive Party in 1912, the year Theodore Roosevelt ran for president on the Bull Moose ticket. Though Roosevelt carried Michigan, Watkins finished third in his race. "Lucius Whitney Watkins"; Watkins, "A Disastrous Season on Pelican Island"; Campbell, "The Bull Moose Movement in Michigan"; Dunbar, *Michigan,* 524–25; Green, "Reflections in the River Raisin," 52. For a list of Watkins's publications, see Barrows, *Michigan Bird Life,* 773.

6. *FLAS,* 5 February 1885, 4.

7. Despite being forced to open before completion and never being a financial success, the World's Industrial and Cotton Centennial Exposition focused the nation's favorable attention on the South more than any previous southern exhibition. The New York *Sun* summarized its impact on the North's attitude toward the South three and a half months following the exposition's opening: "People from the North and West . . . come away with an entirely new impression of the Southern people of to-day, of their shrewdness, their broad executive capacity, and their extraordinary force and energy. Northern visitors see things in a new light, and they have their eyes opened" ("New Orleans and Its Great Show").

8. The orange harvest of 1885 was disastrous. All growers suffered, but it was especially hard on small grove owners. Through most of the harvest season, they received the lowest prices in many years for their fruit. Worse, 1885 ushered in a period of falling prices. Florida's citrus bubble was burst. The year marked a pivotal point in the history of Florida's young citrus industry. Thereafter, growers were forced to address the conditions that precipitated the crisis: increasing orange production, an unreliable marketing system, inadequate transportation, and a reluctance to adopt quality control measures. Weeks, "Florida Gold," 73–104.

9. Hunters did set uncontrolled fires. Twice Dr. Herman Herold recorded starting such blazes. Earlier, he and his guide had found their way back to the boat barred by one such woods fire. Despite their difficulty escaping it, the experience did not deter them from setting similar blazes. Cattlemen also burned underbrush and dead vegetation in the south Florida flatwoods in the winter. A range management technique, it was intended to provide fertilizer for a new growth of grass and reduce cattle ticks. The cattlemen protected their homes and cattle pens against fire damage but otherwise allowed their fires to burn at will. This presented problems when permanent settlers built homes and began to cultivate crops on land bordering or encroaching on traditional cattle range. Herold, "Log Book," 28–29, 37, 40; Mealor and Prunty, "Open-Range Ranching in South Florida," 363–66; Otto, "Florida's Cattle-Ranching Frontier," 55.

10. Stebbins, "Southern Florida."

11. Stebbins, "Sailing South."

12. Stebbins was referring to Ignatius Donnelly's book *Atlantis.*

13. For prevailing explanations of the subject, see Otvos, "Barrier Island Formation," 195; and Johnson and Barbour, "Dunes and Maritime Forests," 429–40.

14. Stebbins had visited Charles Moore and E. N. Dimick, the pioneer from Michigan, in 1882. Albert Geer, Dimick's brother-in-law, was a member of the Michigan colony E. N. Dimick brought to Lake Worth in 1876. Stebbins would have been

interested to know that Geer sold his Florida property and returned to Michigan in 1886. In 1893, Henry Flagler bought the Geer homestead and built the Royal Poinciana Hotel on the site. Pierce, *Pioneer Life in Southeast Florida,* 77–79.

15. Stebbins, "A Traveller's Diary."

16. The weather had been sufficiently rainy that winter to raise the water level in Indian River. Nine years later L. Whitney Watkins recalled the damage high water caused on Pelican Island during the nesting season: "The water had risen several feet higher than had been known for many years, a short time before, and the nests on the ground had been floated away and the great white eggs, wagon-loads of them, were strewn promiscuously over the entire south half of the island, in some places being left in wind-rows, as it were by the receding water. All were spoiled. . . . The only occupied nests, which at this time contained young, were in the stunted Mangroves at the North end of the island" ("A Disastrous Season on Pelican Island," 149).

17. Stebbins, "Northerners in the South."

18. *FLAS,* 5 March 1885, 4.

CHAPTER 10

1. Jacob S. Johnson was an Adrian dentist. William K. Choate was a commission fruit dealer and manager of a sawmill in Adrian. This may have been Dr. Johnson's first Florida trip, but W. K. Choate had been there before. The previous winter he and his daughter Mary had visited his brother C. A. Choate, who permanently resided in Tallahassee, where he sold real estate. *Adrian City Directory 1885–1886,* 70; *Adrian City Directory 1882–83,* 122; *Weekly Floridian,* 19 February 1885, 3.

2. *ADT&E,* 3 February 1886, 3.

3. *ADT&E,* 8 February 1886, 3.

4. The World's Industrial and Cotton Centennial Exposition was a financial failure despite infusions of money from the federal government. It received its best reviews during the 1884–85 season even though many exhibits were assembled after opening. When the exposition reopened under new management in the fall of 1885, its attendance fell below that of the previous season. Jackson, *New Orleans in the Gilded Age,* 93, 204–07.

5. Floridians, hoping to counter exaggerated stories of damage circulating in the northern papers, invited a panel from the National Editorial Association to visit the state and proclaim the actual condition of the groves. A group of editors undertook the task and issued a reassuring joint statement ("The Orange Crop") in early March. This was reprinted in newspapers across the country.

6. As Stebbins noticed, the ocean had been eroding the beach near the lighthouse for several years. One night in April 1886 shortly after Stebbins's visit, the tide came within seventy feet of the base of the tower. The government later appropriated $300,000 to move the lighthouse inland about one and a half miles, and the project was completed in 1893. The removal took eighteen months. Ransom, *A Memoir of Captain Mills Olcott Burnham,* 19, 24–25.

7. Stebbins, "In the Sunny South."

8. Newspapers around the country carried accounts of Florida's fish kill the winter of 1886. A recent immigrant to the New Smyrna area wrote a New Haven, Connecticut, newspaper about local conditions during the freeze, and his story was reprinted in a major New York City paper: "This country has caught it badly. . . . The thermometer was down to 18°, ice made three inches thick, thousands of fish were chilled and came to the surface just alive and floated about and were finally stranded on the shore. . . . The catfish, which no one eats here, were affected the most. Wagon loads of them have been carried away for fertilizing purposes" ("The Florida Freezes").

9. Stebbins, "Florida's Freeze Up."

10. The larger hotel Sutton saw under construction was Henry M. Flagler's Ponce de Leon, which was begun in 1885 but overran schedule and was completed in early 1888. Its success spurred the Standard Oil multimillionaire to look southward for other resort hotel sites. Between extending his rail system, which came to be known as the Florida East Coast Railroad, and erecting palatial hotels ever further south, Flagler opened up the remote Indian River and Lake Worth region to tourists and settlers. The Ponce de Leon, Flagler's first large-scale Florida project, thus symbolized the end of the east coast's isolation, which had made the area appealing to sportsmen and outdoor enthusiasts such as Sutton and Stebbins. Akin, *Flagler,* 118, 120–25, 133.

11. Sutton, "The Sunny South."

12. *ADT&E,* 9 April 1886, 3.

13. *Tecumseh News,* 15 April 1886, 1.

CHAPTER 11

1. Stebbins, "Correspondence."

2. Fred Bury, the son of F. R. Stebbins's friend Richard A. Bury, was considerably younger than the others and just beginning his working life. He was a close friend of Stebbins's two youngest sons, Fred B. and Ed. In 1885 he graduated from Adrian High School and the next year held "a responsible position with a large lumber company at Spring Lake [Michigan]." In 1886 he became treasurer of the newly incorporated Spring Lake Clinker Boat and Manufacturing Company, and the next spring he managed its showroom in Adrian. Both firms were owned by his brother Frank. However, the spring of 1888 after returning from Florida, Bury moved to work for a Chicago lumber business. *ADT&E,* 21 June 1886, 3, 26 March 1887, 3, 7 April 1887, 3; *Weekly Press,* 20 April 1888, 3; "Richard A. Bury"; *Weekly Press,* 16 January 1885, 3; *ADT&E,* 25 August 1885, 3 and 26 September 1885, 3.

3. *ADT&E,* 31 January 1888, 3. Alanson Worden, a retired boot and shoe merchant, was an old friend and neighbor of F. R. Stebbins. They had shared a number of outdoor adventures previously, and both were charter members of the Grand Lake Fishing and Sporting Club in Presque Isle County, Michigan. David Metcalf, a member of another Adrian mercantile family, had lately returned to the city. He had worked in various capacities for the Milwaukee and St. Paul railroad until 1882. In 1883 he opened a dry goods store in Adrian and soon was accepted into the ranks of Adrian's prominent citizens. The businessman participated in the creation of the

Commercial Savings Bank of Adrian and became its director. He became a trustee of Adrian College and of the Bay View Camp Ground Association. To advertise his wealth and community standing, Metcalf built one of the city's showplace residences for his family. *Adrian City Directory, 1882–83,* 122; *Combination Atlas Map of Lenawee County, Michigan,* 132; "David Metcalf"; Feeman, Cargo, and Hay, *The Story of a Noble Devotion,* 145.

4. *ADT&E,* 4 February 1888, 3. Another Adrian editor surmised Worden's fainting spell "betokens an affection of the stomach or heart." *Weekly Press,* 10 February 1888, 3.

5. *ADT&E,* 6 February 1888, 3.

6. *FLAS,* 16 February 1888, 8.

7. While touring the Jacksonville Sub-Tropical Exposition, the party probably gazed upon the paleontological exhibit of their townsman Dr. John Kost. That January the *Adrian Daily Times and Expositor* printed Kost's description of his Florida fossils, and Stebbins and his friends may have wished to examine them. Kost was then professor of moral history and geology at the Florida Agricultural College in Lake City. The fall of 1887, he recovered five mastodon skeletons from the Ichetucknee River and transported the bones to the college museum. One of the five skeletons was virtually complete. This one he selected to reassemble and display at the exposition. *Weekly Floridian,* 9 February 1888, 2; Kost, "Geological Survey of Florida."

8. Stebbins, "Roving on Indian River." The proof of the group's isolation was that they heard nothing about President Grover Cleveland's flying trip to Rockledge on 24 February. Ironically, miles away in Michigan, both the *Detroit Free Press* and the *Adrian Daily Times and Expositor* covered the junket. The Titusville paper had been alerted of Cleveland's coming on the twenty-second and published the news the next day. Word spread quickly among area residents, and they turned out in force to greet the president and his wife at Titusville and Rockledge. So jubilant were the Indian River citizenry to have the Democratic president and his wife among them that when they disembarked at Titusville, souvenir seekers swarmed the steamboat. "The President's Outing"; "The President Coming to Indian River"; and "Our Guests."

9. In 1885 John Minor owned property near Melbourne, which he was reported clearing then. He was listed as an orange grower in the 1886 *Florida State Gazetteer.* He truck gardened extensively as well, proudly exhibiting some of his cabbages at the 1888 Jacksonville Sub-Tropical Exposition. Minor apparently worked for his neighbors also, for an area correspondent reported that he was planting a tomato crop for J. B. Morse in the fall of 1884. His horticultural enterprises brought him sufficient return to purchase the Melbourne area's landmark orange grove, Turkey Creek Grove. *FLAS,* 25 September 1884, 1, 7 July 1887, 8, 1 March 1888, 4, and 8 March 1888, 1; *The South Publishing Company's Florida State Gazetteer and Business Directory,* 1:296.

10. For fifteen more years, pelicans remained at the mercy of tourists and commercial fishermen, who believed the birds were competitors. Then President Theodore Roosevelt rescued all the island's birds in typically dramatic fashion. He extended federal protection to Pelican Island by executive order on 14 March 1903. Roosevelt

found authorization to make this controversial move in the Forest Reservation Crea-
tive Act of 1891. Once he determined the island had undergrowth, thus meeting one
of the act's conditions, Roosevelt made Pelican Island the first National Wildlife Refuge and ensured it a place in the annals of the early conservation movement. Reed
and Drabelle, *The United States Fish and Wildlife Service,* 6–8; Trefethen, *An American
Crusade for Wildlife,* 122–24.

11. Dr. H. C. Sill, whom Stebbins thought a recluse, was listed in the *Florida State
Gazetteer* as a valued member of Sebastian. The only physician for the small community (population 91), Sill also owned a one-acre orange grove. The doctor, like many
of his neighbors, truck gardened for income but apparently was not adept. A *Florida
Star* correspondent remarked, "[S]omehow the vegetables don't understand the Doctor's methods, or the Doctor don't understand the vegetables." *South Publishing Company's Florida State Gazetteer and Business Directory,* 1:405; Spratt, "Narrows."

12. Stebbins, "Balmy Ocean Breezes."

13. *Weekly Press,* 2 March 1888, 3.

14. The next winter, a correspondent and his friends called on Portuguese Joe, as
he was locally known, and related their encounter with Old Cuba's worthy successor.
E.S.W., "A Winter in Florida."

15. J. W. Zellers and his partner were after animals to exhibit at the ongoing Jacksonville Sub-Tropical Exposition. They displayed one of the several they captured on
Wager's Wharf at Titusville. The manatee expired the first afternoon, and a Dr. F. H.
Houghton bought the carcass for the Ohio State Agricultural College. Zellers resumed
searching for a manatee to ship to Jacksonville. He captured two by the end of March;
one he personally transported to the Sub-Tropical Exposition and the second he
planned to exhibit along Indian River. By summer Zellers was back at St. Lucie River
hunting for more to take north. He caught six or seven, but needing only three, he
released the surplus. He confined these animals in tanks just large enough to contain
them for five weeks and then shipped them to New York City. His show did "fairly
well" there, but Zellers had to have food for them shipped up from Indian River. By
late October, two of the manatees were sold and the third was on exhibit at a Baltimore museum. In mid-November, he was showing the remaining manatee in Columbus, Ohio. Zellers returned to Titusville by early December, with or without the
manatee, and rushed to St. Lucie River to capture more of the animals. *FLAS,*
15 March 1888, 8; *FLAS,* 22 March 1888, 8; *FLAS,* 29 March 1888, 8; "Brevard County
Day at the Sub-Tropical," *FLAS,* 22 March 1888, 4; *FLAS,* 28 June 1888, 8; *FLAS,*
2 August 1888, 8; *FLAS,* 6 September 1888, 4; *FLAS,* 25 October 1888, 8; *FLAS,* 15 November 1888, 8; *FLAS,* 6 December 1888, 8; and "Manatees Exhibited in New York."

16. Several men named Bessie were mentioned in contemporary sources. Willis
Bessie resided on the St. Lucie River by the fall of 1884. In 1886 the *Florida State
Gazetteer* listed M. Bessy as a member of the small community of Waveland (popu-
lation 60). He was an orange grower and the owner of a five-acre pineapple plantation.
The summer of 1887, Herbert Bessie's journey to the Dakotas to bring home a wife
was mentioned in the local paper. *FLAS,* 25 September 1884, 1, and 7 July 1887, 8;
South Publishing Company's Florida State Gazetteer and Business Directory, 1:450.

17. The same year a winter visitor to Melbourne reported his observations of the interactions between Seminoles and whites: "It is not an unusual thing for a man at work on his homestead in this vicinity to feel the nearness of a human presence, and look up to find a Seminole Indian standing before him. When saluted the Indian says: 'How, how.' If in a mood for talking he will answer questions for awhile in broken English, but will generally leave you in the midst of your sentences. These Indians often bring in venison" (Stout, "Indians in Florida").

18. In 1885 Charles R. Carlin, anticipating a permanent move to Jupiter from Titusville, purchased ten acres and began constructing a residence. Almost as soon as the family occupied it, they turned the house into a hotel, though at first it was run on a small scale. Mary Carlin and her daughters, finding the site ideal, successfully operated the Carlin House for fifty-three years. Charles R. Carlin retained his post at the life-saving station until it closed in 1896. *FLAS,* 13 October 1887, 7; White, *History of the Carlin House,* 6, 32, 63–64.

19. The Jupiter Signal Service Station was in operation only about a month and a half when Stebbins and his party arrived in the area. The contractor, a Mr. Arnold, started setting poles for the telegraph line from Titusville in July 1887 and finished on 28 December. The wire was strung and the station house erected by mid-January. *FLAS,* 29 December 1887, 8; "Jupiter"; and *FLAS,* 2 February 1888, 8.

20. Part of Stebbins's business was framing and selling pictures, and these were frequently displayed in the store window. He did a large trade in them during the Christmas shopping season. In 1868 he advertised the recent arrival of a chromolithograph of Albert Bierstadt's *Sunset.* The enormously popular and wealthy member of the Hudson River School was famous for his flamboyant landscapes. *Adrian Times and Expositor,* 24 December 1868, 4; Myers, *Encyclopedia of Painting,* 39.

21. M. Quad's "Advice to Boy Terrors" appeared on page eleven of the *Detroit Free Press* on 19 February 1888. M. Quad was Charles Bertrand Lewis, a popular humorist whose pieces were reprinted in newspapers around the country. In this particular article, Lewis explored the "proper" response of a young reader to a surfeit of dime-store novels about the wild west. He aimed his parody of the genre as much at himself as others, for he too had written several dime westerns. Whicher, "Lewis, Charles Bertrand."

22. Sportsmen were spared competition with commercial fishing on the Indian River until relatively late in the nineteenth century. Commercial fishing was not feasible until 1886 when the first railroad reached Titusville. As soon as the rail line was in place, fisheries blossomed along the Indian River. The toll on the lagoon's seemingly endless supply of fish was heavy, and the rate at which they were depleted astonished many. In the mid-1890s, Congress ordered the U.S. Commission of Fish and Fisheries to investigate the extermination of Indian River's migratory fish. No immediate action ensued from this study. The abundance Stebbins and others enjoyed in the 1880s was only a memory at the century's end. A 1901 fishing guide promised only moderate prospects and advised anglers to come south before November when the commercial fishermen began their operations. Brice, "Report on the Fisheries of Indian River, Florida," 224; Evermann and Bean, "Indian River and Its Fishes"; and Wilcox, "Com-

mercial Fisheries of Indian River, Florida," 249; Gregg and Gardner, *Where, When, and How to Catch Fish on the East Coast of Florida,* 190, 194, 198, 202–03.

23. Stebbins, "Fishing and Feasting."

24. *ADT&E,* 19 March 1888, 2.

25. *Weekly Press,* 23 March 1888, 3.

26. Ibid.

27. *ADT&E,* 28 March 1888, 3.

EPILOGUE

1. The probate court appointed F. R. Stebbins and Alfred H. Wood to handle claims against the estate and to appraise its inventory. Worden, Will.

2. For accounts of the 1888 yellow fever epidemic, see Humphreys, *Yellow Fever and the South,* 119–26; Warner, "The Jacksonville Yellow Fever Epidemic of 1888," 25–39; and Fairlie, "The Yellow Fever Epidemic of 1888 in Jacksonville." The editor of *Forest and Stream* printed the entire official plea for help on the front page ("An 'Al Fresco' Fund"). The *Adrian Daily Times and Expositor,* one among many Northern papers following the disease's progress, also announced Jacksonville's entreaty. "Florida Depopulated."

3. "Florida Depopulated"; "Death's Harvest"; "Yellow Jack's Victims"; and "The Fearful Fever."

4. "The Yellow Fever."

5. *FLAS,* 15 November 1888, 8; "Bronze John's Farewell"; F.S.J.C., "Charlotte Harbor," 494.

6. Tom S. Applegate was not only editor and proprietor of the *Adrian Daily Times and Expositor* but also head of the Lenawee County Republican machine. In 1883 he finagled F. R. Stebbins into accepting the Republican nomination for mayor of Adrian in a race against a favored Democratic contender. The reluctant candidate lost but by a surprisingly narrow margin. Stebbins's sterling civic credentials worried the Democrats. Long after his party's victory, the editor of the *Weekly Press* continued to mutter about the illegality of counting the votes of all the Adrian College students, who negotiated a mile of barely passable sidewalks to vote for Stebbins. "A Strong Ticket"; "Republican Nominations"; "Our 'Invalid' Candidate for Mayor"; "Non-Partisan"; *Weekly Press,* 6 April 1883, 3, and 20 April 1883, 3.

7. *ADT&E,* 28 February 1889, 3, 9 March 1889, 3, 25 July 1888, 3, and 5 August 1889, 3.

8. Fred B. Stebbins to Susan Stebbins, 29 April 1888, 25 November 1888, 14 July 1889, 5 August 1890, and 11 November 1890, Stebbins Family Papers, Michigan State University Archives and Historical Collections, East Lansing; *ADT&E,* 29 July 1889, 3, and 13 November 1889, 3; Geddes, "Memoir of Francis R. Stebbins," 216.

9. *ADT&E,* 12 May 1882, 3, 12 May 1883, 3, and 6 June 1883, 3; Fred B. Stebbins to Susan Stebbins, 11 November 1890; Fred B. Stebbins to C. B. Stebbins, 21 September 1892, Stebbins Family Papers, Michigan State University Archives and Historical Collections, East Lansing; Geddes, "Memoir of Francis R. Stebbins," 217; Bonner,

Memoirs of Lenawee County Michigan, 1:554; "A Pioneer Gone"; "Laid to Rest"; and *ADT&E,* 10 May 1892, 3.

10. Stebbins, Will; and Stebbins, Inventory.

11. Fred's interests also extended to photography, philately, and autograph collecting. So broad were his pursuits that he refused to specialize. When asked to state his preferred studies, he entered "curioso, general science." Both Fred and Edwin belonged to the Adrian Scientific Society and served as treasurer and librarian, respectively, in 1890. In 1887 Edwin was the secretary of the city's Agassiz Association. Fred B. Stebbins to Arthur Stebbins, 28 October 1887; Fred B. Stebbins to Susan Stebbins, 29 April 1888 and 23 February 1890, Stebbins Family Papers, Michigan State University Archives and Historical Collections, East Lansing; *Lenawee Record,* 20 January 1887, 6.

Bibliography

ARTICLES BY FRANCIS R. STEBBINS

Stebbins, Francis R. "Among the Mangroves." *Adrian Daily Times and Expositor,* 11 March 1882, 2.

———. "At Jupiter Inlet." *Adrian Daily Times and Expositor,* 15 March 1879, 1.

———. "At Sea." *Adrian Times and Expositor,* 29 August 1867, 4.

———. "Balmy Ocean Breezes." *Adrian Daily Times and Expositor,* 5 March 1888, 2.

———. "Boating in Florida." *Adrian Daily Times and Expositor,* 27 March 1878, 1.

———. "Boating in Florida: Oranges, Lemons, Potatoes, Etc." *Adrian Daily Times and Expositor,* 17 March 1879, 1.

———. "Correspondence." *Florida Star,* 1 February 1888, 1.

———. "Down in Florida." *Adrian Daily Times and Expositor,* 29 March 1880, 1.

———. "Facts from Florida." *Adrian Daily Times and Expositor,* 24 March 1879, 1.

———. "Farewell to Jupiter." *Adrian Daily Times and Expositor,* 27 March 1882, 2.

———. "Fishing and Feasting." *Adrian Daily Times and Expositor,* 20 March 1888, 2.

———. "Florida's Freeze Up." *Adrian Daily Times and Expositor,* 20 March 1886, 2.

———. "From Far Florida." *Adrian Daily Times and Expositor,* 1 April 1878, 2.

———. "From Far Florida: Wintering on the Indian Lagoon." *Adrian Daily Times and Expositor,* 3 March 1882, 2.

———. "From Florida." *Adrian Daily Times and Expositor,* 7 February 1879, 1.

———. "From Florida: Sea Beans and an Epitaph." *Adrian Daily Times and Expositor,* 15 February 1881, 2.

———. "From Florida Home." *Adrian Daily Times and Expositor,* 10 April 1878, 1.

———. "Frosty Weather in Florida." *Adrian Daily Times and Expositor,* 29 January 1884, 3.

———. "Growing the Orange." *Adrian Daily Times and Expositor,* 20 March 1883, 2.

———. "Indian River, Florida." *Adrian Daily Times and Expositor,* 8 March 1879, 1.

———. "Indian River Longings." *Florida Star.* 1 February 1882, 1.

———. "An Interesting Letter from One of Our Michigan Subscribers." *Florida Star,* 15 January 1885, 1.

———. "Interesting Reminiscence." *Adrian Daily Times and Expositor,* 5 February 1884, 2.

———. "In the Sunny South." *Adrian Daily Times and Expositor,* 27 February 1886, 2.

———. "Life on the Lagoons." *Adrian Daily Times and Expositor,* 3 March 1883, 2.

———. "March in Florida." *Adrian Daily Times and Expositor,* 22 March 1882, 2.

———. "Northerners in the South." *Adrian Daily Times and Expositor,* 11 March 1885, 2.

———. "Notes from Florida." *Adrian Daily Times and Expositor,* 14 February 1883, 2.

———. "Notes on the Gulf." *Adrian Daily Times and Expositor,* 16 March 1878, 1.

———. "On the Bounding Billows." *Adrian Daily Times and Expositor,* 7 February 1881, 2.

———. "On Indian River." *Adrian Daily Times and Expositor,* 14 March 1879, 1.

———. "On Indian River: Sailing on Summer Seas." *Adrian Daily Times and Expositor,* 15 March 1880, 1.

———. "On Indian River: More Fishing and Boating." *Adrian Daily Times and Expositor,* 23 March 1880, 1.

———. "On Summer Seas." *Adrian Daily Times and Expositor,* 21 February 1882, 2.

———. "Our Florida Letter." *Adrian Daily Times and Expositor,* 24 February 1880, 2.

———. "Our Florida Letter: Scenes and Incidents." *Adrian Daily Times and Expositor,* 2 March 1880, 1.

———. "Our Florida Letter: Bad Mail Service." *Adrian Daily Times and Expositor,* 7 March 1884, 2.

———. "The Pioneers." *Adrian Daily Times and Expositor,* 26 April 1879, 1–2.

———. "Roving on Indian River." *Adrian Daily Times and Expositor,* 25 February 1888, 2.

———. "Sailing South." *Adrian Daily Times and Expositor,* 27 February 1885, 2.

———. "Seeing Florida." *Adrian Daily Times and Expositor,* 26 January 1881, 2.

———. "Southern Florida." *Adrian Daily Times and Expositor,* 16 February 1885, 2.

———. "Surf and Sea." *Adrian Daily Times and Expositor,* 7 March 1883, 2.

———. "A Traveller's Diary." *Adrian Daily Times and Expositor,* 19 March 1885, 2.

———. "Way Down South." *Adrian Daily Times and Expositor,* 11 March 1878, 1.

———. "Way Down South: Cedar Key and Jacksonville." *Adrian Daily Times and Expositor,* 19 March 1878, 1.

———. "Way Down South: At Savannah and the Journey Thither." *Adrian Daily Times and Expositor,* 3 February 1879, 1.

———. "Way Down South: The Snowy South." *Adrian Daily Times and Expositor,* 20 February 1880, 2.

———. "Weather Bound." *Adrian Daily Times and Expositor,* 27 February 1884, 2.

———. "Where Summer Lives." *Adrian Daily Times and Expositor,* 20 February 1884, 2.

———. "Wintering in Florida." *Adrian Daily Times and Expositor,* 18 February 1879, 1.

MANUSCRIPT COLLECTIONS

Stebbins, Cortland B. Papers. Clarke Historical Library, Central Michigan University, Mt. Pleasant.

Stebbins Family Papers. Michigan State University Archives and Historical Collections, East Lansing.

UNPUBLISHED DOCUMENTS

Fryman, Frank B. "Turtle Mound, 8VO109." Division of Archives, History and Records Management. Submitted to Florida Master Site File. Division of Archives, History and Records Management. Florida Department of State, 22 March 1971.

Herold, Herman. "Log Book of Travels in the Sunny South—1884." P. K. Yonge Library of Florida History. University of Florida, Gainesville.

Hoffman, Kathleen S., and Dan Hughes. "Cultural Resource Assessment of U.S. Coast Guard Exchange Project." Janus Research for K-Con Building Systems. Submitted to Florida Department of State. Division of Historical Resources. 29 July 1998.

Stebbins, Francis R. Inventory. Lenawee County Probate Court. Estate Division. File 6135. Calendar K, p. 91.

———. Will. Lenawee County Probate Court. Estate Division. File 6135. Calendar K, p. 91.

Thomas, Prentice M., and Carol S. Weed. "Jupiter Midden #2, 8PB35." New World Research. Submitted to Florida Master Site File. Division of Archives, History and Record Management. Florida Department of State. 22 October 1981.

Worden, Alan. Will. Lenawee County Probate Court. Estate Division. File 5344. Calendar I, p. 577.

PUBLIC DOCUMENTS

Brice, John J. "Report on the Fish and Fisheries of the Coastal Waters of Florida." In *Report of the Commissioner for the Year Ending June 30, 1896,* 263–342. U.S. Department of the Interior. U.S. Commission of Fish and Fisheries. Washington, DC: GPO, 1898.

———. "Report on the Fisheries of Indian River, Florida." In *Report of the Commissioner for the Year Ending June 30, 1896,* 223–62. U.S. Department of the Interior. U.S. Commission of Fish and Fisheries. Washington, DC: GPO, 1898.

Earll, R. Edward. "Eastern Florida and Its Fisheries." In *The Fisheries and Fishing Industries of the United States,* by George Brown Goode. Section 2. *A Geographical Review of the Fisheries Industries and Fishing Communities for the Year 1880,* 521–31. U.S. Department of the Interior. U.S. Commission of Fish and Fisheries. Washington, DC: GPO, 1887.

Eleventh Annual Report of the Secretary of the State Horticultural Society of Michigan, 1881. Lansing: W. S. George and Company, 1882.

Evermann, Barton W., and Barton A. Bean. "Indian River and Its Fishes." In *Report of the Commissioner for the Year Ending June 30, 1896,* 227–48. U.S. Department of the Interior. U.S. Commission of Fish and Fisheries. Washington, DC: GPO, 1898.

Fifteenth Annual Report of the Secretary of the State Horticultural Society of Michigan, 1885. Lansing: Thorp and Godfrey, 1886.

LeBaron, J. Francis. "Prehistoric Remains in Florida." In *Annual Report for 1882, Smithsonian Institution*, 771–91. Washington, DC: GPO, 1884.

"List of Papers: Spain." No. 533. H. B. Plant to Mr. Bayard, 30 April 1885. *Papers Relating to the Foreign Relations of the United States*, 711–12. U.S. Department of State. Washington, DC: GPO, 1886.

———. No. 533. T. F. Bayard to Mr. Foster, 6 May 1885. *Papers Relating to the Foreign Relations of the United States*, 711. U.S. Department of State. Washington, DC: GPO, 1886.

Sixteenth Annual Report of the Secretary of the State Horticultural Society, 1886. Lansing: Thorp and Godfrey, 1887.

Smith, Hugh M. "Notes on Biscayne Bay, Florida, with References to its Adaptability as the Site of a Marine Hatching and Experiment Station." In *Report of the Commissioner for the Year Ending June 30, 1895*, 169–86. U.S. Department of the Interior. U.S. Commission of Fish and Fisheries. Washington, DC: GPO, 1896.

Smithsonian Institution. *Annual Report for 1881.* "Appendix C.—List of Contributors to the Museum in 1881," 158. Washington, DC: GPO, 1883.

Smithsonian Institution. *Annual Report for 1882.* "Report of the Secretary: Researches and Explorations, Florida," 18–19. Washington, DC: GPO, 1884.

Smithsonian Institution. *Annual Report for 1883.* "Report on National Museum: Appendix C, List of Contributors to the Museum in 1883," 320–60. Washington, DC: GPO, 1885.

Smithsonian Institution. *Annual Report for 1884.* "Report of the Secretary: Miscellaneous, Sonorous Sand," 47. Washington, DC: GPO, 1885.

Stevenson, Charles H. "Utilization of the Skins of Aquatic Animals." In *Report of the Commissioner for the Year Ending June 30, 1902*, 281–352. U.S. Department of the Interior. U.S. Commission of Fish and Fisheries. Washington, DC: GPO, 1904.

Thomas, Cyrus. *Catalogue of Prehistoric Works East of the Rocky Mountains.* Smithsonian Institution. Bureau of Ethnology. Bulletin no. 12. Washington, DC: GPO, 1891.

True, Frederick W. "The Green Turtles." In *The Fisheries and Fishing Industries of the United States*, by George Brown Goode. Section 1. *Natural History of Useful Aquatic Animals*, 150–51. U.S. Department of the Interior. U.S. Commission of Fish and Fisheries. Washington, DC: GPO, 1884.

U.S. Department of the Interior. Census Office. *Compendium of the Ninth Census, 1870: Population.* Washington, DC: GPO, 1872.

U.S. Department of the Interior. Census Office. *Compendium of the Tenth Census, 1880: Population.* Washington, DC: GPO, 1883.

U.S. Department of the Interior. Census Office. *Compendium of the Eleventh Census, 1890: Population.* Part 1. Washington, DC: GPO, 1892.

Wilcox, William A. "Commercial Fisheries of Indian River, Florida." In *Report of the Commissioner for the Year Ending June 30, 1896*, 249–62. U.S. Department of the Interior. U.S. Commission of Fish and Fisheries. Washington, DC: GPO, 1898.

Williams, Robert W. "History of Bird Protection in Florida." In *Florida Bird Life*, by

Arthur H. Howell, 42–58. Department of Game and Fresh Water Fish and Bureau of Biological Survey. U.S. Department of Agriculture, 1932.

Winsberg, Morton D., comp. *Florida's History through Its Places: Properties in the National Register of Historic Places.* Prepared by the Florida Resources and Environmental Analysis Center with the Bureau of Historic Preservation. Division of Historical Resources. Florida Department of State. August 1995.

NEWSPAPERS

Adrian Daily Times and Expositor (Michigan)
Adrian Times and Expositor (Michigan)
Adrian Weekly Times (Michigan)
Atlanta Constitution
Cazenovia Republican (New York)
Daily Morning Democrat (Grand Rapids, Michigan)
Daily News-Herald (Jacksonville)
Detroit Free Press
Evening News (Detroit)
Florida Star (Titusville)
Florida Times-Union (Jacksonville)
Frank Leslie's Illustrated Newspaper (New York)
Grand Rapids Daily Eagle (Michigan)
Grand Rapids Herald (Michigan)
Grand Rapids Press (Michigan)
Hillsdale Standard (Michigan)
Jackson Daily Citizen (Michigan)
Lenawee Record (Adrian, Michigan)
Manchester Enterprise (Michigan)
New York Times
Palatka Daily News (Florida)
Port Huron Daily Times (Michigan)
Sun (New York)
Tecumseh Herald (Michigan)
Tecumseh News (Michigan)
Weekly Floridian (Tallahassee)
Weekly Press (Adrian, Michigan)
Whitehall Forum (Michigan)

BOOKS

Adrian City Directory, 1882–1883. Adrian, MI: Henry H. Chapin, 1882.
Adrian City Directory, 1885–1886. Adrian, MI: Henry H. Chapin, 1885.
Akin, Edward N. *Flagler: Rockefeller Partner and Florida Baron.* Kent: Kent State University Press, 1988.

Atherton, Lewis. *Main Street on the Middle Border.* Bloomington: Indiana University Press, 1954.

Barbour, George M. *Florida for Tourists, Invalids, and Settlers.* New York: D. Appleton and Company, 1882.

Barrows, Walter Bradford. *Michigan Bird Life.* Lansing: Michigan Agricultural College, 1912.

Baxter, Albert. *History of the City of Grand Rapids, Michigan.* New York: Munsell and Company, 1891.

Bonner, Richard Illenden, ed. *Memoirs of Lenawee County, Michigan.* 2 vols. Madison, WI: Western Historical Association, 1909.

Cabell, Branch, and A. J. Hanna. *The St. Johns: A Parade of Diversities.* New York: Rinehart and Company, 1943.

Clark, George P. *Into the Old Northwest: Journeys with Charles H. Titus, 1841–1846.* East Lansing: Michigan State University Press, 1994.

Combination Atlas Map of Lenawee County, Michigan. Chicago: Everts and Steward, 1874.

Coon, James Churchill. *Log of the Cruise of 1889 D.T.S.C., New Smyrna to Lake Worth, East Coast of Florida.* Lake Helen, FL, 1889.

Corse, Carita Doggett, ed. *Florida: A Guide to the Southernmost State.* New York: Oxford University Press, 1939.

DeNovo, John A., ed. *The Gilded Age and After.* New York: Charles Scribner's Sons, 1972.

Donnelly, Ignatius. *Atlantis: The Antediluvian World.* New York: Harper, 1882.

Doughty, Robin W. *Feather Fashions and Bird Preservation: A Study in Nature Protection.* Berkeley: University of California Press, 1975.

Dunbar, Willis F. *Michigan: A History of the Wolverine State.* Rev. and ed. George S. May. Grand Rapids, MI: Eerdmans, 1980.

Feeman, Harlan L., Ruth E. Cargo, and Fannie A. Hay. *The Story of a Noble Devotion, 1845–1945.* Adrian, MI: Adrian College Press, 1945.

Fishburne, Charles C., Jr. *The Cedar Keys in the 19th Century.* Quincy, FL: Sea Hawk Publications, 1993.

Gilman, William H., and Alfred R. Ferguson, eds. *The Journals and Miscellaneous Notebooks of Ralph Waldo Emerson.* 16 vols. Cambridge, MA: Belknap Press of Harvard University Press, 1963.

Gore, E. H. *From Florida Sand to "The City Beautiful": A Historical Record of Orlando, Florida.* Winter Park, FL: Orange Press, 1951.

Gregg, William H., and John Gardner. *Where, When, and How to Catch Fish on the East Coast of Florida.* Buffalo and New York: Matthew-Northrup Works, 1902.

Griffin, Patricia C. *Mullet on the Beach: The Minorcans of Florida, 1768–1788.* Jacksonville: University of North Florida Press, 1991.

———. *Ralph Waldo Emerson in St. Augustine.* St. Augustine: St. Augustine Historical Society and the Museum of Arts and Sciences, St. Augustine Historic Museum Center, 1995.

Hanna, Alfred Jackson, and Kathryn Abbey Hanna. *Florida's Golden Sands.* New York: Bobbs-Merrill, 1950.

Harcourt, Helen [Helen Garnie Warner]. *Florida Fruits and How to Raise Them.* Louisville: John P. Morton and Company, 1886.

Harvey, E. Newton. *Living Light.* New York: Hafner Publishing Company, 1965.

Hawks, John Milton. *The East Coast of Florida: A Descriptive Narrative.* Lynn, MA: Lewis and Winship, 1887.

Hine, C. Vickerstaff. *On the Indian River.* Chicago: Charles H. Sergel and Company, 1891.

History of Jackson County, Michigan. Chicago: Interstate Publishing, 1881.

History of Washtenaw County, Michigan. 2 vols. Chicago: Chas. C. Chapman and Company, 1881.

Humphreys, Margaret. *Yellow Fever and the South.* New Brunswick, NJ: Rutgers University Press, 1992.

Hutchinson, Janet, and Emmeline K. Paige. *History of Martin County.* Hutchinson Island, FL: Gilbert's Bar Press, 1975.

Jackson, Joy J. *New Orleans in the Gilded Age: Politics and Urban Progress, 1880–1896.* Baton Rouge: Louisiana Historical Association, 1969.

Kane, Joseph Nathan. *Facts about the Presidents: A Compilation of Biographical and Historical Data.* New York: H. W. Wilson Company, 1968.

Kjerulff, Georgiana Greene. *Tales of Old Brevard.* Melbourne, FL: Kellerberger Fund of the South Brevard Historical Society, 1972.

Knapp, John I., and R. I. Bonner. *Illustrated History and Biographical Record of Lenawee County, Mich.* Adrian, MI: Times Printing Company, 1903.

Lanier, Sidney. *Florida: Its Scenery, Climate, and History.* Philadelphia: J. B. Lippincott and Company, 1875.

Lockwood, Charlotte. *Florida's Historic Indian River County.* Vero Beach, FL: Media Tronics, 1975.

McKelvey, Blake. *The Urbanization of America, 1860–1915.* New Brunswick, NJ: Rutgers University Press, 1963.

Manning, Thomas C. *U.S. Coast Survey vs. Naval Hydrographic Office: A 19th-Century Rivalry In Science and Politics.* Tuscaloosa: University of Alabama Press, 1988.

Michigan State Gazetteer and Business Directory, 1879. Detroit: R. L. Polk, 1879.

Michigan State Gazetteer and Business Directory, 1883. Detroit: R. L. Polk, 1883.

Myers, Bernard S., ed. *Encyclopedia of Painting.* New York: Crown, 1955.

Ober, F[rederick] A. *The Knockabout Club in the Everglades: The Adventures of the Club in Exploring Lake Okeechobee.* Boston: Estes and Lauriat, 1887.

O'Neal, W. R. *Memoirs of a Pioneer.* Orlando: Orlando Sentinel-Star, c. 1932.

Perez, Louis A., Jr. *Cuba and the United States: Ties of Singular Intimacy.* Athens: University of Georgia Press, 1990.

Pierce, Charles W. *Pioneer Life in Southeast Florida.* Ed. Donald Walter Curl. Coral Gables: University of Miami Press, 1970.

Proctor, Samuel. "The University of Florida: Its Early Years, 1853–1906." Ph.D. diss., University of Florida, 1958.

Rambler. *Guide to Florida.* New York: American News Company, 1875.

Ransom, Robert. *A Memoir of Captain Mills Olcott Burnham: A Florida Pioneer.* St. Augustine, FL, 1926.

Reed, Nathaniel P., and Dennis Drabelle. *The United States Fish and Wildlife Service.* Boulder: Westview Press, 1984.

Rinhart, Floyd, and Marion Rinhart. *Victorian Florida: America's Last Frontier.* Atlanta: Peachtree Publishers, 1986.

Shofner, Jerrell H. *History of Brevard County.* 3 vols. [Melbourne, FL]: Brevard County Historical Commission, 1995.

———. *Nor Is It Over Yet: Florida in the Era of Reconstruction, 1863–1877.* Gainesville: University Presses of Florida, 1974.

Silvia Sunshine [Abbie M. Brooks]. *Petals Plucked from Sunny Climes.* Nashville: Southern Methodist Publishing House, 1880.

The South Publishing Company's Florida State Gazetteer and Business Directory 1886–7. Vol. 1. New York: South Publishing Company, 1886.

Tebeau, Charlton W. *A History of Florida.* Coral Gables: University of Miami Press, 1975.

Trefethen, James B. *An American Crusade for Wildlife.* New York: Winchester Press and the Boone and Crockett Club, 1975.

Waldron, Clara. *One Hundred Years a Country Town: The Village of Tecumseh, Michigan, 1824–1924.* Tecumseh, MI: Thomas A. Riordan, 1968.

Warner, Joseph Lacy. "The Jacksonville Yellow Fever Epidemic of 1888: A Case Study of the Affect of Natural Disaster upon Growth." Master's thesis, University of Florida, 1976.

Weber, Gustavus A. *The Coast and Geodetic Survey: Its History, Activities and Organization.* Service Monographs of the United States Government No. 16, Institute for Government Research. Baltimore: Johns Hopkins Press, 1923.

Weeks, Jerry Woods. "Florida Gold: The Emergence of the Florida Citrus Industry, 1865–1895." Ph.D. diss., University of North Carolina, 1977.

White, William Carlin. *History of the Carlin House.* N.p., 1988.

Whitney, W. A., and Bonner, R. I. *History and Biographical Record of Lenawee County, Michigan.* 2 vols. Adrian, MI: W. Stearns and Company, 1879.

Williams, Ada Coats. *A Brief History of Saint Lucie County.* Fort Pierce, FL: Theresa M. Field, 1963.

Williamson, Edward C. *Florida Politics in the Gilded Age, 1877–1893.* Gainesville: University Presses of Florida, 1976.

ARTICLES

Abrahamson, Warren G., and David C. Hartnett. "Pine Flatwoods and Dry Prairies." In *Ecosystems of Florida,* ed. Ronald L. Myers and John J. Ewel, 103–49. Orlando: University of Central Florida Press, 1990.

Adams, B.C. "A Delayed Letter." *Adrian Daily Times and Expositor,* 23 July 1883, 2.

———. "Educating the Negro." *Adrian Daily Times and Expositor,* 2 June 1883, 2.

———. "The Land of the Sky." *Adrian Daily Times and Expositor,* 20 January 1883, 2.

"Adrian Fruit-Growers." *Adrian Weekly Times,* 21 January 1875, 4.

Al. I. Gator [J. Francis Le Baron]. "Florida." *Forest and Stream* 12 (12 June 1879): 374.

Al Fresco [Charles J. Kenworthy]. "Florida Again—VI." *Forest and Stream* 23 (15 November 1884): 303.

———. "Southwest Florida—No. 4: Being Notes of a Tour of Exploration—by Our Own Commissioner." *Forest and Stream* 4 (8 April 1875): 137.

"Alfred H. Wood." *Portrait and Biographical Album of Lenawee County, Mich.,* 494–95. Chicago: Chapman Brothers, 1880.

"The Alligator Satchel." *Forest and Stream* 40 (8 June 1893): 489.

"An 'Al Fresco' Fund." *Forest and Stream* 31 (13 September 1888): 141.

"Answers to Correspondents." *Forest and Stream* 12 (26 June 1879): 409.

"Arrivals at the Titus House." *Florida Star,* 26 February 1881, 4.

Avast. "Jupiter." *Florida Star,* 22 March 1888, 1.

B.P.S. [Benjamin P. Shepard]. "Another Letter from Florida." *Hillsdale Standard,* 8 March 1881, 2.

"Beautiful Merritt's Isle." *Florida Star,* 22 November 1888, 1, 4.

Beverly, Fred [Frederick A. Ober]. "Our Okeechobee Expedition." *Forest and Stream* 2 (7 May 1874): 194.

"Brevard County Day at the Sub-Tropical." *Florida Star,* 22 March 1888, 4.

"Bronze John's Farewell." *Florida Star,* 29 November 1888, 4.

Campbell, Alice Porter. "The Bull Moose Movement in Michigan." *Michigan History Magazine* 25 (Winter 1941): 34–47.

Cash, W. T. "The Lower East Coast, 1870–1890." *Tequesta* 8 (1948): 57–71.

"Chaffee, Jerome Bunty." In *American Legislative Leaders, 1850–1910,* ed. Charles F. Ritter and Jon L. Wakelyn, 112. New York: Greenwood, 1989.

"Chaffee, Jerome Bunty." In *Biographical Directory of the United States Congress 1774–1989,* 759–60. Bicentennial edition. Washington, DC: GPO, 1989.

Crow, C. L. "Florida University (1883)." *Florida Historical Quarterly* 15 (October 1936): 96–112.

"Cruise of the May: Capron, St. Lucie, Homeward Bound." *Florida Star,* 21 May 1885, 1.

"David Metcalf." In *Illustrated History and Biographical Record of Lenawee, County, Michigan,* ed. John I. Knapp and R. I. Bonner, 307–09. Adrian, MI: Times Printing Company, 1903.

"Death Claims William Gunn." *Grand Rapids Press,* 28 June 1933, 1.

"Death of Mr. Charles W. Gunn." *Grand Rapids Daily Eagle,* 16 January 1886, 7.

"Death's Harvest." *Adrian Daily Times and Expositor,* 7 September 1888, 4.

"Disston's Million Dollar I.O.U. Rescued Florida from Bankruptcy." In *Florida's Promoters: Men Who Made It Big,* by Charles E. Harner, 12–17. Tampa: Trend House, 1973.

Dubois, Bessie Wilson. "Jupiter Inlet." *Tequesta* 28 (1968): 19–35.

———. "Jupiter Lighthouse." *Tequesta* 20 (1960): 5–17.

"The Duchess del Castilluccia Sues a Roslyn Yacht Builder for Damages." *Florida Star,* 1 February 1883, 1.

"The Dummitt Grove." *Florida Star,* 15 December 1886, 2.

Duncan, John T. "Church Notice for Titusville." *Florida Star,* 4 September 1884, 8.

E. S. W. "A Winter in Florida." *Forest and Stream* 33 (21 November 1889): 342.

E. W. H. "Orange County Enterprise." *Florida Times-Union,* 31 May 1888, 2.

F.S.J.C. "Charlotte Harbor: Fourth Paper." *Forest and Stream* 33 (9 January 1890): 494–96.

"Facts from Florida: Done into Rhyme by a Lady for Readers of the Times." *Adrian Daily Times and Expositor,* 27 February 1886: 2.

Fairlie, Margaret C. "The Yellow Fever Epidemic of 1888 in Jacksonville." *Floriday Historical Quarterly* 19 (October 1940): 97–108.

"The Fearful Fever." *Adrian Daily Times and Expositor,* 21 September 1888, 3.

"A Few Dots about Indian River." *Florida Star,* 17 March 1886, 4.

"Florida." *Adrian Daily Times and Expositor,* 29 January 1879, 1.

"Florida Depopulated." *Adrian Daily Times and Expositor,* 6 September 1888, 3.

"The Florida Freezes." *Sun,* 27 February 1886, 3.

"Francis R. Stebbins, Memorial Paper Read by Hon. Norman Geddes at the Meeting of the State Pioneer Society." *Adrian Daily Times and Expositor,* 10 June 1893, 2.

"Francois Rene Stebbins (Francis R. Stebbins)." In *The Stebbins Genealogy,* ed. Ralph Stebbins Greenlee and Robert Lemuel Greenlee, 1:542–47. Chicago: N.p., 1904.

"Frank W. Clay." In *Portrait and Biographical Album of Lenawee County, Mich.,* 866–67. Chicago: Chapman Brothers, 1888.

Friar Tuck [Milton E. Card]. "A Winter's Cruise in Eastern and Southern Florida." *Cazenovia Republican,* 9 September 1880, 1.

G. "Chas. W. Gunn." *Ornithologist and Oologist* 11 (May 1886): 73.

"'Gators' Getting Scarce." *Adrian Daily Times and Expositor,* 24 March 1898, 2.

Geddes, Hon. Norman. "Memoir of Francis R. Stebbins." *Michigan Pioneer and Historical Collections* 22 (1894): 214–17.

Green, Marian Palmer. "Reflections in the River Raisin." *Michigan History* 33 (March 1949): 47–64.

Gunn, Charles W. "A Collector in Florida." *Ornithologist and Oologist* 7 (March 1882): 103–04.

"The Halifax Fish and Fertilizing Co." *Florida Star,* 23 November 1882, 1.

Hastings, John Woodland. "Bioluminescence in Bacteria and Dinoflagellates." In *Light Emission by Plants and Bacteria,* ed. Jan Amaesz and David Charles Fork, 363–98. Orlando: Academic Press, 1986.

Hause, E. "The Land of Flowers." *Tecumseh Herald,* 25 October 1883, 1.

Henshall, James A. "Around the Coast of Florida." *Forest and Stream* 20 (1 February 1883): 3–4.

———. "A Winter in East Florida: Fourth Paper." *Forest and Stream* 13 (16 October 1879): 724.

———. "A Winter in East Florida: Sixth Paper." *Forest and Stream* 13 (30 October 1879): 763–64.

———. "A Winter in East Florida: Seventh Paper." *Forest and Stream* 13 (6 November 1879): 783–84.

———. "A Winter in East Florida: Ninth Paper." *Forest and Stream* 13 (20 November 1879): 823–24.

"Hon. Jerome B. Chaffee." In *History and Biographical Record of Lenawee County, Michigan,* ed. W. A. Whitney and R. I. Bonner, 1:120–23. Adrian, MI: W. Stearns and Company, 1879.

Howard, H. "To Florida." *Port Huron Daily Times,* 13 March 1883, 2.

"Indian River." *Florida Star,* 23 February 1881, 1.

"Indian River, as Seen by an Editor." *Florida Star,* 31 March 1886, 4.

Irishman. "A Trip to Indian River." *Florida Star,* 20 August 1885, 1.

J. W. "The Homosassa River (Hernando Co., Fla.)." *American Angler* 2 (25 February 1882): 137.

———. "Notes from Florida—Fly Fishing, Etc." *American Angler* 2 (29 July 1882): 68–69.

"James H. White." In *Early History of Michigan with Biographies of State Officers, Members of Congress, Judges and Legislators,* 686–87. Lansing: Thorp and Godfrey, 1888.

Johnson, Ann F., and Michael G. Barbour. "Dunes and Maritime Forests." In *Ecosystems of Florida,* ed. Ronald L. Myers and John J. Ewel, 429–80. Orlando: University of Central Florida Press, 1990.

"Jupiter." *Florida Star,* 19 January 1888, 1.

Kost, [John]. "Geological Survey of Florida." *Adrian Daily Times and Expositor,* 17 January 1888, 2.

L.D.W. [Lucius D. Watkins]. "From the Land of Flowers." *Manchester Enterprise,* 28 February 1884, 2.

L. W. L. "Florida Sketches—Yachting Down South." *Forest and Stream* 2 (19 March 1874): 82–83.

———. "Yachting in Florida.—No. 1." *Forest and Stream* 5 (7 January 1875): 347.

"Laid to Rest." *Adrian Daily Times and Expositor,* 3 October 1892, 3.

Lamb, Martha J. "The American Life-Saving Service." *Harper's New Monthly Magazine* 64 (February 1882): 357–73.

"Lenawee County Horticulturalists." *Michigan Farmer* 16 (14 July 1885): 3.

Lewes, G. H. "The Phosphorescence of the Sea." *American Naturalist* 1 (1868): 316–17.

Lewis, Carolyn Baker. "Agricultural Evolution on Secondary Frontiers: A Florida Model." In *The Frontier: Comparative Studies,* ed. William W. Savage, Jr. and Stephen I. Thompson, 205–33. Norman: University of Oklahoma Press, 1979.

"Loveliest Village of the Plain." *Tecumseh Herald Anniversary Supplement,* 31 May 1895, 1.

"Lucius Whitney Watkins." *Michigan Biographies,* 2:412. Lansing: Michigan Historical Commission, 1924.

M. "From Kissimmee City." *Florida Times-Union,* 29 May 1883, 1.

"Manatees Exhibited in New York." *Forest and Stream* 31 (6 September 1888): 123.

"Manufacturers of Fish Fertilizer." *Florida Star,* 12 July 1883, 1.

Mealor, W. Theodore Jr., and Merle C. Prunty. "Open-Range Ranching in South Florida." *Annals of the Association of American Geographers* 66 (September 1976): 360–76.

"Melbourne and Vicinity." *Florida Star,* 30 December 1885, 1.

Merchandise List. Jacksonville, FL: Alvord, Kellogg, and Campbell, c. 1878.

Mrs. A. H. [Mary Howell]. "The Captive Redskins." *Adrian Daily Times and Expositor,* 15 May 1886, 2.

———. [H.]. "In the Florida Pines." *Adrian Daily Times and Expositor,* 24 April 1882, 2.

———. [Mrs. H.]. "The Prairies of Florida." *Adrian Daily Times and Expositor,* 1 May 1882, 1.

———. [Mrs. H.]. "The Sunny South." *Adrian Daily Times and Expositor,* 12 May 1885, 2.

"Nehemiah M. Sutton," *Portrait and Biographical Album of Lenawee County, Mich.,* 478–79. Chicago: Chapman Brothers, 1888.

"New Orleans and Its Great Show." *Sun,* 30 March 1885, 2.

"Non-Partisan." *Adrian Daily Times and Expositor,* 3 April 1883, 2.

Ober, Frederick A. "Ten Days with the Seminoles." *Appleton's Journal* 14 (July 1875): 142–44.

"The Orange Crop." *Atlanta Constitution,* 7 March 1886, 5.

Otto, John Solomon. "Florida's Cattle-Ranching Frontier: Manatee and Brevard Counties (1860)." *Florida Historical Quarterly* 64 (July 1985): 48–61.

———. "Open-Range Cattle Herding in Southern Florida." *Florida Historical Quarterly* 65 (January 1987): 317–34.

Otvos, Ervin G. "Barrier Island Formation through Near Shore Aggradation— Stratigraphic and Field Evidence." *Marine Geology* 43 (1981): 195–243.

"Our Guests." *Florida Star,* 1 March 1888, 1.

"Our 'Invalid' Candidate for Mayor." *Adrian Daily Times and Expositor,* 31 March 1883, 2.

P. H. A. "Alligator Shooting in Florida." *Forest and Stream* 6 (1 June 1876): 264.

Perejda, Andrew D. "Sources and Dispersal of Michigan's Population." *Michigan History* 32 (December 1948): 355–66.

"A Pioneer Gone: Hon. F. R. Stebbins Passes Peacefully Away." *Adrian Daily Times and Expositor,* 30 September 1892, 3.

"Preserve the Ancient." *Forest and Stream* 12 (20 March 1879): 130.

"The President Coming to Indian River." *Florida Star,* 23 February 1888, 1.

"The President's Outing." *Detroit Free Press,* 25 February 1888, 1.

Proctor, Samuel. "The Early Years of the Florida Experiment Station, 1888–1906." *Agricultural History* 36 (October 1962): 213–21.

Quad, M. [Charles Bertrand Lewis]. "Advice to Boy Terrors." *Detroit Free Press,* 19 February 1888, 11.

"Republican Nominations." *Weekly Press,* 30 March 1883, 6.

"Richard A. Bury." In *Illustrated History and Biographical Record of Lenawee County, Michigan,* ed. John I. Knapp and R. I. Bonner, 276–77. Adrian, MI: Times Printing Company, 1903.

"Rockledge, the Beautiful, the Palmetto Grove Town." *Florida Star,* 16 December 1885, 1.

S. "Bits of Florida Experience." *Forest and Stream* 18 (22 June 1882), 407.

S.C.C. [Samuel C. Clarke]. "Canine Madness." *Forest and Stream* 10 (27 June 1878):
400.

"Sad Death of Miss Anna Chaffee." *Adrian Daily Times and Expositor*, 28 December
1876, 1.

Scott, W.E.D. "The Present Condition of Some of the Bird Rookeries of the Gulf
Coast of Florida." *Auk* 4 (October 1887): 273–83.

"The Shake Up!" *Adrian Daily Times and Expositor*, 2 April 1878, 1.

"The Shark Fisheries at New Smyrna, Florida." *Frank Leslie's Illustrated Newspaper*,
11 February 1882, 435, 437.

Sherman. "Observations of a Massachusetts Yankee on Indian River." *Florida Star*,
24 May 1883, 1.

"Sir Mark Sykes." In *Salutation to Five*, by Shane Leslie, 133–56. Freeport, NY: Books
for Libraries Press, 1951.

Smith, Edward J. "Editorial Ramblings in the South: XI." *Whitehall Forum*, 25 March
1886, 4.

Sojourner. "Down the Indian River." *Daily News-Herald*, 4 April 1888, 2.

"A Southern Memory." *Adrian Daily Times and Expositor*, 21 January 1879, 1.

Spratt, Jack. "Narrows." *Florida Star*, 22 March 1888, 1.

"Stebbins, Francis Ranna." *American Biographical History of Eminent and Self-Made
Men: Michigan Volume*, Congressional District 2, 66–67. Cincinnati: Western Biographical Publishing, 1876.

Stonehouse, Merlin. "The Michigan Excursion for the Founding of Riverside, California." *Michigan History* 45 (September 1961): 193–209.

Stones, Wm. "From Florida: An Adrian Man in an Orange Grove." *Adrian Daily
Times and Expositor*, 19 October 1883, 2.

Stout, E. C. "Indians in Florida." *Detroit Free Press*, 25 November 1888, 12.

"A Strong Ticket." *Adrian Daily Times and Expositor*, 27 March 1883, 3.

[Sutton, Nehemiah M.]. "Letter from Florida." *Tecumseh Herald*, 1 April 1880, 2.

———. "The Sunny South." *Tecumseh Herald*, 1 April 1886, 2.

"Tecumseh Topics." *Adrian Daily Times and Expositor*, 8 January 1879, 1.

"Thomas New." In *Tales of Sebastian*, by George Keyes, 33–34. Craftsman Litho for
the Sebastian River Area Historical Society, 1990.

Thurlow, Sandra Henderson. "Lonely Vigils: Houses of Refuge on Florida's East
Coast." *Florida Historical Quarterly* 76 (Fall 1997): 152–71.

True, F. W. "Porpoise Steak." *Forest and Stream* 24 (18 June 1885): 411–12.

Waterbury, Jean Parker. "The Castillo Years, 1668–1763." In *The Oldest City: St. Augustine Saga of Survival*, ed. Jean Parker Waterbury, 57–89. St. Augustine, FL:
St. Augustine Historical Society, 1983.

Watkins, L. Whitney. "A Disastrous Season on Pelican Island." *The Oologist* 11 (April
1894): 148–50.

"What Sweet Potatoes to Grow for Northern Markets." *Weekly Floridian*, 7 November
1882, 2.

Whicher, George F. "Lewis, Charles Bertrand." In *Dictionary of American Biography*,
ed. Dumas Malone, 6:207–08. New York: Charles Scribner's Sons, 1933.

White, J[ames] H. "Florida: A Trip along the East Coast." *Port Huron Daily Times,* 16 March 1883, 2.

"Wintering in Florida." *Adrian Daily Times and Expositor,* 16 May 1881, 2.

"Wm. S. Gunn Dies Abroad." *Grand Rapids Herald,* 3 January 1909, 1.

Woodward, C. Vann. "The Southern Ethic in a Puritan World." *William and Mary Quarterly* 25 (July 1968): 343–70.

Wyman, Jeffries. "Fresh-Water Shell Mounds of the St. John's River, Florida." *Memoirs of the Peabody Academy of Science* 1 (December 1875): i–94.

"The Yellow Fever: It Still Has Its Grip on Florida Towns." *Adrian Daily Times and Expositor,* 30 October 1888, 3.

"Yellow Jack's Victims." *Adrian Daily Times and Expositor,* 10 September 1888, 4.

Ziska [Amos J. Cummings]. "Adventures in Florida." *Sun,* 28 August 1874, 3.

———. "The Farming in Florida." *Sun,* 28 May 1873, 2.

———. "Florida's Indian Mounds." *Sun,* 17 April 1873, 2.

———. "Florida's Orange Groves." *Sun,* 24 March 1873, 3.

———. "The Home of the Turtles." *Sun,* 6 August 1874, 3.

Index